UPDATED EDITION

WAMPUS CAT FOOTBALL HISTORY

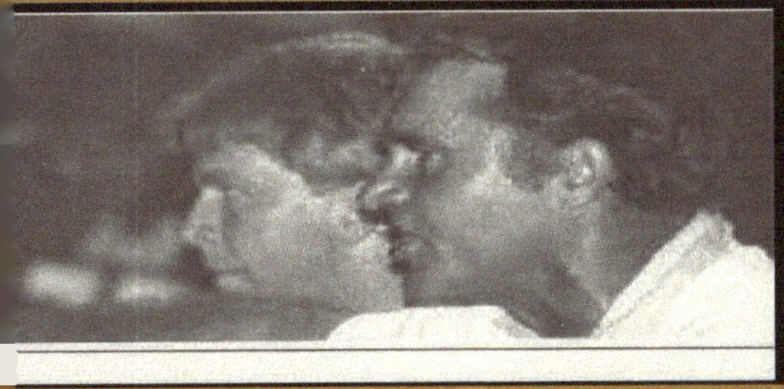

Charles A. Owen

UPDATED - 2023

FOREWORD

"Once A Wampus Cat, Always A Wampus Cat"

If I had a dollar for every time someone has asked me, "What's a Wampus Cat?" I would have more money than Elon Musk. Is there such a creature as a Wampus Cat? Are they for real? All I know for sure is that I am a bona fide, for-real Wampus Cat! and so are the hundreds of the Cats fans who have followed Leesville High School football for decades.

Tigers, Eagles, Bulldogs, Panthers, Lions and Wildcats are common names for high school athletic teams. But there is nothing at all common about being a Wampus Cat from Leesville!

But how could it be any other way? For the town of Leesville, though small, has a kind of greatness which makes it a most unique place to build a home, raise a family, go to school, or coach a team. Home to Fort Polk, one of the largest military facilities in the United States, the Leesville community is comprised not only of "old timers" and "locals" who have lived here for generations, but also of military families who have lived in places all over the world. As the principal of this large, diverse, and exceptional high school in the heart of town, I experienced the most exciting and inspiring nine years of my life as a professional educator—and as a number one Cats fan!

Wampus Cats football, with successive seasons of genius coaches and outstanding athletes, played no small part in that excitement! Wampus Cat football was the source of immense pride and joy, and it continues to be, not only for our students, faculty, and staff, but also for this enthusiastic principal. Rarely did I miss a game, even when they were out-of-town. Never did I fail to enjoy every moment of the Cats' amazing display of high school football fervor, both on the field and in the stands. To this day, the LHS Wampus Cat season is my favorite to follow. "Once A Wampus Cat, Always A Wampus Cat"!

In the Foreword to Charles Owen's previous publication, Wampus Cat Football History, former Coach Danny Smith wrote, "Charles Owen has created a book that captures the passion of Wampus Cat football and his love for the Black and Gold." Since the publication of this first volume in 2020, Charles has continued his exhaustive research and has captured even more memories that will surely swell your pride and joy. And they may even, as Danny Smith first suggested, "bring a tear" to your Wampus Cat eyes!

Billy Crawford

Principal of Leesville High School (1989-95)
Classroom Teacher and Coach (1969-78)
Student (Class of 1964)

Copyright @ Fiddle-Dee-Dee Entertainment Group, LLC 2020 &, Charles A. Owen
All Rights Reserved. No part of this publication may be reproduced in any form
without written permission of the publisher.
Layout and Typesetting: Julisa Sandra Marquez
http://imageandcreativity.com

ial History

CHARLES A. OWEN

2023 Update

Table of Contents

Prologue ... 5
The Written History ... 7
Team Records ... 35
Offensive Stat Leaders ... 57
Defenders, 100 Tackle Club ... 68
All Time Results ... 83
Hooper Trophy History ...111
All State Selections ...119
Old Timer's Game ... 129
Rich History of Leesville High School ... 135
For the Love of Box Scores ... 139
First Golden Age of LHS Football 155
1995: LHSAA State Runner Up Season ...175
Teams in Pictures ...183
Players And Coaches ...223
Head Coaches 235
LHS Sports Hall of Fame ... 243
Dedication ..248
Epilogue ...253

PROLOGUE

This book is written as a tribute to the people of Leesville who have supported high school football in this great city since at least 1910. Football in Leesville is special because of the community and the pride the community takes in its teams. Most football games in our town have been played under the banner of "Wampus Cats," but we've also had "Bob Cats" and Vernon "Lions" who have generated interest, a sense of community and a camaraderie that is inexplicable. Football is made great because of the players, the band members, the cheerleaders, the entire student body, the teachers and staff at Leesville High School and the city that loves this sport.

This book is an updated and unofficial chronicle of the history of Leesville football. The first book was published in 2020, and it's time for an update. The book contains the written history, team/ individual records, and a litany of pictures of the teams, players, coaches and fans who have been a part of LHS football for many decades. Of note in this year's edition is the list of games and scores---all scores, every year we could find.

I emphasize the point that these are "unofficial" records. To my knowledge, there's no such thing as an official record keeper at the State or Parish level for high school sports. If records are kept, they are done so at the initiative of the school or private citizens. There is no protocol and there are no rules. The lists you see here were compiled essentially by two people: Former Leesville Leader Editor Brian Trahan and me. Brian started this project some years back and handed it off to me in about 2014. Brian's work was stupendous and was mainly focused on the Leesville-DeRidder rivalry and individual statistics back through the late 1970s. I undertook the project of expanding out the list to include seasonal win/loss records and to gather individual records where they could be found. Sports reporter and local educator Daniel Green also has contributed significantly to this effort and he has helped me with stat protocols and other nuances of recording sports history.

I've spent a lot of time digging through Leesville Leaders, Wampus Cat Annual Yearbooks, old Alexandria Town Talks, Shreveport Times, and other papers around Louisiana. Fortunately, most of this digging was electronic. The Vernon Digital Archives are a great online resource and am thankful for the fact that old Leesville Leaders are digitized. Sincere thanks to the library in my beloved hometown and Mr. Howard Coy for having the vision to digitize their holdings. The pictures of photographer Eddie Wise from his days at the Leesville Leader added a great flair to the publication.

As with any historical project, the product is only as good as the data. This "look" goes back to 1910. There are holes early and from 1910 – the early 30s. Information and data are pretty well archived from the 30s going forward. The win-loss list includes wins, losses, and ties in the regular and post seasons. Some seasons had little or no data in the early years, and I included what I could find. Coaches are identified and relevant notes and honors are included where they could be found. Any year I could find an "All District" or "All State" list, I included the info in notes. Athletes who signed to play or did play at the college and pro level are identified.

I am a Wampus Cat, but I am a Leesville native more than anything. Since the previous edition of this book, I have published a book on the Vernon Lions and the Hooper Trophy, both of which add to the body of work related to football in Leesville and Vernon Parish. Once a Wampus Cat, always a Wampus Cat.

THE WRITTEN HISTORY

In the ensuing pages and paragraphs, you see will see the history of football in Leesville. This history was crafted through the review of news accounts, yearbooks, and individual knowledge of the sport in the City of Leesville, primarily at Leesville High School. The history is generally told in the context of decades or periods of time. Much research could still be done, and any help in correcting or adding to this story is appreciated. There is no agenda, other than to chronicle the story of Wampus Cat football. Many names and accomplishments are listed, as are coaches. Maybe someday, we'll have a list of every player, coach, and manager. This body of work has been updated since the 2020 edition, but much more needs to be done.

PRE 1929

Scant info is available on football in Leesville prior to 1929. The earliest reference to football and the City of Leesville actually goes back to 1907. Louisiana State University's (LSU's) All Time Letterman list contains the names of a William Lyles and Pleasant Ferguson, both of who lettered for LSU in 1907. Another person identified as a Leesville native was Wee Willie Wintle, who lettered in 1921 and 1922. Mr. Ferguson was an attorney who passed away in 1931; he was a member of the Nona Mills Lumber company. Buffalo Lyles was from an old Vernon Parish family with direct ties to the Burr family of Burr Ferry. Mr. Wintle, the son of a former Leesville Mayor, passed away in 1967 and his headstone in Fort Worth indicates he served in World War I.

The first games recorded for Leesville playing football dates back to 1910, in our inaugural meeting with Deridder. Prior to the establishment of a mascot called "Wampus Cats," the team from Leesville is noted as playing against DeRidder a number of times and against other teams in this area. Leesville had games against Hornbeck, Florien, & Glenmora. Something caused football to come to an end in 1922, but ground truth on why the school stopped playing the sport is undetermined. In 1920, there was a shooting after a game in Glenmora, when two Leesville residents got into a fight over expenses related to the game. One of the residents

1907 LSU Tigers

died, and the other, whose name was listed in the press at "Mr. Henry Beason" was investigated but not charged in the murder. Football stopped in 1922 and re-commenced in 1929. Beason was listed in the news as the Assistant Principal of Leesville High School and the "manager" of the football team. A coach by the name of Beason appeared as the school's head coach in the 30s.

1929 TO 1944: THE EARLY YEARS

In the fall of 1929, the Wampus Cats suited up for the first time. Leesville native & son of Vernon Parish Sheriff, W.C. Turner, was the first coach. As the story goes, Coach Turner paid for the team's uniforms and equipment in this inaugural season. The team initially had some success, going 5-3-1. In ensuing years, WH Beason became the head coach & Turner served as an assistant coach of the Leesville team. For 3 years (30 – 32), the team was referred to as the "Bobcats". Beason's team was successful through the mid-30s, with no losing records identified. Some key players of this era were the Fertitta brothers, Sam, Fatty & Anthony, Fred Rowzee, Julien Stevens, Jake Armes, Percy Cabra, Buddy Hadnot, Bill Anderson, Louis Moses, and others.

In the mid 1930s, the team came under the guidance of a coach named Wood Osborne, and Osborne led the squad through roughly 1944. Little info is available on the teams in 42 and 43, but it is assumed Osborne remained with the squad. Some of the prominent players in this era were Alfred Dunn, TB Porter, CA Hughes, Bobby Pinchback, Johnny Moses, Carl Babin, Glen McRae, Mickey Cohen, Kemp Tucker, Derry Smart, Cotton McClure, and John Sepeda. In 2019, TB Porter was inducted into the LHS Sports Hall of Fame. The World Champion Cowboy was also inducted into the Louisiana Sports Hall of Fame in the same year and into the National Rodeo Hall of Fame in 2015.

During the induction of Mr. Porter into the LHS Sports Hall of Fame, the Leesville native told the crowd that the football program was so poor players had to share cleats. When the offense came off the field, the players took off their cleats and gave them to the defense to wear. He said that he didn't have to take his off, however, because he was a 2-way player, plus he played in the band for the half-time show.

Due to US involvement in the World War II, football was abandoned for the 1944 season, but re-started in 1945. The town again turned to Coach Turner as he organized the Cats and was the head coach for a brief time.

Coach Wood Osbourne

POST WORLD WAR II

The period after WWII has some deficiencies in data, but not many. The teams saw no winning records in the years 1945 -1950, but football was back. In 1949, Zolon Stiles was hired as head coach and he put the Cats back on a winning track.

The 1950s would usher in a number of firsts and renowned moments for football in Leesville. In 1951, Ted Paris became LHS's first athlete to be named "All State" & was signed to play at LSU. While at LSU, Paris would earn 3 varsity letters, playing for Coaches Gayness Tinsley earn 3 varsity letters, playing both on offense & defense for Coaches and Tiger legend Paul Dietzel. At the end of the 1951 season, a local booster club held a banquet for the successful team, which went 8-4 on the year. One of the merchants (Cain Motor Company) was so enamored with Paris' play and accomplishments that they gave him a *Ted Paris* watch that contained "21 jewels"

Ted Paris

In 1951 and 52, the Cats saw their first post season play. In consecutive years, LHS traveled to Oakdale to play in what was called "the Hardwood Bowl." The Bowl was a tournament of sorts, with Oakdale acting as a host. In one year, the Cats played a single game, and in another year, they played two. INo wins were notched, but Leesville went into a post season environment for the first time. The 1952 team recorded 9 wins on the season, with 5 losses.

Pat Riser was hired as head coach in 1952 and lead the Cats to a number of successful years. Riser's team just missed a playoff spot, going 7-3 in 1954. 1953 was a banner year for the Cats as a 14-year losing streak to DeRidder was broken. A number of the stars from the mid-50s included James Coburn, George Fisher, Jerry Skinner, Harles Smart, Edwin Smart, Jerry Gregg, Bucky Tuminello, Wallace McRae, TL Berry, Dick Berry, Kenneth Magee, Lynn McClain and Julien Stevens, Jr. Coburn was a 1,000-yard rusher in 1954 and played for a year on LSU's freshman team.

Coach Pat Riser

The late 50s were led by Coach Dalton Faircloth who had some success and near misses in terms of making the post season. Faircloth's 1958 squad went 9-2 and were led by LHS's second-ever All State performer, Robert Pynes, Sr. Pynes also was a signee of LSU. Johnny Hall, John Simonelli, Doug Marshall, Sam Piranio, Joe Scogin, Chris Bagents, Billy Lewis, and John Terry were some of the stars from these years. At the conclusion of the 1959 season, the Cats returned again to Oakdale for an unofficial post season game, this time in the "Lions Club Bowl" against the Oakdale Warriors. The decade ended with the return of Leesville's most famous player to date—Ted Paris. The 1952 LHS grad and LSU letterman accepted the job as Head Coach prior to the start of the 1959 season.

Coach Dalton Faircloth

Robert Pynes, Leesville's fine halfback for the past three years, culminated his great football career by being picked for the Associated Press Double "A" All-State team for 1958. This is indeed an honor for Robert and Leesville High School, since Robert is the first back in the history of Leesville High and the second player from Leesville to ever make the All-State team.

Much expectation and hope go with Robert to L.S.U. next fall where he will continue his football career.

James Coburn   *Sam Piranio*   *Roy Hooker*   *Robert Pynes*

THE 1960's

In 1959, LHS and LSU great Ted Paris returned home to coach his high school alma mater. His tenure as coach turned out just as the townsfolk and fans would have hoped—a venture into success that was unprecedented to that time.

Paris' teams were always competitive, with the first few years teetering in the .500 percent range. By his fourth year, he had built a program that would propel the Cats over the edge and into the high school playoffs. One of the stars of those years was George Smith, a star running back who would gain over 1,000 yards in 1961 and go on to star at Tulane University.

The 1963 team was filled with great players and achieved something none other had done—a district title and a berth in the State Playoffs. Coach Paris' team had great players such as Paul Nicholas, RJ Fertitta, Jack Ashfield, Roy Trahan, Richard Schwartz, Ronald Holsomback, James Well, Billy Salim, John Martinez and Jackie Self.

The first ever playoff game in LHS history was played at Wampus Cat Stadium on Saturday, 23 Nov, 1963. Leesville lost to rival DeRidder a week after beating the Dragons in the season finale. Some controversy had swirled around the fight for the Hooper Trophy in the regular season, as Deridder was accused of playing its second string, anticipating a playoff the ensuing week. DeRidder came into the regular season game with a record of 8-0-1, and upon losing, added a blemish to their season mark, while the Cats moved their record to 9-2.

1963 District Champions   *R. J. Fertita*   *Ronald Holsomback*

The Dragons would get their revenge the following week, beating the Cats 34-19 in front of probably the largest crowd in LHS history. Portable benches were brought in from Fort Polk and placed in the end zones to allow for the overflow crowd. This game was recorded on tape and maintained and has been digitized. It can be viewed on Youtube. In the game, Richard Schwartz threw 2 touchdowns to John Martinez and running back sensation Paul Nicholas scored the other touchdown on a short run. Nicholas gained over 1,000 yards on the season for the Cats.

Sadly, both Martinez and Nicholas would lose their lives in Vietnam, both as Marines, and both in 1967. In 2016, through an initiative by State Representative James Armes (LHS Class of 1969 and Wampus Cat player) Highway 171 in Leesville was re-named after Paul Nicholas

RJ Fertitta from the class of 1964 played for Louisiana College and earned multiple years of All- District, All-Region, and Honorable Mention All-State honors.

Paul Nicholas   *John Martinez*

History has many peculiar intersections and the first LHS playoff game had more than one. The game was actually played on a Saturday, because US President John F. Kennedy had been assassinated on Friday, November 22 and the contest was delayed. Further, on the day that LHS's loss was reported in the local media, the first Vernon Lions' State football Championship was being reported. The articles appeared next to each other in the Leesville Leader. Coach Foster Thomas' Lions would win 3 state championships during his time at Vernon. Carl Howard was listed as the star of the Lions in 1963. Carl had touchdown runs of 68 and 25 yards for the undefeated Lions in the championship game. The story of the Lions' team is chronicled in its own book "The Heart of the Lions", available on Amazon and via Claitor's Books in Baton Rouge. In the ensuing year (1964), the Cats also made an appearance in the playoffs. Coach Paris' team compiled a 4-4-2 record & were included in the post season. Jimmy Skinner, Billy Salim, Don Jackson, Keith Carver, Dickie Bailies, Roger Causey, Larry Jeane and Dwayne Palmer were some of the stars of the 1964 team. The Cats traveled to Eunice and experienced a first round loss.

Coach Paris' tenure as a player and coach were honored in 2014, when he was installed as a member of the Leesville High School Sports Hall of Fame; his name resides on a bronze colored plaque at the entrance to Leesville High School.

The remainder of the 1960s saw a number of solid teams & Leesville experienced success, but the period ushered in a drought of playoff appearances, yet again. The 1966 4-4-2 Wampus Cat team was in a playoff hunt until the last game of the season and lost a heart breaker to Natchitoches to keep the team at home. The 1968 & 69 teams were also "near misses" and fell out of playoff contention in the last or second to last game of the year. Some of the other stars from the 60s included Doug Goldsby (who played for Northwestern), Jack Ashfield (NSU) and Johnson Driscoll (who played for McNeese).

Coach Foster Thomas

Thad and Dickie Bailes, Ronnie Morrow, Jimmy Funderburk, Wayne Cavanaugh, Jimmy Auvill, Quarterback Donnie Gill, Dennis Karamales, Darwin Davis, Vic Ortiz, Joe Gendron (who played for Tulane) and Bobby Craft.

Pat Garner

George Smith

Vic Ortiz

Jimmy Funderburk

Don Jackson

Donnie Gill

Brown Word

John Driscoll

THE 1970's

The 1970s ushered in a new era of LHS football. The fall of 1970 would see the Cats playing on a truly integrated team. In November of 1969, Vernon High School and Leesville High School were merged into a single school and the parish was integrated, as per Federal mandates. The tumult of those days is a topic for another historical page, but let it suffice to say here that the inclusion of African American athletes forever changed and improved the landscape of Wampus Cat football. The 70s brought no victories over DeRidder and no playoff appearances for the Cats. For the entire decade, the Cats scratched out only two winning seasons (1972 and 1977).

1971 Coaches: Charles Jackson, George Smith, Foster Thomas, Bob Lash, Roland Warren, Richard Schwartz, Douglas Creamer, Head Coach.

Lorenzo Garner

Despite the shortage of wins, LHS football in the 70s was an exciting and intense brand of football. In the early 70s, the Mapu brothers (Jimmy, Raymond, John, and Jackson) roamed the field and sidelines and All District teams for what seemed like years. Lorenzo Garner, in the first class of Vernon-Leesville students to go all four years at Leesville High School, was a star and exciting running back. Garner would be the first African-American athlete to earn "All District" Honors as a Wampus Cat. Vernon coaching legend Foster Thomas worked as an assistant coach for two years, making him the first African American coach at LHS. Thomas would serve many years as Assistant Principal and is credited by many for helping Leesville transition through the turbulent days of integration. He was inducted into the Hall of Fame in 2022. A bone crushing linebacker/offensive lineman named Charlie Hanks played with Garner and was a two-way All District selection in 1972 and was signed by the University of Houston to play at the college level. Some other key players from the early 70s included Jerry Haynes, Joe and Donnie Gilbert, Paul Sliman, Glover Carter, Perry Morrow, JT Buckley and Ronald Fertitta. The coach in the late 60s and early 70s was Guy Barr.

Dennis Driscoll

Doug Creamer was hired as head coach in 1971 and took the Cats to 1 winning season in 3 attempts. Creamer resigned in the late Fall of 1973 & was replaced by Julius "Gerry" Robichaux. In 2 seasons, the Cats were 3-17 under the Cajun coach, & went 0-10 in 1975, losing to DeRidder in a downpour 50-0. Creamer & Robichaux's teams were loaded with talent, but wins were few in the first 5 years of the decade. Julien Stevens III, Sam Fertitta, Hubert Knight, Max Antony, Mike Anderson, the West brothers (Bill and Rick), Dennis Driscoll, Ray Macias, Greg Stracner, Lou Moses, Leo Casearez & Ralph Ortiz were key players and award winners in those days. Anderson, Driscoll, and Bill West were named all district in multiple years, as was Jimmy Mapu.

Sam Fertita

Footnote to the Class of 71: Bo Harris grew up in Leesville, but moved to Shreveport as he was starting high school. Bo was an impactful star in Junior High, playing under CA Hughes and alongside teammates Steve

Bo Harris

Woods, Bimbo West, Mike Karamales, and others. Bo grew early and was a man among boys and everyone was excited for him to get to high school. He DID get to high school, but it was in Shreveport, playing at Captain Shreve under coaching legend Lee Hedges. After making All State as a Defensive End, Bo signed with LSU, where he had a stellar career, playing under famed coach Charlie McClendon and earning All-SEC honors as a Linebacker in 1973. Bo was drafted into the NFL, played for 9 years, and was a starter for the Cincinnati Bengals' in the 1981 Super Bowl. While Bo isn't a graduate of LHS, we claim him as forever a Wampus Cat; he still comes to LHS Homecomings and can be spotted stepping into the woods to hunt turkey with Bimbo every spring.

Like Ted Paris, Richard Schwartz was a star at Leesville & was able to return home to coach the Wampus Cats. The mess he inherited from Robichaux was turned around in 2 years, and the Cats achieved a 6-4 season in 1977, just missing the playoffs. Schwartz assembled a team of former star Wampus Cats and a Vernon Lion to lead the Cats for his 3 year tenure; star running back George Smith, dual threat quarterback Vic Ortiz and Vernon Lion All State quarterback Mike Mallet were assistants for the Cats, as was Rolf Kuhlow, an intense native of Germany who served as defensive coordinator.

Jimmy Mapu

Don Jones from Sterlington replaced Schwartz as head coach after a controversial move by the school board that removed the popular and successful coach. Jones had a brief tenure at LHS, being hired in January of resigning in May of 1979r. Ironically, Jones went on to greatness at other schools, earning over 200 wins as a head coach at Plaquemine, Abbeville, and Woodlawn of Baton Rouge and an induction into the LHSAA Hall of Fame. Ronnie Stephens, the former head coach at Wisner, was hired in the summer of 1979; his two-year tenure saw records of 2-8 (1979) and 4-6 (1980).

Some of the stars of the late 1970s included Terry Holt, Robert Gaines, Tommy Driscoll, Bobby Bordelon, Harles Smart, Bobby Stephens, Robert Freshley, Roland Stallings, Michael Deans, Bruce Payton, Jim Tucker, James Johnson, Curt Mitchell, Mike Liscicki, Steve Morrison, and Mark Smith. Holt (2016) and Gaines (2015) would both be inducted to the LHS Sports Hall of Fame; Holt signed to play college ball the USL (now ULL) and Gaines signed with McNeese and both were track All Americans at LHS. 1980 graduate Matt Oliver played collegiately at West Point and Tony Jones played for Glendale Community College.

Richard Schwartz & Terry Holt

Schwartz at Holt's Hall of Fame Induction

Coaches Schwartz & Kuhlow and Bruce Payton

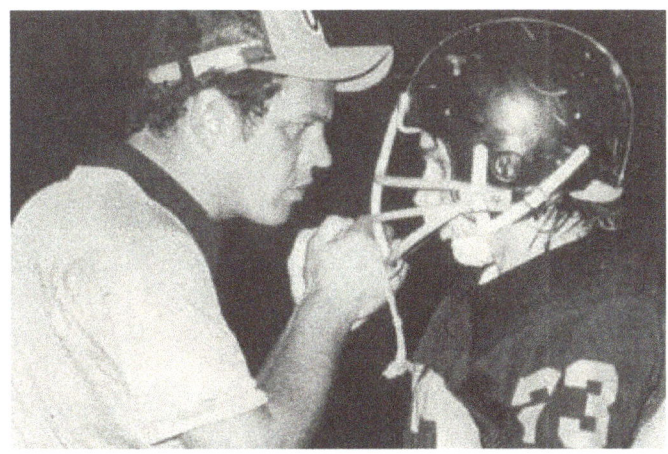

Coach Rolf Kuhlow & Mark Smith

Roland Stallings

Robert Gaines

THE BIG 1980's

The decade of the 80s produced big and new things for Wampus Cat football. In the second game of the year in 1980, the Cats broke a 10-year losing streak to DeRidder. On a hot night in DeRidder, future LSU signee Oscar Joiner would return a punt 88 yards and dash 77 yards for another touchdown to lead the Cats out of the Hooper Trophy desert. The game was a big enough deal that Superintendent of Schools C. Creighton Owen allowed LHS Principal H. Lynn Russell to close the school the ensuing Monday. 1981 graduate Moe Pointer would become a letterman at Southern University and earn a tryout in the Canadian Football League.

The spring of 1981 was a turning point for LHS football. The decade of the 80s would be an inverted image of the 70s in many ways, with winning becoming the rule and losing the exception. Jerry Foshee was hired after Ronnie Stephens was relieved in May of 1981. Foshee turned the tide quickly and enjoyed two winning seasons. The Cats went 13-7 in his two years and established themselves as a contender in AAA football in Louisiana. In his junior campaign, Oscar Joiner averaged over 12 yards a carry and pushed himself on to the national stage of recruiting as a prized running back.

Coah Jerry Foshee

Also during Foshee's tenure was a controversy involving the Lake Charles press corps tinkering with All District selections and nominations voted on by coaches in order to justify their own nominations of a player from Jennings. Wampus Cat Melvin Maxwell was robbed of an award that probably would have catapulted him to "All State" status; Foshee was angered to the degree that he published letters to the editors of a number of papers in Louisiana, calling out the sportswriters for shenanigans. Other star players for Foshee were Robert Pynes, Jr., TJ Moore, Pat Mahoney, James Walters, Richard Scott, Maxwell, Joiner, Jimbo Shapkoff, Kevin West, David Bonner, and David Deans. Shapkoff signed to play at the collegiate level with Delta State University.

Jerry Foshee retired from coaching in the Spring of 83 and was replaced by Jack Andre. The first golden era of Wampus Cat football began when Andre accepted the post. Coach Andre assembled a team of coaches that would assist in some of the finest seasons in school history. Names like Tom Neubert, James Williams, Rick Wilson, Hub Jordan, Roger Causey, and Danny Smith were added to the coaching roles and they would all have lasting impacts for the school. The 1983 season saw LHS return to the playoffs for the first time since 1964.

History always has a context & this is important to note: For many years, the Louisiana High School Athletic Association post season was a scarce event. Until the late 1990s, playoff appearances were rare. The first two or sometimes only the first place team in a district would advance to the post season. The Cats had many winning seasons where in which they didn't get into any official post season simply because they weren't first or second in their district. Since the late 1990s with a power ranking system, the playoffs are still important, but much less scarce.

In Andre's first year, the Cats went 8-3 and tied for first in the district. On a momentous November day in 1983, the Wampus Cats won their first-ever post season game against Abbeville The team was led by Percy Burns, Sam Hoecker, Al Capello, Mark Clay, Odell Miller, Dexter

Dexter Gatewood, Steve Gunn, Chris Robertson and a host other Cats who reached a pinnacle unmatched by any others since football began in Leesville.

The 1984 season took a near repeat path, with the Cats tying for the district and making it to the second round of the post season. The first round of the playoffs was a bye, so the Cats had a week to prepare for the second round. True fans will remember the Rayne Wolves ending the Wampus Cat playoff run by pulling off two "fumble-ruskie" plays to stun the favored Cats on the 16th of November. Andre's team in 84 had similar & familiar names, including the standouts Hoecker and Gunn, both of whom signed to play at the collegiate level. The year also resulted in staggering offensive statistics from the ground game, with two athletes, Charles Buckley and Jeff Steele both breaking the 1,000-yard barrier. Other stars from the year included Lowell Green, Tony Phillips, Jimmy Chamberlain, Craig Pierce, Bo Cryer, Al Capello, Arnold McPherson, and Tom Crosby. Buckley and Gunn were both named First Team All State by the Louisiana Sports Writers Association.

In the early/mid 1980s, the Vernon Parish School Board and a group of citizens decided to get behind football in a new and useful way. Resources were provided from both the public and private sector and the LHS Fieldhouse was built adjacent to the Wampus Cat gymnasium and across the street from the Stadium. The "Wampus Cat" Club was reformed after several years of dormancy; some years later, the club would morph into its current state of "The Gridiron Club." Prior to the construction of the fieldhouse, the Cats dressed underneath the stadium in make-shift dressing rooms and space-constrained workout facilities.

Mark Smith & Steve Morrison

Robert Pynes

Oscar Joiner

Melvin "Muppet" Maxwell

1982 Team

Steve Gunn

1983 Coachimg Staff

1985 was a landmark year for the Cats. Leesville won the district again, and they advanced to the quarterfinals of the LHSAA playoffs. Future LHS Sports Hall of Famer Eddie Fuller attended Leesville for a single year—his senior year—but it was a momentous year. Fuller gained over 1,800 yards on the ground and joined with Rayford Clayton to give LHS its second, consecutive year of a 1,000-yard duo in the backfield. The Cats defeated West Monroe in the first round and Huntington in the second round of the playoffs, before losing to St. Martinville in what many remember as the "fog bowl" in the quarterfinals. Roger Anderson, Earl Wallace, Mike Smith, Raymond Smoot, Nick Gatewood, Clayton, James Adams, Robert Gonzales, Dickie Fetting, Vince Fuller, and Jeff Steele were standouts on the season. Eddie Fuller went on to star at LSU, and was drafted to play in the NFL for the Buffalo Bills. Of note: the selfless Steele moved from being a standout, high profile running back to the defensive backfield. Coach Andre was named District Coach of the Year.

Success continued in 1986 & 87. In 86, the Cats won the district outright & advanced to the quarterfinals, losing to Ruston at home on the Friday after Thanksgiving. Coach Andre's team was filled with stars and intense competitors. Brian Estep & Robert Jenkins were named First Team All State; Estep signed a National Letter of Intent (NLI) to play with Tulane & Jenkins signed with Grambling. Other key players on the 86 team included Dennis Mitchell, Teddy Berry, Clint Batteford, Vince Fuller, Jeff Mitcham, Mike Smith, Warren Estey, Stacy Cooper, Demetrius Payton. Tony Rush, Chuck Abrams, Cliff Buckner, and Sean Mayfield. In February of 1987, Coach Jack Andre resigned and reclaimed his former position at Patterson High School. Brownie Parmeley was hired to replace Andre.

In 1987, the Cats achieved their highest win total to date, finishing the season at 11-2, again advancing the state quarterfinals. The Cats won the district and slashed through the playoffs, again falling to Ruston in the quarterfinals, only this time in Lincoln

Eddie Fuller

1983 Playoff Team

Parish, and not at Wampus Cat Stadium. The "program" of Wampus Cat football had become strong, achieving seven straight winning seasons. The 87 season saw two athletes sign with LSU (Vincent Fuller and Raymond Smoot), one with Northwestern State (John Mawae) and one with Northeast Louisiana (Andy Belamy). Other stars of the team included Joe Williams, Stan Watley, Wayne Martin, Andre Page, Jason Guintini. It should also be noted that enrollment at LHS in those days was heading towards a high point of 1,200 students; Fort Polk had its largest contingent of soldiers and most families in those days chose to attend Leesville when the Army brought them to Polk. These high numbers would eventually drive Leesville to be classified at the 5A level, which changed the landscape of competition.

1985 Team

Kevin Mawae

1988 and 89 saw the Cats begin to take a step backwards. In 88, Parmee's team finished at 5-5 & the 89 team finished 4-6. Stars of the years included All State performers Kevin Mawae (G) & Chip Clark (P). Other stars included Corey Thompkins, Erwin Brown, Buck Lewis, Bobby Smith and Ellis Garner. Mawae would go on t a 4-year letterman at LSU, then spend 17 years in the NFL, playing for Seattle, the New York Jets and the Tennessee. Kevin would later be named to the LHSAA Hall of Fame, the Louisiana Sports Hall of Fame, the Pro Football Hall of Fame, and was also the first person inducted into the Leesville High School Sports Hall of Fame (2012).

The 1980s saw many triumphs. The Wampus Cats record for the decade was an astounding 77-34; the team participated in and saw 7 wins in the post season and made LHSAA Quarterfinals on 3 consecutive occasions. Most prominently, the Cats began a culture of winning that continues to this day. The players and coaches deserve much credit for the accomplishments in this era.

THE 1990's: CHANGING LANDSCAPE AND A NIGHT AT THE DOME

Coach Danny Smith

Mark Mawae

The decade began with a hope for a return to the glory days of the mid-80s, but the 1990 season didn't quite work out that way. Jack Andre was hired for a second time to be the head coach but results were markedly different this time around. The Cats finished with a 3-7 record in Andre's fifth year as the Cat's coach. Ray Mason, Willie Williams, John Brown, Cornelius Jones, Anthony Borner, Robert Nunez, Tyron Smith, Jeff Falifea, Ellis Garner, and Ronnie Snap were key players for the Cats in this season. Andre's second tour at Leesville was uneventful, other than an important shut out win against DeRidder and retention of the Hooper Trophy.

In 1991, long time assistant Danny Smith was hired as the coach for the Wampus Cats. Sadly, things got worse for the Cats. Leesville went 0-10 for the season. This was the only the second time since 1929 that the Cats had a winless season, the other being in 1975. Unlike 1975, when the School Board gave up on the head coach, leadership decided to stick with Smith, and it proved to be a wise decision. Kavika Pittman was a genuine star in the 1991 season, earning All District MVP and Honorable Mention All-State honors. Pittman would sign with McNeese, have a stellar career and go on to a 9-year career in the NFL. Other key players on the team were Tyrone Smith, Ronnie Snapp, Heggie Smith, Rodney Gardner, Antoine Shaw, Derrick Smart and Ellis Gardner.

An important point about the 91 season was the LHSAA forcing LHS to move up to play at the 5A level. In those days, the LHSAA computed classification size by using a two year average of enrollment. In the ensuing year, LHS's population decreased significantly as the 5th Infantry Division was moved out of Fort Polk and the force size was cut by roughly half.

In 1992, the cats went 2-7 and 0-4 in their 5A district. On the upside, Leesville won the DeRidder game, claiming the Hooper Trophy on the 30th anniversary of the establishment of the award. Of note during the year was the leadership at Fort Polk intervening on behalf of LHS by leading a party down to the LHSAA Headquarters to explain the complexities and error-riddled way that classification methods

were hurting schools in military communities. Garrison Fort Polk Garrison Commander Colonel Tom Tucker flew to Baton Rouge with LHS LHS Principal Billy Crawford and appealed to the Association to change rules, which allowed Leesville to re-classify back to 4A. in 1992 key Wampus Cat players included Anthony Gill, Mike Fuller, Derrick Smart, Tyrone Simms and future LHS Principal Mark Mawae.

In 1993, the Cats achieved a 6-4 record in the regular season and finished in a three-way tie for the district title. Due to tie-breaker rules, LHS won the district. In the playoffs, Leesville defeated Pineville 39-7 in the first round. Sophomore sensation Cecil Collins ran for 221 yards on 19 carries to a sold-out Wampus Cat Stadium.

Leesville bowed out in the second round to the Abbeville Wildcats but the stage was being set for real excitement in the next two years. Other key players for the year were Andre Middlebrooks, Andre Mageo, Matt Morrow, Willie McNutt, Alton Harris, C-Micah Wilson, Tyrone Sims, Lawrence Powell, Mark Mawae, Jason Collions, Clinton King, Joe Rosen, and Anthony Ford. LHS was re-classified to 4A.

For 1994, the season record was 7-3 and LHS tied for champions of the District. The black and gold finished the year ranked # 10 in the Louisiana Sports Writer's Association poll. Cecil Collins finished his second year rushing for over, 1,000 yards and was on the All State team for the second year. In the playoffs, the Cats beat Haughton in the first round and Collins recorded 230 yards on the ground. Wossman eliminated the Wampus Cats in the second round. Other stars for the season were Andrew Mageo, Matt Morrow, Antountel Goza, Shermaine Jones, Anthony Ford, Dennis Fetting, Matt Glasper, Virgil Ruffin, Andre Middlebrooks.

1995 was a year for the record books. The Wampus Cats would go 13-2 on the year and make their first and still the only appearance in the State Championship game. Coach Danny Smith's Cats ran through the first four rounds of the playoffs with little trouble, trouncing Opelousas, Carroll, DeRidder, and Breaux Bridge. Salmen of Slidell defeated the Wampus Cats soundly in the State title game, but the year was a great success. Cecil Collins was named "Mr. Football" for the year in Louisiana and finished his career with

Greg Rone

Cecil Collins & Denni Fetting

a 3,000 yard senior year and almost 8,000 yards for his career as a Cat. Cecil would sign a scholarship with LSU and would go on to burn brightly, but briefly in the SEC. Collins had a short time at McNeese and was drafted by the NFL's Miami Dolphins. Collins stands to this day as the greatest, most successful, and most decorated running back in Wampus Cat history. Cecil remains in the top 5 all-time of running backs in the State of Louisiana.

But, Mr. Collins was not alone in the 1995 campaign. He was joined on the All-State team by Greg Rone, a bruising, two-way athlete who earned his All-State honors as a linebacker. Dennis Fetting also earned All-State accolades as an offensive lineman. Shermaine Jones, Robert Carter, Sig Milerski, and Ced Clemons were some of the other key players on the 95's squad. Clemons would go on to play at Tulane as a 3-year letterman and later return to LHS as a football and track coach.

Odd intersections of history occurred in the 1995 season. The Cats were able to revenge the 1963 loss to the DeRidder Dragons in the playoffs. And on the night of the State Championship game, the last remaining member of the first class of Wampus Cats —Sam Fertitta—passed away at his home in Leesville.

Keith Smith

In the year after the state title run, the Cats fell off, but still had a winning season and made the playoffs. The senior laden team of the previous year left quite a void, but Danny Smith's Cats kept winning. Key players in 1996 were Adrian Burns, Xavier Burrell, Mike Lewis, Wes Bailey, Greg Manns, and LeMarcus Thurman. Burrell would finish his career with over 2,000 yards on the ground and remains in the top 10 all-time of Wampus Cat running backs; Xavier earned two varsity letters at Louisville.

In 1997 and 1998, the Wampus Cats took a significant dip in terms of winning and losing. Back to back 3-7 seasons would end the career of Danny Smith as a Wampus Cat head coach. The departure of Danny Smith would be a landmark event, as he had been on staff since 1982. For 97's season, key players were Ronnie Robinson, Robert Carter, Andre Thurman, Dwayne Thibodeaux and Derek Jones. Thurman had over 100 tackles on the season, and Carter had 90. Quarterback Dustin Smith passed for over 1400 yards and 11 touchdowns.

In 1998, Keith Smith earned All-State honors and was signed by McNeese. Smith would become an All-Conference player for the blue and gold in Lake Charles and would be drafted into the NFL and play for eight years. Demond and Deshun McNeely were stars and both were signed by Northwestern. Other key players were Dwayne Thibodeaux, Sam Cobb, Sam Scott, and Lemond Leasure. Smith was the team's leading tackler with 125 on the season. Deshun McNeely had over 1,300 yards rushing in 1998; he finished his career in black and gold with over 2,500 yards on the ground.

In 1999, former coach Jerry Foshee came out of retirement for a single year. The team went 4-7 and made the playoffs, where they Cats were defeated in the first round. Some key players in 1999 included Lamond Leasure, Justin Brown, William Dudley, Kenny Jones, James White and Mark Dowden.

2000's

The 21st Century started with excitement for the black and gold. Coach Kevin Magee was hired in 2000 and took the Cats through some tumultuous and exciting times. The 2000 season saw a jaw dropping playoff run for the team from Leesville.

Some fans and coaches disparage the "Power Rankings" system that allows for and creates a playoff system wherein which most teams over .500 gain entry. In brief, a 32 team, post season tournament is created and usually, a handful of 5-5, 4-6 and even 3-7 teams gain entry, based on a number of variables. In 2000, the Cats finished their inaugural season under Coach Magee with a 4-6 record and were seeded 28th in the group of 32. Teams with losing records tipically don't last very long in the post season, if at all, in the post season. Coach Magee's Cats won not one, but TWO playoff games, upsetting a #5 and a #12 seed, en route to a quarterfinal berth that was played at Wampus Cat Stadium on a cold night in November. LHS did fall to Assumption and future NFL star Brandon Jacobs, but their wins at Walker and Woodlawn of Baton Rouge were awe-inspiring. and remain the stuff of legend.

Justin Brown

All Stater Justin Brown was a multi-purpose threat for the Cats and signed a National Letter of Intent to play for Northwestern State University. Brown earned All-District honors on offense, defense and as a kick returner. Other stars on the team were Kenny Hughes (grandson of 40s star and Junior High coaching legend CA Hughes), Chris O'Bryan, Tommy Edwards, Cody McKenzie, Darnell Thompkins, Kenny Jones, Lorenzo Garner (son of 73 graduate and star running back Lorenzo Garner, Sr), Roderick Lawhorn and, Martin Driscoll (son of 70 graduate and McNeese signee John Driscoll).

The Cats made the post season again in 2001, but this time, the State's elite were waiting on them. Neville ended the post season journey quickly and LHS finished 5-6 on the year. On the 2001 squad were a number of players who would go on to compete at the next level, including most prominently Keith (Alleger) Zinger. Keith would be a two time All-State tight end, making him only the second athlete (with Cecil Collins) to earn All-State honors more than once. Quarterback Martin Driscoll went on to play for Nicholls State University. Other key players in the 2001 season were Cody McKenzie, Chris Nash,

Coach Kevin Magee

Martin Driscoll

Keith Zinger

2000 State Quarterfinalists

Dante Williamson, Roderick Lawhorn, Gilbert Franca, Josh Chaney, Darnell Thompson, Jeremy Burkes, Derek Skidmore, Casey Vinson, Marcus Johnson and Michael Toney.

The 2002 team season saw the Cats achieve a winning record & make another trip to the post season. The season saw a 1st round exit, this time at the hands perennial power John Curtis. Keith Zinger continued to gain State and national acclaim as he was named All-State for the second year; Keith had a long career at LSU, playing first for Coach Nick Saban and then Coach Les Miles. Zinger was one of only two players to play on both national championship squads (2003 and 2007). Chris White, Cordell Upshaw, Josh Quayhagen, Gilbert Franca, Andy Hughes, Chris Nash, James Burkes, Michael Toney, Michael Cools, and Justin Goins were other standouts for the Wampus Cats in the 2002 season.

History seemed to repeat itself in 2003, with the Cats finishing 4-6, only this time not making the playoffs. Linebacker Josh Quayhagen was an inadvertent participant in a still fresh Wampus Cat legend. As the story goes, Josh was holding his right forearm on the sideline, wincing in pain during a timeout and one of his coaches "encouraged" him to stop complaining about pain & get back in the game. The next day, Josh was discovered to have a broken forearm, but played much of the game with the badly broken bone. Key players on the 2003 squad included Quayhagen, Wes

Josh Quayhagen

Wes Tunuufi Sauvao

Michael Ford

Trevante Stallworth

Harvey, Justin Harris, Jared James, Andy Hughes, Danny Williamson, Quintiza Scott, Marcus Williams, Bernardo Henry, Tommy Neubert. Quayhagen would be the team's leading tackler on the season and go on to earn a varsity letter at McNeese.

In 2004, Magee's Cats pulled of a 9-1 regular season, winning the district outright and drumming DeRidder 46-7 at Cecil Doyle field. Senior quarterback and 3-year starter Justin Goins had a strong year under center, throwing for nearly 900 yards & 11 touchdowns; Edwin Ivory cracked the 1,000 yard barrier for the Cats. The Cats went out in the first round of the playoffs against the Opelousas Tigers. Stars for the team included Matt Morrison, Kevin McCavey, Bobby Cummings, Casey Vinson, Wes Tunuufi Sauvao, Tommy Neubert, Larry Frank, Daryl Joiner, Mike Nelson, Jacoby Kaima, and Tyler Gill. Sauvao would go on to a collegiate career at the University of Central Florida. Josh Andrews played at the collegiate level for the University of Louisiana-Monroe.

Disruptions from Hurricanes Rita and Katrina put the 2005 season in turmoil. The annual fete with DeRidder was canceled because of the impact of Rita. On the year, LHS finished 3-6 and Coach Magee resigned to take a position elsewhere at the end of the season. Justin Ford, Bernardo Henry, Frank Larry, Wes Bouves, future LSU letterman David Detz, and Brandon Sharper were some of the top Wampus Cats during the season. No playoff appearance was earned during the 2005 year.

Parish coaching icon Johnny Cryer was Leesville's coach for a single year, 2006. Coach Cryer had seen many levels of success coaching around southwest Louisiana, including prominently in Pickering & Rosepine. In his year at Leesville, the Cats had a winning record, going 6-4 in the regular season & losing in the first round of the State playoffs to Breaux Bridge. Cryer's stars from the 2006 team included his son Josh Cryer, an All-District performer on both sides of the ball, Jacoby Kaiama, Damion Smith, Michael Harris, Cornelius Jackson, Michael Smith, David Detz and a sophomore running back named Michael Ford. In Ford's sophomore season, he would rush for over 1,300 yards and catch the attention of coaches around the country. Cryer would go on to a successful college baseball career at Southeastern Louisiana University.

The 2007 and 2008 seasons were led by Coach Terence Williams. The Cats in these years were explosive on the offensive side of the ball and produced some of the most staggering stats ever recorded (at the time) in Leesville history. Future LSU star Michael Ford was injured for part of 2007 but the Cats compensated well and achieved a district title and a playoff berth. Trevante Stallworth shined during the year as a dual-threat quarterback, rushing for 940 yards and passing for over 1,300, including 10 touchdowns. Some of Stallworth's targets were Allen Muse who caught 54 balls and Dejuan Taylor who caught 40 passes. Defensively, David Detz finished out his great career at LHS as an All-District and All-State honoree. Detz would become a walk-on and letter at LSU and Muse starred for Arkansas State, catching nearly 100 passes in his career and earning All-Conference honors. Adron Hackett earned a sport at NSU as a walk-on, as well. Other stars from the 2007 team included Cole Parker, James Baker, Keyon Henry, Alan Harshaw, Dejan Taylor, Devin Moran, Michael Ramsey, Michael Harris, and Chris Brown.

In 2008, the Cats achieved their first 10-win season since 1995. LHS won the district outright and won their first round playoff game against St Michael The Archangel of Baton Rouge. The Cats lost in the second round to Zachary amidst questionable officiating. The explosiveness from the previous year continued and on fast forward with the healthy return of Michael Ford. On the season, Ford rushed for over 2,900 yards; he put up mind-boggling numbers in single games, rushing for 448 against Tioga---the top single game efforts in Wampus Cat history. Trevante Stallworth threw for over 1,400 yard and tossed 14 touchdowns on the season, finding Mark Demetrius and Levander Liggins as his top targets on the year. Ford and Linebacker Devin Moran both earned All-State honors on the year. A number of Cats would go on to play at the collegiate level. Ford signed with LSU, and had a great career, playing a key role in LSU's national runner up team in 2011 and being drafted into the NFL. Trevante Stallworth signed with Auburn & was a 3-year letterman. Casetti Brown signed to play collegiately at Louisiana Tech.

Levander Liggins   *Coach Davis Feaster*

Other key players were Demetrius O'Bryant, Allen Perry, Rob Tunuufi Sauvao, Devon Brown, Tyler Anders, Michael Maldanado, Terrell Turner, Emanuel Long, Eddie McTear, Chad Parker. Michael Ford was named Offensive MVP and Devin Moran Defensive MVP and Coach Williams was named District Coach of the Year. Tunuufi Sauvao earned a varsity letter at the University of Central Florida. Coach Williams resigned in June of 2009 and David Feaster was hired.

The 2009 season was not a winning season, but it was not a disaster. The Cats finished the regular season at 4-6 and made the playoffs, bowing out in the first round. Feaster knew the talent he inherited and began building a plan for the ensuing year. For 2009 the top players were Je'ron Hamms who signed with ULM and had a great college career in Monroe, earning a free agent contract with Saints. Tremayne Freeman signed with McNeese and later transferred to Northwestern where he earned a letter with the Demons. Other key players were Javal Chancy, Levander Liggins, Allen Perry, Kendrick Mitchell, Tiasham Burnett, Cody Lefort, Michael Dennis, Daniel Winnfield, and Demetrius Atwater. Quarterback Zach Squyres threw for over 2,400 yards and 26 touchdowns on the year.

2010's: THE SECOND DECADE

The second decade of the 2000s saw some of the highest highs in Wampus Cat football history. The decade also had a few low moments, but they were overshadowed by the successes. In his second year as head coach at LHS, David Feaster's team set the scoreboards of local fields on fire. Feaster, known as an audacious offensive genius, brought a brand of aggressive football that fans had been craving. The Bossier native assembled a strong suite of coaches to help him guide the Cats both on and off the field. Long time assistants Robert Causey and Sed Clemons remained with the Cats and Justin Scogin, a former baseball standout began to emerge as an offensive guru under Feaster's mentorship.

The 2010 team put up never-before-seen passing numbers as they piled up 9 wins against only 3 losses. The Cats won the district and first round playoff game and lost in the second round to a formidable

Franklinton team. Junior quarterback Zack Squyres threw for over 2,700 yards. He also tossed 26 touchdowns. His favorite target was Levander Liggins, who caught 57 passes for over 1,300 yards and 11 touchdowns. For his efforts, Liggins would be named first team All-State and would receive a scholarship offer to play at Louisiana Tech, where he lettered for four years. Other offensive targets on the year were Jeval Chancey who caught 31 passes, Clinton Thurman who caught 30, and Diantay Thurman who caught 30 passes. Liggins also nearly cracked the 1,000 yard barrier on the season, reaching 978 on the year.

Other stars in this 2010 season were Jevon Leday, Bobby Mace, Dan Winnfield, Demetrius Atwater, Jacob Chambers, Joe Horlacher, Dylan Gaskill, AJ Green, Cotton Honeycutt, and Logan Morrison. As a footnote: Morrison's selection made him the third member of his household to be named an All-District Center (brother Matt (2003) and father Steve (79 and 80)).

Bobby Mace

Diontay Thurman

After the 2010 season, Feaster took a job at a larger school, & Jimmy Adams was hired as the head coach; the 2011 team went 4-6. In his senior year, Zach Squyers continued to put up impressive passing numbers; the strong armed Leesville native put up 1,800 yards and 11 TDs. Squyers finished his career at LHS with almost 7,000 yards and 75 touchdowns through the air, making him the most prolific passer in LHS history. His favorite target would be Clinton Thurman, who equaled Levander Liggins' single season record of 57 catches.

Some of the stars of the 2011 season included All Stater Clinton Thurman, Diontay Thurman, Adam Woods, Colton Honeycutt, Jeremiah Cross, Jacob Chambers, Derrick Blackshire, Juwan Lewtry, Jamall Harris, Dalton Harville and Mason Delapp. Tight End Adam Woods earned a walk-on spot at Louisiana Tech as a long-snapper.

In 2012 and 2013, the Cats took a significant detour from success. Records of 1-9 and 2-8 were disheartening for the team and the fans. The intensity and fight by the Cats were as it always has been, but wins were few and far between and the Cats went on a 3-year drought from playoff participation. Some key players from these years were Jamal Harral, Jacob Chambers, Roger Luafelemana, Kole Smith, Elbert Marbury, Solomon Cross, Deval Lewis, Logan Kreynbuhl, Moses Tolbert, Elbert Marbury, Kory Jones, and Jonathan Price. Adams tenure ended as head coach in 2012 and Tommy Moore was hired before the 2013 season.

Tommy Moore had a 3-year tenure at Wampus Cat Stadium. He took the Cats to the post season once, after the 2014 season. Leesville went 6-5 on the season and lost to Rayne on the road in the first round of the playoffs. Some of the top players during Moore's three years included Cory McCoy, Garrett Rogers, Kory Jones, Solomon Cross, Davion Clemons, E.J. Ane, Antonio Tharp, Jacob Adams, Dantrell Lewis, Jaelyn Edwards, Tywann Brown, Tucker Wann, and Caden Wheeler. Moore resigned in the summer of 2016, and former LHS Assistant Robert Causey was hired as the 27th coach in Wampus Cat history.

In Causey's first year (2016), the team went 6-4 in the regular season and earned a hard fought playoff win from Beau Chene on the road, giving the Cats their first playoff victory since 2010. The season was full of ups and downs, but a seminal moment comes to mind that should be recorded for

Corey McCoy

the storybooks. In the Homecoming game against Lagrange, the Cats were down 14-0 early in the 4th quarter, and pulled out a dramatic come-from-behind-win, turning the season on a dime. The Cats went on a 3 game winning streak and earned the playoff bid; more importantly, the team bought into Causey's broader game plan. Stars from the 2016 team included: Cory McCoy, who finished his career with over 4,000 yards rushing and signed a National Letter of Intent to play with McNeese State University. McCoy would earn multiple varsity letters and earned All-Conference accolades for the Cowboys. Other key players included: Elijah Mundy, Jaelyn Edwards, Jacob Adams, Daquan Davis, Andrew Croker, and Theron Westerchil.

Coach Justin Scogin

Theron Westerchil

Sabian atu Dre Croker

att Pa inag

Pancake Possee

Noah Allain

D'Ante Gallashaw

Talyn Adams

    The 2017 team took the District outright and compiled a 10-2 record on the season. A single blemish to Rayne in the 4th game of the year and then again to Rayne in the post season were the only losses in an outstanding season. Chris Vargas, a 3-year back up at quarterback took advantage of his single year under center and put up dizzying numbers, tossing for over 2,000 yards and 17 touchdowns. Andrew Croker, a dynamic, multi-talented athlete played both ways and was a fixture in the offensive backfield & as a receiver. Cat fans can attest to the exciting game-breaker who collected 68 receptions during his career at LHS, including 39 in his senior campaign. Nine Wampus Cats would sign National Letters of Intent, including Croker (McNeese), Mackenzie Jackson (Naval Academy), Vargas (Louisiana College), and Kobe Joiner (ULL). Other stars from this team were All-State Linebacker Matt Pajinang, D'Ante Gallashaw, Matthew Anderson, Brett Pope, Michael Ciachelli, Xavier Reyes, Donald Smith, Sabian Matu, Gabe Ellis, Derek Hurt, Montae Lynch, Steven Thomas, Talyn Adams, Jordan Dowden, Demarcus McCord. Coach Causey was named Coach of the Year for the District.

    The 2018 season was one for the ages. The Wampus Cats ran the table in the regular season, winning all 10 games, then won three games in the playoffs, decimating strong teams from Woodlawn and Assumption and winning a heart-stopping come-from-behind game against St. Martinville. At the quarterfinal game, the Wampus Cats went at St. Martinville like prize fighters, trading body and head blows. LHS recovered two second half onside kicks on a rainy night and on the road and pulled out one of the most dramatic wins in the school's history. Leesville made it to the Semi-finals for only the second time in school history and won 13 games for only the second time. The Cats fell to Warren Easton on a rainy night in New Orleans but had more fans in the stands than the home team. Coach Causey's defensive team was led again by Matt Pajinang, and the offense was led on the field by sophomore quarterback Jacob Mount, who, like Vargas, put up eye popping numbers. The offense was dynamic, however, with D'Ante Gallashaw gaining over 1,400 yards on the year, and earning All-District, All CENLA and all SW Louisiana honors. The team was filled with talented athletes and gritty fighters. Of note in this year was the offensive line, nicknamed the "Pancake Posse", and the focal point for giving Mount the time he needed to run Offensive Coordinator Justin Scogin's offense. The line created holes for both D'Ante Gallashaw and his younger brother, Caleb. Three of the starters on the line signed national letters of intent to play at the next level. Starting tackle Matthew Anderson was named First Team All-State and signed with the University of Nebraska. Other notable stars form the team included Montae Lynch, Duwon Tolbert, Brett Pope, Noah Allain, Khrystian Hoffpauir, Peyton Lipps, Caleb Westfall, Ben Ward, Talyn Adams, Nick Green, Darius Allen, Aaron Hunter, Ruben

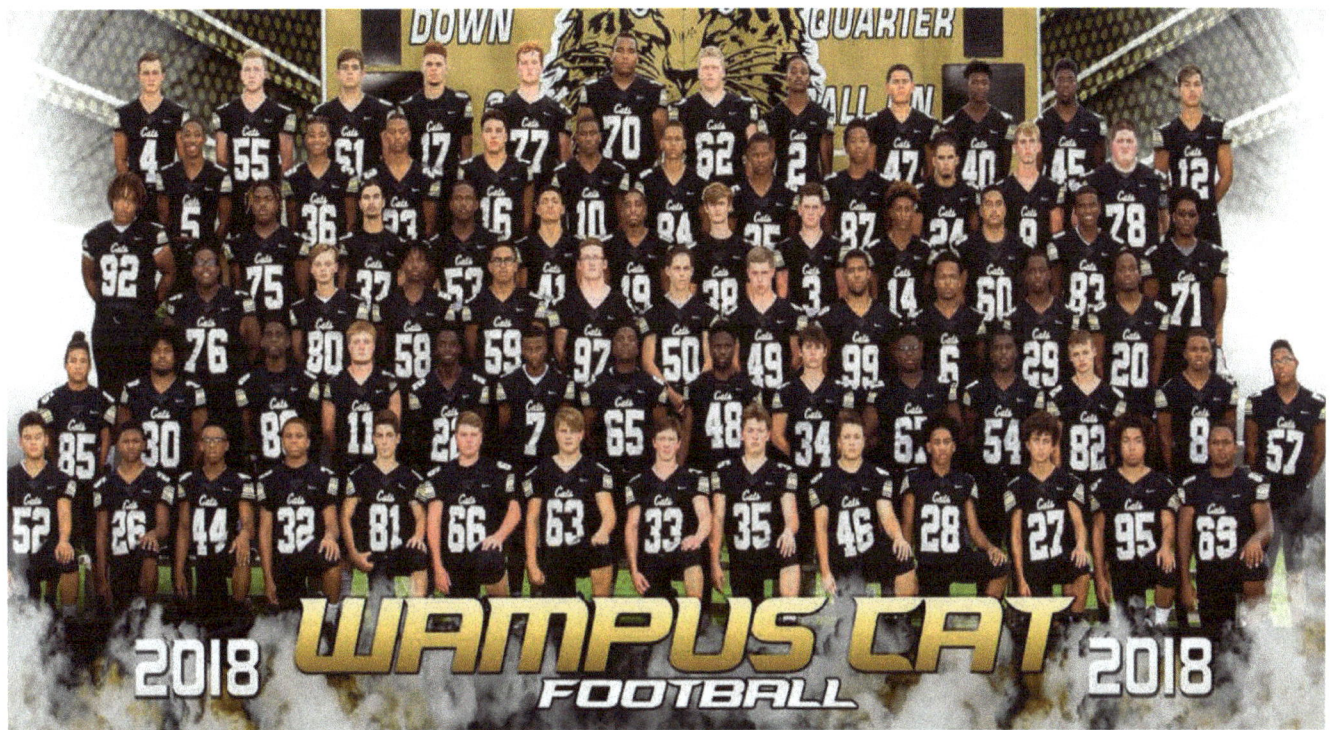

Jeane, Jacob Feliciano, Nigel McCoy, Darius Sawyer, and Efosa Evbuowon. Lynch and Tolbert signed at the collegiate level with Tyler Community College, and Brett Pope signed with Louisiana Tech. Coach Causey was named State and District Coach of the Year.

The 2019 season started with great promise as the Cats jumped out to a 4-0 start, and extended a regular season winning streak to 20 games, going all the way back to the Rayne game in 2017.

Leesville would finish the year 6-4 in the regular season, losing close games to DeRidder and Tioga. In the playoffs, Causey's squad got a big first round win on the road at Pearl River and came home to face the #1 seed, Lakeshore. The second round exit was painful, but the season record of 7-5 was nothing in which to find shame. Efosa Evbuowon signed a National Letter of Intent to play for Lamar University. Stars from the team included Caleb Gallashaw, Darius Sawyer, Noah Allain, Darius Allen, Quan Williams, Jacob Mount, D'Ante Gallashaw. Khrystian Hoffpauir, Steven Winslow, Christian Sage, and Chris Davis. Four straight winning seasons for Causey and playoff wins in 4 years was quite a way to end the decade.

The 2020's

The 2020 season was marred by presence and reactions to the COVID-19 virus and pandemic that swept the nation for the entirety of the year. With spring sports and summer conditioning put on hold as the nation and the state came to grips with how to manage the virus, the Cat's season seemed to be in jeopardy for much of the year. The Louisiana High School Athletic Association (LHSAA) made a hard, controversial but very bold decision by deciding to have the season in August of 2020. The start of the season was delayed by a month, and the Cats began play in early October of 2020.

The season saw many ups and down, as each school, each parish and each district seemingly had a different set of challenges related to the virus. The first game was initially scheduled against long time foe Jennings, but the Bulldogs from Jeff Davis Parish canceled the game on Monday of the playing week because of too many players lost to the virus. Neville of Monroe faced a similar fate when their week 1 opponent was forced to cancel. On Tuesday of the game week, the coaches discovered the mutual conundrum and decided to suit up and play in Ouachita Parish. Neville took the win, 29-7, but the season was underway. Of note about the game: The son of former LHS quarterback Clint Batteford was the signal caller for the Neville Tigers. Clint made time for an interview with the KJAE radio crew and relayed his fond memories of playing for the black and gold of Leesville. Batteford played in the Jack Andre era and was part of some extraordinary teams.

Clint Batteford

The remainder of the season was an up and down affair. The annual game with DeRidder was cancelled due to COVID, delaying the much anticipated 100th meeting between the schools. The Homecoming game was canceled, as well, at 3:00 PM on game day, as Northwood of Shreveport found out on the way to Leesville that their team had been exposed to COVID and were thus forced to turn around on I-49 and go home. Leesville was able to reschedule the game with Jennings and wound up, during one week of strange cancellations, to find a game with a team from East Texas (Elysian Fields).

Frank Ford   Lane Self   Jeff Keys

LHS would finish the season in 2nd place in the district and Coach Causey's Cats made the playoffs for the fifth consecutive season. Leesville won a first-round playoff game against Northwood, but lost in the second round in a wild, overtime affair with Minden. The team from Webster Parish tied the Cats on the last play of regulation and would prevail in a single overtime stanza. Of note during the game was the loss of star running back Caleb Gallashaw, who was kept out by COVID guidelines. It turned out later that Gallashaw was not sick and never had symptoms, but state guidelines ruled the day, which no doubt effected the outcome of the game. A litany of Cat players pulled in All District honors for the year. Gallashaw, Khrystian Hoffpauir, 3-year signal caller Jacob Mount, and Jeff Keys were key players for the Cat offense in the 2020 campaign. On defense, some of the stars included Deshawn Grooms, Frank Ford and Kehmari Pruitt.

The real bottom line on the season was that the Cats KEPT winning and that football happened, despite of the presence of virus.

2021: The 2021 season took on more of a routine feel for the Wampus Cats. Coach Causey's team finished the season with an 8-3 record (only 9 regular season games scheduled) and would advance to the second round of the playoffs. The season began with a big win over Jennings and culminated with the Cat's 4th district title in six years. A close loss to Pineville and a lopsided setback to Captain Shreve (at Independence Stadium in Shreveport) were the only negatives in the LHS ledger in the regular season. The Cats won a decisive first round victory over Assumption and lost to eventual State Champions Westgate 16-7 in the regional round of the playoffs.

Caleb Gallashaw

Parker Maks

Mustafaa Dhiia

About halfway through the year, Leesville and DeRidder faced off for the 100th time in the rivalry. Caleb Gallashaw rushed for over 230 yards and scored six touchdowns (4 on the ground, 2 in the air) as the Dragons and Cats fought valiantly for the Hooper Trophy. Leesville took a close victory and brought home the Hooper Trophy for the year.

Other big moments on the year included Coach Causey becoming the winningest coach in LHS History. After registering an 8-3 on the season (7-2 regular season, 1-1 playoffs), Causey had accumulated 50 wins as head man for the Cats. Danny Smith is 2nd all time with 44 wins and Jack Andre is 3rd. Sadly, Coach Andre passed away in the spring of 2021, but his legacy of winning and commitment to excellence remains with the Wampus Cats, to this day.

Caleb Gallashaw finished his career in black and gold as the third, all time leader in rushing yards with 4,204 yards and second all-time in receptions with 105 catches. Caden Bealer and Frank Ford eclipsed the 100-tackle barrier for the season and JaShawn Mayberry was named Defensive MVP of the district.

Key players on the year for Leesville were Gallashaw, Parker Maks, Lane Self, Kemhari Pruitt, Davion Grubb, Caden Bealer, Frank Ford, JaShawn Mayberry and Caden Catron.

2022---7th Visit to the Quarterfinals

The 2022 season was one for the record-books, in a lot of ways. The Wampus Cats achieved their 7th consecutive playoff appearance and notched wins in the post season for the 7th year, as well. The Wampus Cats advanced to the LHSAA State Quarterfinals for the 7th time in school history---a tremendous accomplishment for the program.

The wins and the co-district championship were not expected by all as the season started. Coach Robert Causey's team lost 26 seniors and 16 starters after the 2021 season and had a significant turnover in the coaching staff. Gone from the sideline was long-time offensive guru Justin Scogin who took a head coaching job at Airline High School in Bossier City. A number of other assistants also went in other directions and the bulk of the staff was brand new as the summer and fall practices approached. Replacing Scogin on the sideline as the Offensive Coordinator was an experienced hand, Winnfield native Chad Harkins. Coach Harkins brought a 30+ year coaching resume to the job and the Cat offense took up where it left off in previous years---putting up impressive numbers in a fast-paced system not seen in Leesville for many years.

The Wampus Cats achieved an 8-2 record in the regular season, finishing the year as co-district champions with Eunice. Big wins over perennial powers Iowa, Jennings and Jena got the year off on the right foot.

Leesville took the Hooper Trophy yet again from rival DeRidder. 2022 marked the 60th Anniversary of the establishment of the Trophy. Prior to the game between LHS and DeRidder, a special ceremony was held at midfield to commemorate the significance of the trophy. Co-Author of "History of the Hooper Trophy" book and Hooper Family nephew, Samuel Lewis, former Leesville player (and All-District Quarterback) Louis Magee and former DHS player and son of Dragon Coaching Legend Cecil Doyle (David Doyle) were honored as the big game and history of the trophy were commemorated.

At this printing, the Dragons lead the all time series between the schools 54-43-4 and the Cats hold the advantage in Hooper Trophy contests 33-24-1. A full rundown of the Hooper Series appears later in this book.

L-R: Samuel Staples Lewis, David Doyle, Louis Magee
Hooper Trophy 60th Anniversary Commemoration

Xavier Ford

The 2022 season saw the continuance of high powered offense and fundamentally sound and physical defense for the black and gold. Sophomore running back Xavier Ford rushed for 2,581 yard and 34 touchdowns for the season. Ford became only the third athlete in LHS history to surpass the 2,000 yard barrier in rushing yards for the season; he joined his uncle, Michael Ford (2008) and Cecil Collins (1994 and 1995) in this elite club. Quarterback Parker Maks threw for over 1,000 yards and rushed for almost 700 yards in his senior campaign and finished his career as the fourth leading passer in LHS history. A key to the dizzying numbers put up on the ground and in the air was a consistent and strong offensive line. Daniel Cheatam, Terry Evans, and Andrew Lewis, Jacob Smith and Harvey Denni opened holes all year long for the Cat offense.

Defensively, the Cats were dominant in nearly every game. Linebacker Frank Ford was one of the top 2 tacklers on the team for the third consecutive year. Safety Stefan James led the team in tackles and interceptions. JaSahwn Mabry, Christian Henderson and Simon Allain anchored the hard-hitting defense. Other key players for the Cats in the 2022 season were H-Back Carter Causey, receivers Marshawn Graham and Izaiah Farley and defensive backs Evan Combs, Derrick Beebee and Jeremiah Lee.

Derrick Beebee, Stefan James, Simon Allain

Marshawn Graham

Evan Combs

TEAM RECORDS

The Totals

Though the Cats have never won a State title, the team is a winner, just like the city & parish are winners. For every game that is accounted for, the Cats have won 489, lost 456, tied 21. In post season games, the Cats are 28 and 33.

In time, I hope to fill the holes of unaccounted for and lost seasons and maybe provide a complete picture. What I have provided to date is anything and everything that is available. There are few things more exciting than a Friday night at Wampus Cat stadium and there isn't a town or a community anywhere that loves its team more than Leesville.

True fans hope for a state championship, and the truest fans will continue to flock to the old school on the hill. LHS has accomplished many things, recorded many wins, graduated many stars, many college players, produced a fair share of NFL players and a member of the Pro Football Hall of Fame. It has been good.

Once a Wampus Cat, ALWAYS a Wampus Cat. The story will continue!

Season (Fall)	Wins	Losses	Ties	vs DeRidder	Head Coach	District Champ	PLAYOFF GAMES
2022	10	3		Leesville 42, DeRidder 16, at LHS	Robert Causey	Yes	Yes, won first round vs Pearl River; won second round at Jennings lost uarterffinal to owa
2021	8	3		Leesville 49, DeRidder 41, at LHS	Robert Causey	Yes	Yes. Won first round vs Assumption. Lost 2nd round to Westgate
2020	5	4		No DeRidder Game;--COVID	Robert Causey	No	Yes. Won first round vs Northwood. Lost second round vs. Minden
2019	7	5		DeRidder 30, Leesville 28; at DHS	Robert Causey	No	Yes. Won first round at Pearl River; lost second round to Lake Shore
2018	13	1		Leesville 26, DeRidder 7; at LHS, Homecoming	Robert Causey	Yes	Yes. State Semi Finalists. First round defeated Woodlawn; 2nd round defeated Assumption; quarterfinals defeated St. Martinville; lost Semi-Finals to Warren Easton.
2017	10	2		Leesville 27, Deridder 0; at DHS	Robert Causey	Yes	Yes. Won first round, lost second round to Rayne

Post Season Win	Post Season Loss	Notes
2	1	Cats advanced to Quarterfinals. Xavier Ford rushed for 2,581 yards. All Dist (Dist): Xavier Ford (RB); Terry Evans (OL) Parker Lowe (K); Parker Maks (ATH); Christian Henderson (DL), Jayshawn Mabary-Liles (DL), Frank Ford (LB), Stefon James (DB). Offensive MVP; Xavier Ford. Defensive MVP Jayshawn Mabary-Liles 2nd year in a row. Coach Causey picks up 60th win as head coach
1	1	Caleb Gallashaw signs with Bellhaven Academy. All Dist: FIRST TEAM OFFENSE: QB Parker Maks; RB Caleb Gallashaw; WR Daveion Grubbs; WR Kehmari Pruitt; TE Layne Self; OL Mason Fitzgerald; OL Derrion Beebe; DEFENSE: DL JayShawn Mabry; LB Caden Bealer; LB Frank Ford ; DB DJ Beebe. SECOND TEAM: Offense; WR Aj Bush; OL Mason Champan; OL Terry Evans; K Caden Catron; Defense: DL Jaymeion Henderson; LB Nathan Mawae; DB Mustafaa Dhiaa; Flex Stefan James; Defensive MVP: JayShawn Mabry; Coach of the Year: Robbie Causey
1	1	Jeff Keys signs with LaGrange College (GA). Deshawn Grooms signs with Louisiana College. 8 regular season games were scheduled 7 were played. Several games were scheduled in mid week because of teams that dropped out due to COVID. First game against at a Texas team (Elysian Fields) in many years. Team finished 4-3 in regular season, and 1-1 in playoffs. All Dist: Caleb Gallashaw, RB; Khrystian Hoffpauir, WR; Braeden Bradley, TE; Mason Fitzgerald, OL; Christian Sage, DL; Layne Self, RB' AJ Bush, WR; Jacob Mount, QB; Jeff Keys, OL' Dante Milton, OL; Dashawn Grooms, DL; Frank Ford, LB; Kehmari Pruitt, DB; Chris Tyler, DB; Caleb Gallashaw, Return Specialist; Jacob Mount, Punter; Caden Catron, Kicker. NOTE: Hoffpauir scored 3 x TDs in a single game (catches) vs Peabody.
1	1	Efosa Evbuomwan signs with Lamar University All Dist: Caleb Gallashaw (RB); Darius Sawyer (WR); Noah Allain (TE): Darius Allen (DB); Quan Williams (DB); Jacob Mount (QB & P); D'Ante Gallashaw (RB); Khrystian Hoffpauir (WR): Steven Winslow (OL); Christian Sage (DL); Chris Davis (DB). .
3	1	Matthew Anderson, First Team All-State. Coach Causey, State Coach of the Year. Montae Lynch (Tyler CC), Duwon Tolbert (Tyler CC), Matthew Anderson (Nebraska), and Brett Pope (La Tech) all signed to play at next level. Matt Pajinag earned preferred walk on at Northwestern. All Dist: Caleb Gallashaw (RB); D'ante Gallashaw (RB & Offensive MVP); Montae Lynch (OL); Matthew Anderson (OL); Brett Pope (C); Darius Sawyer (ATH); Jacob Mount (QB); Noah Allain (TE); Khrystian Hoffpauir (WR); Peyton Lipps (OL): Ben Ward (P): Talyn Adams (DL): Nick Green (DL); Matt Pajinag (LB): Darius Allen (LB): Aaron Hunter (DL): Ruben Jeane (DL); Jacob Feliciano (DB): Nigel McCoy (DB): Darius Sawyer (KR); Efosa Evbuomwan (FLEX)
1	1	9 players sign national letters of intent. Andrew Croker signs with and earns varsity letters at McNeese Matt Pajinag Second Team All-State Linebacker. All Dist: Chris Vargas (QB and Dist Offensive MVP); D'Ante Gallashaw (RB); Andrew Croker (RB); Kobe Joiner (TE); Matthew Anderson (OL); Brett Pope (OL); Michael Ciachelli (OL); Xavier Reyes (K & P); Donald Smith (DL); Sabian Matu (LB); Matthew Pajinag (LB); Gabe Ellis (LB); McKenzie Jackson (DB); Derek Hurt (FLEX); Montae Lynch (OL): Steven Thomas (DL); Talyn Adams (DL); Jordan Dowden (DB); Demarcus McCord (DB). Coach Causey named Coach of the Year

Season (Fall)	Wins	Losses	Ties	vs DeRidder	Head Coach	District Champ	PLAYOFF GAME
2016	7	5		Leesville 42, DeRidder 28; at LHS	Robbie Causey	Yes	Yes. Won First round vs Beau Chene, lost second round to Edna Karr.
2015	3	7		DeRidder 56, Leesville 20; at DHS	Tommy Moore	No	No
2014	6	5		Leesville 21, Deridder 6; at LHS	Tommy Moore	No	Yes; lost to Rayne in first round
2013	2	8		DeRidder 49, Leesville 0; at DHS	Tommy Moore	No	No
2012	1	9		DeRidder 49, Leesville 0; at DHS	Jimmy Adams	No	No
2011	4	6		DeRidder 42, Leesville 14; at LHS	Jimmy Adams	No	No
2010				Leesville 34, DeRidder 20; at LHS	David Feaster		
2010	9	3		Leesville 27, DeRidder 17; at DHS	David Feaster	Yes	Yes. Won first round at DeRidder, lost to Franklinton in second round
2009	4	7		DeRidder 37, Leesville 18; at LHS	David Feaster		Yes.
2008	10	2		Leesville 68, DeRidder 29; at DHS	Terrance Williams	Yes	Yes. Won First round vs St. Michael. Lost second round to Zachary

Post Season Win	Post Season Loss	Notes
1	1	Cory McCoy becomes only 3rd Cat to break 4,000 yard rushing barrier, signs with McNeese and letters multiple years, plays 5th year at Marshall, earns NFL free agent contract at New England All Dist: Cory McCoy (RB); Elijah Mundy (DL); Jaelyn Edwards (LB); Jacob Adams (P and PK); Daquan Davis (RB); Andrew Croker (WR & DB)
		All Dist:. Cory McCoy (RB): Caden Wheeler (QB); Jaelyn Edwards (LB). NOTE: Coach Moore resigns in the summer of 2016.
	1	All Dist: Cory McCoy (RB & KR); Garrett Rogers (OL): Kory Jones (DL); Solomon Cross (LB): Davion Clemons (LB); E.J. Ane (TE): Antonio Tharp (OL); Jacob Adams (PK); Dantrell Lewis (DL); Jaelyn Edwards (LB); Tywann Brown (FLEX). Note: Cory McCoy scored six TDs in a single game vs Peabody. Ane played collegiately at San Jose State—letterman.
		All Dist: Logan Kreynbuhl (OL); Moses Tolbert (RB): Elbert Marbury (OL); Kory Jones (LB); Jonathan Price (P)
		All Dist: Jamal Harral (OL); Jacob Chambers (P); Roger Luafelemana (LB); Kole Smith (TE); Elbert Marbury (DL); Solomon Cross (LB); Deval Lewis (DB)
		All State: Clinton Thurman. All Dist: Diontay Thurman (RB); Adam Woods (TE); Clinton Thurman (WR & DB); Colton Honeycutt (K); Zach Squyres (QB & ATH); Jeremiah Cross (DL); Jacob Chambers (P); Derrick Blackshire (RB); Juwan Lewtry (OL); Jamall Harris (OL); Dalton Harville (DL); Mason Daelapp (LB):
		Playoff Game. Mulitple scores by Liggins
1	1	All State: Levander Liggins. Levander Liggins signs with La Tech, letters 4 years, gets NFL tryout with Houston Texans. Liggins scored 20+ touchdowns on the season. All Dist: Zach Squyres (QB); Levander Liggins (ATH & WR); Clinton Thurman (WR); Jeval Chancy (TE); Jevon Leday (OL): Bobby Mace (OL); Daniel Winnfield (DL); Demetrius Atwater (DB); Jacob Chambers (P); Joe Horlacher (RB); Logan Morrison (OL); Dylan Gaskill (OL); AJ Green (OL); Cotton Honeycutt (K); Deshawn Short (DL); Jeremiah Cross (DL); Thomas Medina (LB): Mason Detz (LB): Marshall Smith (DB) . Bobby Mace played in college in Rochester, MN.
	1	Lost in first round of playoffs. Je'ron Hamms signs with ULM; has great career, free agent contract with Saints. Tremayne Freeman signs with McNeese, later transfer to NSU. All Dist: Javal Chancy (TE); Je'ron Hamm (WR); Levander Liggins (ATH); Allen Perry (K); Keedrick Mitchell (RB & DB); Tiasham Burnett (RB);Cody Lefort (OL); Michael Dennis (OL); Daniel Winnfied (LB); Demetrius Atwater (DB);
1	1	All State: Michael Ford and Devin Moran. Ford signs with LSU; played on 2011 national runner up team, later signs with Chicago Bears and Atlanta Falcons. Trevante Stallworth signed with Auburn. All Dist: Michael Ford (RB & KR & P); Trev Stallworth (QB); Demetrius Woods (RB): Allen Perry (PK); Rob Saovao (DL); Devon Brown (DB); Cassetti Brown (DB) (Brown signed with La Tech); Levander Liggins (WR); Tyler Anders (C); Michael Maldanado (OL); Terrell Turner (OL); Emanuel Long (DL); Eddie McTear (LB); Chad Parker (LB); Ford Offensive MVP; Moran Defensive MVP; Terrence Williams Coach of the Year

Season (Fall)	Wins	Losses	Ties	vs DeRidder	Head Coach	District Champ	PLAYOFF GAME
2007	6	5		Leesville 43, DeRidder 13; at LHS	Terrance Wlliams	Yes	Yes; Lost to Vandebilt Catholic 34-6 on the road
2006	6	5		Leesville 33, DeRidder 7; at DHS	Johnny Cryer	No	Yes; lost to Breaux Bridge in opening round on the road
2005	3	6		Did Not play due to Hurricane Rita	Kevin Magee	No	No
2004	9	2		Leesville 46, DeRidder 7; at DHS	Kevin Magee	Yes	Yes; Lost to Opelousas in first round, at home
2003	4	6		Leesville 21, DeRidder 14; at LHS	Kevin Magee	No	
2002	6	5		Leesville 14, DeRidder 6; at LHS	Kevin Magee	No	Yes. Lost to John Curtis in the first round
2001	6	5		Leesville 14, DeRidder 3; at DHS	Kevin Magee	No	Yes; Lost to Neville in first round
2000	6	7		Leesville 40, DeRidder 0; at LHS	Kevin Magee	No	Yes; made quarterfinals as a 28 seed. Defeated Walker (5 seed) and Woodlawn BR (12 Seed). Lost to Assumption and NFL star Brandon Jacobs in Quarter Finals
1999	4	7		Leesville 30, DeRidder 8; at DHS	Jerry Foshee	No	Yes; lost to Abbeville in first round

Post Season Win	Post Season Loss	Notes
	1	All State: Trev Stallworth. David Detz signs with and letters at LSU. All Dist: Alan Muse (WR); Cole Parker (DL); Trevante Stallworth (QB); David Detz (LB, also Hon Men All State); James Baker (WR); Keyon Henry (DL); Alan Harshaw (DL); Adron Hackett (LB); Dejan Taylor (KR); Devin Moran (DL); Michael Ramsey (LB); Michael Harris (LB); Chris Brown (DB).
	1	All Dist: Michael Ford (RB); Josh Cryer (RB & LB); Jacoby Kaiama (OL); Damion Smith (KR); Michael Harris (DL); Cornelius Jackson (DB); Michael Smith (DB); David Detz (DB)
		All Dist: Justin Ford (RB); Bernardo Henry (ATH); Frank Larry (LB); Wes Bouves (LB); David Detz (LB); Brandon Sharper (DB). Wes Tunnufu-Sauvo signs/letters with Central Florida; Frank Larry and Bernardo Henry sign with McNeese State. Henry letters at McNeese
	1	All Dist: Bernardo Henry Offensive MVP: Edwin Ivory (RB); Matt Morrison (C); Kevin McCavey (OL); Bobby Cummings (OL): Casey Vinson (DL); Wes Tunnufu-Sauvo (DL); Tommy Neubert (LB); Larry Frank (LB); Daryl Joiner (DB); Mike Nelson (DB); Justin Goins (QB); Jacoby Kaima (OL); Tyler Gill (DL)
		All Dist: Josh Quayhagen (S): Wes Harvey (DL); Justin Harris (LB), Jared James (DB); Andy Hughes (C); Danny Williamson (OL); Quintiza Scott (RB); Marcus Williams (WR); Bernardo Henry (WR); Tommy Neubert (TE). Quayhagen had 109 tackles and 3 INTs.
	1	Keith Zinger All State; signs with LSU. Zinger won 2 national championships at LSU. Zinger (Alleger) named All State (only LHS athlete besides Cecil Collins named more than once). Cordell Upshaw signs with Southern Arkansas University (SAU) and was a 3 year letterman, later becoming a collegiate coach. James Burkes signs with SAU. All Dist: Zinger (TE); Chris White (DE); Upshaw (LB); Josh Quayhagen (DB); Gilbert Frances (OL); Andy Hughes (C); Chris Nash (RB); James Burkes (LB); Michael Toney (P); Michael Cools (K)
	1	Keith Zinger named All State First Team. Martin Driscoll signs with Nicholls State. All dist: Keith (Alleger) Zinger (TE); Cody McKenzie (OL); Chris Nash (RB); Dante Williamson (LB); Roderick Lawhorn (DB); Gilbert Francis (OL); Josh Chaney (DL); Darnell Thompson (DL); Jeremy Burkes (LB); Marcus Johnson (DB); Michael Toney (P)
2	1	All State Justin Brown; signs with Northwestern. All Dist: Justin Brown (DB, WR & PR); Kenny Hughes (OL); Chris O'Bryan (DL & K); Tommy Edwards (OL); Cody McKenzie (OL): Kenny Jones (RB); Lorenzo Garner (LB); Roberick Lawhorn (DB).
	1	All Dist: Lamond Leasure (C); Justin Brown (DB and PR); William Dudley (DL); Kenny Jones (LB); James White (DB); Mark Dowden (P).

Season (Fall)	Wins	Losses	Ties	vs DeRidder	Head Coach	District Champ	PLAYOFF GAME
1998	3	8		Leesville 36, DeRidder 34, OT; at DHS	Danny Smith	No	Yes; lost to Tioga in first round
1997	3	7		DeRidder 14, Leesville 12; at LHS	Danny Smith	No	No
1996	7	5		DeRidder 25, Leesville 7; at LHS	Danny Smith	No	Yes.. Won first round vs Northwood. Lost second round vs Wossman
1995				Leesville 29, DeRidder 0; at DHS (State quarterfinals)			
1995	13	2		Leesville 15, DeRidder 6; at DHS;	Danny Smith	Yes	Yes. State Finalist. Defeated Breaux Bridge semi. Defeated DeRidder quarter finals. Defeated Carrol in second round. Opelousas in first round
1994	8	4		Leesville 28, DeRidder 0; at LHS	Danny Smith	Co-Dist Champ	Yes; defeated Haughton first round, lost to Wossman 2nd round
1993	8	4		DeRidder 24, Leesville 14; at DHS	Danny Smith	Co-Dist Champ	Yes; defeated Pineville first round, lost to Abbeville 2nd round
1992	2	7		Leesville 13, DeRidder 12; at LHS	Danny Smith	No	No
1991	0	10		DeRidder 26, Leesville 12; at DHS	Danny Smith	No	No
1990	3	7		Leesville 15, DeRidder 0; at LHS	Jack Andre	No	No

Post Season Win	Post Season Loss	Notes
	1	All State: Keith Smith. Smith signed with McNeese; would become an all conf player and NFL player (Detroit). Demond and Deshun McNeely both signed with Northwestern. All Dist: Deshun McNeely (RB); Demond McNeely (WR); Dwayne Thibodeaux (OL); Keith Smith (DB); Sam Cobb (LB); Sam Scott (TE); Lemond Leasure (OL); Smith was team's leading tackler with 125. Deshun McNeely had over 1,300 yards rushing.
		All Dist: Ronnie Robinson (WR); Robert Carter (DL); Andre Thurman (DB); Dwayne Thibodeaux (OL); Derek Jones (DL) Thurman had over 100 tackles on the season, and Carter had 90. Dustin Smith named All Vernon Parish, throwing for 1492 yards and 11 touchdowns
1	1	All Dist: Adrian Burns (OL), Xavier Burrell (RB & Punter); Mike Lewis (DB): Wes Bailey (DL); Greg Manns (OL); LeMarcus Thurman (WR)
4	1	Team State Runner up. All State: Cecil Collins, Greg Rone and Dennis Fetting. Cecil Collins named LHSAA Mr. Football. All State. Signed with LSU, played in NFL. All CENLA: Ced Clemons (LB), Dennis Fetting (OL). All Dist: Dennis Fetting (OL); Cecil Collins (RB); Greg Rone (LB); Shermaine Jones (DB); Robert Carter (DL); Sig Milerski (DL); Ced Clemons (LB); Mike Lewis (DB). Clemons was 3 year letterman with Tulane. Coach of the Year Danny Smith.
1	1	All State Cecil Collins (RB) and Andrew Mageo (OL). Collins gained 2488 yards for the season. Cats advanced to 2nd round of playoffs, losing to Wossman. All Dist: Andrew Mageo (OL); Matt Morrow (C); Cecil Collins (RB & KR); Antountel Goza (DL); Shermaine Jones (DB); Anthony Ford (WR): Dennis Fetting (OL); Matt Glasper (RB); Virgil Ruffin, (DL); Andre Middlebrooks (P). Danny Smith Coach of the Year.
1	1	Cecil Collins (RB) All State and All Dist RB; Coach Smith Coach of the Year. Other All Dist: Andre Middlebrooks (WR); Andre Mageo (OL); Matt Morrow (OL); Willie McNutt (DL); Alton Harris (LB); C-Micah Wilson (DB); Tyrone Sims (DB). Lawrence Powell (WR); Mark Mawae (OL); Jason Collions (RB); Clinton King (DL); Joe Rosen (LB); Anthony Ford (DB). LHS re-classified to 4A. Danny Smith named Coach of the year.
		All Dist: Anthony Gill (TE); Mike Fuller (KR & WR); Derrick Smart (LB): Tyrone Simms (DB). Future LHS Principal Mark Mawae recovered fumble late in the game to seal Deridder game.
		Kavika Pitman signs with McNeese, letters multi year, conference defensive MVP; drafted into NFL (Broncos), played nine years in NFL. Pittman also was All State in track. LHS was forced to move to play at the 5A level. All Dist: Pittman (DL); Ronnie Sapp (OL); Rodney Gardner (DL); Antoine Shaw (DB); Ellis Garner (P)
		All Dist: Willie Williams (OL); John Turner (KR); Cornelius Jones (WR); Anthony Boerner (TE); Robert Nunez (OL); Tyrone Smith (DL); Jeff Falifea (DL); John Brown (DL) Ellis Garner (P)

Season (Fall)	Wins	Losses	Ties	vs DeRidder	Head Coach	District Champ	PLAYOFF GAME
1989	4	6		DeRidder 14, Leesville 7; at DHS	Brownie Parmeley	No	No
1988	6	4		DeRidder 17, Leesville 16; at LHS	Brownie Parmeley	No	No
1987	11	2		Leesville 23, DeRidder 14; at DHS	Brownie Parmeley	Yes	Yes; defeated Acadiana in first round, St. Amant in 2nd round; lost in quarterfinals at Ruston
1986	10	2		Leesville 45, DeRidder 14; at DHS	Jack Andre	Yes	Yes; defeated Carencro first round, Broadmoor 2nd round; lost in quarterfinals at home to Ruston
1985	10	2		Leesville 36, DeRidder 0; at LHS	Jack Andre	Co-Dist Champ	Yes; defeated West Monroe in first round, Huntington in 2nd round; Cats lost to St. Martinville at home in quarterfinals
1984	10	3		DeRidder 14, Leesville 12; at DHS	Jack Andre	Yes	Yes: Received first round bye; lost to Rayne in 2nd round
1983	8	3		Leesville 37, DeRidder 26; at LHS	Jack Andre	No	Yes; defeated Abbeville in first round, lost to Wossman in second round
1982	6	4		DeRidder 37, Leesville 12; at DHS	Jerry Foshee	No	No
1981	7	3		Leesville 21, DeRidder 7; at LHS	Jerry Foshee	No	No

Post Season Win	Post Season Loss	Notes
		Chip Clark sigs with Tulane. Erwin Brown signs with McNeese All Dist: Erwin Brown (RB) (Dist MVP); Dwayne Johnson (DB); Anthony Johnson (DE)
		All State: Kevin Mawae and Chip Clark. Kevin Mawae signs with LSU; 4 year letterman at LSU; becomes all pro center, enters LSU. LHSAA, State and Pro Football Hall of Fame. Mawae All Dist and All State. Other All Dist: Chip Clark (P); Corey Thompkins (LB); Irwin Brown (RB); Buck Lewis (DL); Bobby Smith (OL). Cats lost last game and were kept out of playoffs
2	1	All State: Vince Fuller and Raymond Smoot; both sign with LSU. Both were multiple year lettermen. All Dist: Vince Fuller (RB); Joe Williams (RB); Kevin Mawae (C); Raymond Smoot (T); Stan Watley (DB); Wayne Martin (DE); Andre Page (DT); Jason Guintini (P); Fuller Offensive MVP. Any Bellamy signs with NLU (later became ULM). John Mawae signs with NSU, later transfers to LSU and letters in 1992.
2	1	All State: Brian Estep and Robert Jenkins. Estep signs to play with Tulane. Jenkins signs to play with Grambling. All Dist: Brian Estep (G); Dennis Mitchell (G); Teddy Berry (C); Clint Batteford (QB); Vince Fuller (RB); Jeff Mitcham (K); Robert Jenkins (DT); Mike Smith (LB): Warren Estey (LB): Stacy Cooper (DB); Demetrius Payton (TE); Tony Rush (RB); Chuck Abrams (DT); Cliff Buckner (DE);Sean Mayfield (P) NOTE: Only 9 regular season games scheduled
2	1	All State Eddie Fuller. Eddie Fuller signed with LSU; letters 4 years; caught "earthquake" pass vs Auburn in 88; played in NFL Buffalo Bills. All Dist: Roger Anderson (C); Eddie Fuller (RB); Earl Wallace (DE): Mike Smith (DB); Raymond Smoot (OL); Nick Gatewood (TE); Rayford Clayton (RB); James Adams (DL); Robert Gonzales (DL); Dickie Fetting (LB); Vince Fuller and Jeff Steele (DB). Coach Andre was coach of the year. Eddie Fuller Offensive MVP. NOTE: 9 regular season games scheduled
	1	All State: Charles Buckley and Steve Gunn. All Dist: Lowell Green (C); Tony Phillips (G); Jimmy Chamberlain (T); Charles Buckley (RB); Sam Hoecker (DE); Steve Gunn (LB); Craig Pierce (DB); Al Capello (QB); Arnold McPherson (TE); Jeff Steele (RB); Tom Crosby (DT);. Gunn Defensive MVP Sam Hoecker and Steve Gunn sign NLIs. Jeff Steele and Charles Buckley rushed for over 1,000 yards on the season. This was the "fumble roosky" game vs Rayne in playoffs.
1	1	All Dist: Percy Burns (TE), Sam Hoecker (OL); Al Capello (QB); Mark Clay (RB); Odell Miller (DT); Dexter Gatewood (DE); Steve Gunn (LB); Chris Robertson (DB) All Dist.
		Oscar Joiner signs with LSU. Daniel Aboutboul (PK) signs with Northwestern State, earns a varisty letter. All Dist: Sam Hoecker (OL); Jimbo Shapkoff (LB), Melvin Maxwell (DE); TJ Moore (QB); Kevin West (DE)
		Tommy Peevey signs with La Tech. All Dist: Jimbo Shapkoff (LB); Oscar Joiner (RB); Lyle Kerry (OL); Richard Scott (OL); Clint Ensley, Chris Roberson; David Bonner (DBs); Robert Pynes (DL); Melvin Maxwell (NG); Steve Gunn (DL) All Dist

Season (Fall)	Wins	Losses	Ties	vs DeRidder	Head Coach	District Champ	PLAYOFF GAME
1980	4	6		Leesville 26, DeRidder 15; at DHS	Ronnie Stephens	No	No
1979	2	8		DeRidder 22, Leesville 14; at LHS	Ronnie Stephens	No	No
1978	5	5		1978: DeRidder 23, Leesville 6; at DHS	Richard Schwartz	No	No
1977	6	4		DeRidder 6, Leesville 0, OT; at LHS	Richard Schwartz	No	No
1976	2	7	1	DeRidder 42, Leesville 6; at DHS	Richard Schwartz	No	No
1975	0	10		DeRidder 50, Leesville 0; at LHS	Gerry Robichaux	No	No
1974	3	7		DeRidder 28, Leesville 6; at DHS	Gerry Robichaux	No	No
1973	2	6	1	tie, DeRidder 6, Leesville 6; at LHS	Doug Creamer	No	No
1972	7	3		DeRidder 14, Leesville 0; at DHS LHS Won by forfeit	Doug Creamer	No	No
1971	3	7		DeRidder 21, Leesville 6; at LHS	Doug Creamer	No	No
1970	2	6	2		Guy Barr	No	No
1969	7	2	1	Leesville 25, DeRidder 0; at DHS	Guy Barr	No	No
1968	7	3		Leesville 26, DeRidder 20; at LHS	Charlie Edwards	Tied for 2nd	No

Post Season Win	Post Season Loss	Notes
		LHS breaks 10 year losing streak to Deridder. Mo Pointer played at Southern Univ and in CFL; All Dist: Earnest Bess (RB & DB); Michael Deans (OL & DL); Oscar Joiner (RB); Steve Morrison (C); Mark Smith (LB); Tommy Peevy (OL); Charles Owen (TE); Robert Pynes (DL); Pat Mahoney (LB)
		Stephens hired in June before schools year; head coach, Don Jones on site from Feb - June and left for Plaquemine. Matt Oliver (QB) played at West Point for 4 years. Tony Jones played at Glendale CC. All Dist: Robert Gaines (DB); James Johnson (OL); Michael Deans (OL); Steve Morrison (OL); Stacy Williams (DE); Tony Jones (RB).
		Terry Holt signs with USL (ULL). All Dist: Terry Holt (RB); Mike Williams (C); Terry Williams (OL); Robert Gaines (TE and DB). Gaines inducted into LHS Sports Hall of Fame in 2015
		Terry Holt, 1,000 yard + RB. All Dist: Joe Mastracchio (LB); Richard Bastedo (DE); Harles Smart (OT); Bruce Payton (LB); Holt (RB). Holt inducted into LHS Sports Hall of Fame in 2016
		Terry Holt (RB); All Dist: Eddie Herndon (DB); Tommy Driscoll (NG); Bill West (DT); William Garner (TE). 20 game losing streak is broken on Homecoming night 1976, heroics by Terry Holt and Eddie Herndon
		Sam Fertitta (DE) and Butch Stevens (DB) first team all Dist
		All Dist: Dennis Driscoll (RB); Mike Anderson (C); Ray Macias (TE); Ralph Ortiz (DB); Hubert Knight (LB); Bill West (DT); William Dowden (DT)
		All Dist: Raymond Mapu (RB); Hubert Knight (NG); Larry Wilson (DB); Dennis Driscoll (QB); Mike Anderson (C); Danny Turick (DT). Head coach resigned in May of 74, Robichaux hired.
		All Dist: Johnny Mapu, (NG); Charlie Hanks (OT and LB); Lorenzo Garner (RB). Hanks signed NLI to play with University of Houston. Coach Creamer was named Coach of the year for the Dist. Garner first African American to be named All-Dist at LHS
		All Dist: Jimmy Mapu (RB & DT). Mapu signed with McNeese; played collegiately for Ricks College in Idaho
		All Dist Paul Sliman (S); Sam Burnley (LB); Dennis Davis (DT); Jimmy Mapu (NG). First season of LHS Football after merger with Vernon High School
		Started season 7-0-1; lost last two, did not make playoffs. All Dist: Doug Goldsby (E); John Driscoll (OL and DL: Jimmy Anderson (FB): Larry Johnson (DL): Jack Ashfield (RB & S): Steve Hays (DB): Johnny Moore (DB). Goldsby and Ashfield played for Northwestern. Driscoll signed with McNeese; All State 2nd Team Offense/ Defense
		Leesville Leader declared "best season ever" at the end of the season. Future LHSAA Basketball coaching Hall of Famer Vic Ortiz was star player. Larry Carr (DL) All Dist; Vic Ortiz All Dist QB; Leroy Treme All Dist DB. Larry Laurent (E and DL); Joe Ewing (OL); John Driscoll (DL)

Season (Fall)	Wins	Losses	Ties	vs DeRidder	Head Coach	District Champ	PLAYOFF GAME
1967	5	4	1	Leesville 21, DeRidder 0; at DHS	Charlie Edwards	No	No
1966	4	4	2	Leesville 21, DeRidder 7; at LHS	William Hickman	No	No
1965	4	6		DeRidder 13, Leesville 0; at LHS	Ted Paris	No	No
1964	4	5	2	DeRidder 39, Leesville 13; at DHS	Ted Paris	No	Yes
1963				DeRidder 34, Leesville 19; at LHS	Ted Paris		PLAYOFF GAME
1963	9	3		Leesville 28, DeRidder 6; at LHS	Ted Paris	Yes	Yes
1962	7	2	1	DeRidder 12, Leesville 0; at DHS	Ted Paris	No	No
1961	4	6		DeRidder 47, Leesville 7; at LHS	Ted Paris	No	No
1960	4	6		DeRidder 13, Leesville 12; at DHS	Ted Paris	No	No
1959	5	4	1	DeRidder 7, Leesville 6; at LHS	Ted Paris	No	No
1958	9	2		DeRidder 14, Leesville 0; at DHS	Dalton Faircloth	No	No
1957	7	4		Leesville 33, DeRidder 6; at LHS	Dalton Faircloth	No	No
1956	1	10		DeRidder 34, Leesville 7; at DHS	Dalton Faircloth	No	No
1955	1	9		DeRidder 32, Leesville 6; at LHS	Pat Riser		
1954	7	3		DeRidder 12, Leesville 6; at DHS	Pat Riser	No	No

Post Season Win	Post Season Loss	Notes
		All Dist: Thad Bailes, Bobby Craft, Donnie Gill (QB)
		All Dist: Dickie Bailes (OL & DL), Jimmy Auvil, Wayne Cavanaugh
		All Dist: Keith Carver (FB); Joe Gendron €; Allen Nickerson (G). Gendron signed with Tulane
	1	Lost to Eunice at Eunice in first round of playoffs. .Named to "All Star" team (All Dist) were Jimmy Skinner (End), Dwayne Palmer (Center), Billy Salim (QB). Salim played for Northwestern State, Skinner played for Blinn Jr. College.
		Game on Youtube at https://www.youtube.com/watch?v=6jX1ZRhVCwY
	1	First Dist title in school history; lost to DeRidder in first round; RJ Fertitta and Larry Jeane played at Louisiana College; Paul Nicholas played at NSU. All Dist: RJ Fertitta (OL & LB); Paul Nicholas (RB); Richard Schwartz (E); James Well (T): Roy Trahan (RB); Ronald Holsomback (E). Ted Paris Coach of the Year. Paul Nichols and John Martinez died in Vietnam in 1967.
		Team finished 9th in State rankings; All Dist: Louis Magee (QB); Roy Trahan (HB); RJ Fertitta (G); John Millner (C). Ted Paris Dist Coach of the year
		George Smith signs with Tulane; gains over 1,000 yards on the ground. All Dist: Bobby Craft (E): George Smith (RB); Ronnie McRae (T); RJ Fertitta (G);
		All Dist: Mike Wego (T); George Smith (RB); Charles Wilson (C); Sid Morris (RB):
	1	Cats played a voluntary post season game vs Oakdale. The "Lions Club Bowl" was played a week after the conclusion of the season. LHS lost the charity event 19-7. All Dist: John Simonelli (G); Doug Marshall (C): John Terry (DB);
		Robert Pynes, All State; signs with LSU. All Dist: Robert Pynes (RB): Johnny Hall (FB); John Simonelli (G); Roy Hooker (E); Joe Scogin, Chris Bagents were team captains. Billy Lewis "Most Improved". Cats invited to play Morgan City in the Tidelands Bowl after the season, but did not make the trip.
		Finished second in Dist to Landry Memorial; Sam Piranio All Dist QB, Johnny Hall, All Dist FB; JC Welch All Dist End; Robert Pynes All Dist HB
		All Dist: Bobby Arthur (E); Junior Coburn (G); Sam Piranio (QB)
		Wallace McRae played for La Tech. All Dist: Morris Jean McRae; Lewis Reid Brown; Harles Smart
		James Coburn played for US Army Team. All State Hon Men: All Dist: James Coburn, George Fisher, Jerry Skinner, Harles Smart; Bucky Tuminello, Wallace McRae, Lynn McClain. Fisher played at LSU

Season (Fall)	Wins	Losses	Ties	vs DeRidder	Head Coach	District Champ	PLAYOFF GAME
1953	8	3		Leesville 18, DeRidder 7; at LHS	Pat Riser	No	No
1952	8	4		DeRidder 39, Leesville 0; at DHS	Pat Riser	No	No*
1951	8	4		DeRidder 28, Leesville 7; at DHS	Zolon Stiles	No	No*
1950	1	10		DeRidder 7, Leesville 6; at LHS	Zolon Stiles	No	No
1949	2	7		DeRidder 20, Leesville 19; at LHS	Zolon Stiles	No	No
1948	3	7		DeRidder 20, Leesville 6; at DHS	William Noonan	No	No
1947	1	10		DeRidder 25, Leesville 0; at LHS	William Noonan	No	No
1946	2	7	1	DeRidder 53, Leesville 0; at DHS	Pete Hendricks	No	No
1945				DeRidder 27, Leesville 7	Pete Hendricks		
1945	3	5		DeRidder 61, Leesville 7	Pete Hendricks	No	No
1944				No Football			
1943	4	4	1	Leesville 7, DeRidder 6	Bill Turner	No	No
1942		4		DeRidder 13, Leesville 7; at DHS		No	No
1941		3		DeRidder 14, Leesville 6		No	No
1940	4	7		DeRidder 39, Leesville 0; at LHS	Wood Osborne	No	No
1939	1	6		DeRidder 33, Leesville 0; at DHS	Wood Osborne	No	No

Post Season Win	Post Season Loss	Notes
		Broke a 14 year losing streak to DeRidder. All Dist: Wallace McRae; Jerry Gregg; Edwin Smart; Dawin Smart
	1	Played in "Hardwood Bowl" against Oakdale and Marion after the end of the regular season. 8-3 in regular season, 0-1 in the post season. Mitch Nicholas and Joe Moses listed as star players in the media
	1	Played in "Hardwood Bowl" against Oakdale. Lost 7-0. Ted Paris named All State. Paris was presented a 21 jewel watch from Cain Motor Company for his performance. First known post season appearance for an LHS team. Paris and Lamar Clark were team captains.
		Cats were shut out in six of 11 games. Only two games saw LHS score in double digits.
		Albert Smart, Joe Pollard, Red Smith and Teddy Berry listed as captains; Defeat Winnfield 13-6
		Football highlights were filmed and presented at post season banquet. Team played a game in Mexico City in front of 30,000 fans. Lost to Ville Platte, Sacred Heart, Menard and Winnfield, Natchitoches, DeRidder and Vivian. Beat Many and Merryville and Mexico City American High School. Jimmy Grafton listed as a key player Bill Beavers, Albert Smart, Hank Berwick also key lettermen
		Buddy Conley and Billy Blackburn were captains. Team was shut out six times. Single win over Many, 13-12
		Team was shut out 7 times
		2nd game against DeRidder
		Seven games scheduled; Coach Hendricks hired on 4 Sep. Team Captains were Ralph Hooks and Frank Haynie. Played DeRidder twice. Beat St Marys twice and Many once
		NO FOOTBALL AT LHS
		Prominent players: Alfred Dunn, TB Porter, Captain CA Hughes, Bobby Pinchback, Johnny Moses, Carl Babin, Glen McRae, Mickey Cohen. Significant fund raising done through local merchants to pay for equipment for the team.
		Marginal DOCUMENTATION IN MEDIA NOR YEARBOOKS. Lost to Eunice, per Towntalk. Also lost to DeQuincy and Ville Platte.
		Lost to Jennings 73-0; Ville Platte 26-7
		Lost to Oakdale 1-0; coach forfeited game because of poor referee work. Defeated St. Mary's of Natchitoches, Port Arthur, Merryville, Pelican. Lost to DeRidder, Crowley, Natchitoches, Port Arthur and Oakdale.
		Kemp Tucker was team captain. Lost to Oakdale; Lost to Port Arthur; Lake Charles; Lost to Natchitoches; won in Mexico City

Season (Fall)	Wins	Losses	Ties	vs DeRidder	Head Coach	District Champ	PLAYOFF GAME
1938	7	2	1	Leesville 49, DeRidder 0; at LHS	Wood Osborne	No	No
1937	7	1	1	Tie, DeRidder 7, Leesville 7; at DHS	Wood Osborne	No	No
1936	6	2		Leesville 7, DeRidder 0; at LHS	Wood Osborne	No	No
1935	4	2	1	DeRidder 25, Leesville 0	Wood Osborne	No	No
1934	5	3		Leesville 25, DeRidder 13	Wood Osborne	No	No
1933	6	2		DeRidder 13, Leesville 0; at DHS	Hanna	No	No
1932	1	1	1	Tie, DeRidder 19, Leesville 19		No	No
1931	5	2		Leesville 7, DeRidder 6; at DHS	Beeson	No	No
1930	6	4		DeRidder 13, Leesville 0; at LHS	Beeson	No	No
1929	5	3	1	DeRidder 13, Leesville 0	WC Turner	No	No
1922	0	2		DeRidder 53, Leesville 0	Unknown	No	No
1921	0	1		DeRidder 49, Leesville 0	Unknown	No	No
1921	0	1		DeRidder 19, Leesville 7	Unknown	No	No
1920	0	1	1	Tie, DeRidder 6, Leesville 6	Unknown	No	No

Post Season Win	Post Season Loss	Notes
		Cats outscored opponents 163-50. Played game in Mexico City. Homer Robinson and John Sepeda were captains. Kemp Tucker later nominated for LHS Sports Hall of Fame by 42 grad Ted Castillo in 2016. Defeat Mexico City 12-8
		Cats outscored opponents 184-55. Team traveled to Mexico City to play Mexico-American High School. Derry Smart, Cottom McClure, John Sepeda team captains. Coach Osborne said in final news report of the season that he was pessimistic about the upcoming year.
		Lost to Glenmora & Normal; Beat DeRidder, Winnfield, Boyce, Oakdale, Merryville, Hemphill. Lost to NSU (Normal) Freshmen team. Game initially scheduled with Mexico City American school cancelled due to health outbreak
		Defeated Mexico American team (6-0), Hemphill, Winnfield, and DeQuincy. Tied Sulphur. Lost to DeRidder, Normal and Jennings. Played Oakdale & Natchitoches, but no scores or reports located
		Bill Adams. Fatty Fertitta, James Anderson key players. Media identifies Coach Osborne as a former "star" from Centenary." Defeated Merryville, Oakdale, DeRidder; Dequincy, Sulphur; lost to Bossier, Lake Charles, Jennings
		Listed as undefeated through 25 Nov in Shreveport Times, played Bossier on 25 Nov. Lost to Bossier. Valentine listed at QB. The Times reported an "Air Raid" offense implemented by the Leesville team. NO mascot was listed in media.
		Beat Oberlin
		Lost to two college teams. Defeated Natch, Sulphur, Pelican, DeRidder. Coach Beeson writes editorial in Leesville Leader, complaining about prioritization of funds and how lack of funds is hurting athletics. He suggested spending less money on the agricultural exhibits at the fall fair and more money to buy uniforms and fund activities. He noted during previous basketball season, the LHS team had to travel and play at state tournament without uniforms. Two players from basketball were named all state, John Pelt and Fred Rowzee
		Team listed as "Bobcats" in the 30, 31 and 32 seasons. Team Captain Anthony Fertitta. 6-4 record annotated in Leesville Leader 4 Dec but results for only 3 games can be found
		Inaugural game as Wampus Cats. First game was 0-0 tie vs Merryville. Sam Fertitta, Anthony Fertitta. JR Stevens, Percy Cabra, Leftt Nicholas (QB), Fred Rowzee, Dunlap, Fisher were some of the players
		No documentation available as to why football stopped after this season. One rumor was there was a knife fight after a game in Mamou. Lost to Mansfield, DeRidder
		After Glenmora game, a shooting occurred. Teacher named Beason got into a fight with person over game proceeds. Oscar Mcelven died as a result. Event was ruled an accident

Season (Fall)	Wins	Losses	Ties	vs DeRidder	Head Coach	District Champ	PLAYOFF GAME
1919	0	1		No Game with DeRidder	Unknown	No	No
1917			1	No Game with DeRidder	KS Thompson	No	No
1915	1	2		DeRidder 6, Leesville 0	Unknown	No	No
1913	0	1		DeRidder 24, Leesville 0	Unknown	No	No
1912	1	0		No Game with DeRidder	Unknown	No	No
1910	1	1		DeRidder 35, Leesville 0	Unknown	No	No
	Wins	**Losses**	**Ties**				
	489	456	21				

Post Season Win	Post Season Loss	Notes
		Lost to Glenmora
		Tied Glenmore 0-0
		Defeated Florien; James Wintle signs with LSU; letters 21-22.
		One game recorded, 22-0 victory over Oakdale
		Defeated Hornbeck 21-0;
		Pleasant Ferguson and William Lyles sign with LSU; both earn letters 1907
Post Season Wins	Post Season Losses	
28	33	

Offensive Stat Leaders

In the following pages, you'll see the leaders in passing, rushing and receiving statistics for the Leesville Wampus Cats. As noted in the previous book, this effort was started by Brian Trahan, former editor of the Leesville Leader in the 2010 time-frame. Brian's initial work gathered available and discoverable stats back to the late 1970s, but no further. I made a conscious decision to gather this data for any year that could be found. It's taken the better part of eight years to get where we are now.

Readers should understand the limitations with football stats at the high school (or any) level. There is no such thing as "official" records at the school or parish level. I'm pretty sure I've never heard of official records at the state level, when you're talking about things like passing, rushing and receiving accomplishments. It's all done, or NOT done at the local level. In Leesville, there has one thing that has been consistent---inconsistency. Every coach and athletic director have had their method or NO method for tracking stats. All data that was found was discovered in media and yearbooks. Some people have said "those records have to be somewhere." No, they don't. In fairness to coaches and A s, they're busy and undermanned. It's just the way it is.

It is worth noting that the past 8 years of stats are chronicled on MaxPreps website Prior to THOSE 8 years, it has been a foraging effort. I was able to find good and I think interesting stats as far back as the 1950s, chroniclin the first 1,000-yard rushers and passers. A lot of stats have been added in recent years because of the prolific nature of LHS offenses. I've also included some notable achievements by Vernon High athletes. Also of note in this year's book is the addition of defensive stats---somewhat. They appear after the offensive ection and some explanations are provided.

Cecil Collins
Rushing Leader

Zach Squyres
Passing Leader

Levander Liggins
Receiving Leader

CAREER RUSHING LEADERS

First Name	Last Name	Years	Attempts	Yards	Avg	TDs
Cecil	Collins	1992-95	1033	7834	7.6	93
Michael	Ford	2005-08	613	4971	8.1	52
Caleb	Gallashaw	2018-21	588	4204	7.1	60
Cory	McCoy	2013-16	604	4111	6.8	43
Vincent	Fuller	1985-87	517	3454	6.7	35
D'Ante	Gallashaw	2017-19	431	3210	7.2	44
Terry	Holt	1975-78	491	3069	6.2	24
Erwin	Brown	1987-89	415	2938	7.1	32
Xavier	Ford	2021-Pres	384	2704	7	34
DeShun	McNeely	1996-98	467	2502	5.4	22
Robert	Pynes	1957-58		2216		24
Oscar	Joiner	1980-82	214	2050	9.6	22
Carl	Howard (Vernon)	1962-65		1939		32
Rayford	Clayton	1984=86		1857		17
Eddie	Fuller	1985	238	1829	7.7	26
Geroge	Smith	1960-61		1775		20
Paul	Nicholas	1962-63	238	1571	6.6	18
Heggie	Reynolds	1990-92	253	1568	6.2	10
Travante	Stallworth	2006-08	300	1485	5	31
Diontay	Thurman	2008-11	210	1416	6.7	21
Justin	Ford	2003-06	295	1416	4.8	12
Charles	Buckley	1983-85	202	1360	6.7	21
Levander	Liggins	2008-10	183	1321	7.2	21

Cory McCoy   **Terry Holt**   **Justin Ford**   **Rayford Clayton**

SINGLE SEASON RUSHING LEADERS

First Name	Last Name	Year	Attempts	Yards	Avg	TDs
Cecil	Collins	1995	396	3045	7.7	40
Michael	Ford	2008	340	2953	8.7	29
Xavier	Ford	2022	375	2581	6.8	34
Cecil	Collins	1994	268	2441	9.1	29
Vincent	Fuller	1987	271	1890	7	22
Xavier	Burrell	1996	311	1831	5.9	19
Eddie	Fuller	1985	238	1829	7.7	26
Cecil	Collins	1993	246	1758	7.1	21
Caleb	Gallashaw	2021	191	1736	9.1	18
Corey	McCoy	2015	203	1502	7.2	22
D'Ante	Gallashaw	2018	200	1488	7.4	9
DeShun	McNeely	1998	231	1415	6.1	14
Erwin	Brown	1989	188	1371	7.3	12
Rayford	Clayton	1985	182	1367	7.5	10
Vincent	Fuller	1986	220	1362	6.2	12
Michael	Ford	2006	181	1334	7.4	18
Oscar	Joiner	1981	92	1235	13.4	15
Charles	Buckley	1984	175	1228	7	19
Jeff	Steel	1984	157	1198	7.6	10
John	Hall	1957		1181		19
Erwin	Brown	1988	157	1156	7.4	14
Carl	Howard (VHS)	1963		1151		9
Robert	Pynes	1958		1131		16
Joe	Williams	1987	140	1098	6.9	9
Robert	Pynes	1957		1085		10
Andrew	Croker	2017	126	1055	8.3	9
George	Smith	1961	170	1050	6.2	13
James	Coburn	1954	139	1048	7.5	16
Paul	Nicholas	1963	116	1025	8.8	9
Mark	Clay	1983	193	1017	5.3	10
Terry	Holt	1978	143	1009	7.1	10
Edwin	Ivory	2004	162	1001	6.2	13
D'ante	Gallashaw	2019	155	1001	6.5	9
Levander	Liggins	2010	103	978	9.5	17
Corey	McCoy	2016	103	956	8.3	11
Tony	Rush	1986	141	953	6.8	7
Travante	Stallworth	2007	165	940	5.7	17
Terry	Holt	1976	141	907	6.4	
DeShun	McNeely	1997	188	884	4.7	6

SINGLE GAME RUSHING LEADERS

First Name	Last Name	Year	Opponent	Attempts	Yards
Michael	Ford	2008	Tioga	37	443
Xavier	Ford	2022	Pearl River	37	374
Xavier	Ford	2022	Washington-Marion	32	359
Michael	Ford	2008	Sam Houston	30	335
Cecil	Collins	1994	BTW-Shreveport	28	332
Cecil	Collins	1994	Sam Houston	25	332
Cecil	Collins	1995	Sam Houston	37	325
Eddie	Fuller	1985	Pineville	27	314
Cecil	Collins	1994	Alexandria	15	309
Michael	Ford	2006	LaGrange	38	303
Michael	Ford	2008	Zachary	38	299
Cecil	Collins	1995	Breaux Bridge	37	294
Cecil	Collins	1995	ASH	33	292
Vincent	Fuller	1987	LaGrange	36	292
Xavier	Ford	2022	Catholic-New Iberia	30	282
Robert	Pynes	1958	Westlake	23	285
Caleb	Gallashaw	2021	DeRidder	25	278
Michael	Ford	2008	DeRidder	28	274
Cecil	Collins	1995	Crowley	32	265
Xavier	Ford	2022	Iowa	41	257
Cecil	Collins	1994	DeRidder	21	257
Cecil	Collins	1995	Washington-Marion	26	249
Caleb	Gallashaw	2021	Tioga	29	248
Michael	Ford	2008	LaGrange	28	248
Cecil	Collins	1995	DeRidder	28	247
Cecil	Collins	1993	ASH	19	245
Tony	Rush	1986	DeRidder	17	245
Caleb	Gallashaw	2021	Minden	24	240
Caleb	Gallashaw	2021	Assumption	28	238
Xavier	Ford	2022	Jena	25	235
Vincent	Fuller	1986	Barbe	15	234
DeShun	McNeely	1998	Peabody	27	231
Michael	Ford	2008	Abbeville	35	230
Cecil	Collins	1994	Crowley	24	230
Cecil	Collins	1994	Haughton	28	230
Glover	Carter	1970	Jena	14	228
Edwin	Ivory	2004	Peabody	20	227
Levander	Liggins	2010	ASH	13	226
Rayford	Clayton	1985	Pineville	21	224
Keith	Carver	1964	Natchitoches	25	223

Cecil	Collins	1993	Pineville	19	221
D'Ante	Gallashaw	2018	St. Martinville	27	220
Cecil	Collins	1993	Washington-Marion	28	219
Xavier	Burrell	1996	Eunice	28	219
Michael	Ford	2008	Peabody	31	218
Erwin	Brown	1989	Bastrop	23	218
Erwin	Brown	1989	Parkway	27	216
Xavier	Burrell	1996	ASH	28	216
Mark	Clay	1983	St Louis	17	215
Terry	Holt	1978	Welsh	21	215
Charles	Buckley	1984	Sam Houston	18	214
Calvin	Wilson (Vernon)	1967	W. Livingston		213
Lorenzo	Garner	1972	Pineville	27	212
Oscar	Joiner	1981	Many	7	212
Carl	Howard (Vernon)	1965	St. Marys	7	215
Michael	Ford	2008	Grant	17	210
Jeff	Steel	1984	Sam Houston	17	210
Cecil	Collins	1993	Sam Houston	32	210
Cecil	Collins	1993	BTW-Shreveport	22	209
Michael	Ford	2008	St Michael	34	207
Erwin	Brown	1988	Peabody	9	206
Erwin	Brown	1989	Carencro	21	205
Joe	Williams	1987	ASH	15	202
DeShun	McNeely	1997	Peabody	20	200

Mark Clay   Xavier Burrell   Carl Howard   Erwin Brown

CAREER PASSING LEADERS

First Name	Last Name	Years	Yards	TDs
Zack	Squyres	2009-11	6970	75
Jacob	Mount`	2017-20	6053	68
Dustin	Smith	1996-98	3193	23
Parker	Maks	2021-22	2909	27
Travante	Stallworth	2006-08	2679	24
Justin	Goins	2001-04	2597	25
Martin	Driscoll	1999-01	2263	10
Al	Capello	1981-84	2216	23
Chris	Vargas	2015-17	2108	17
Caden	Wheeler	2013-15	2016	22
Billy	Salim	1963-64	1864	19
Clint	Batteford	1985-96	1656	14
T.J.	Moore	1980-82	1305	11

CChris Vargas

SINGLE SEASON PASSING LEADERS

First Name	Last Name	Year	Yards	TD
Zack	Squyres	2010	2736	30
Zack	Squyres	2009	2431	26
Jacob	Mount	2019	2147	24
Chris	Vargas	2017	2108	17
Jacob	Mount	2018	2077	24
Zack	Squyres	2011	1803	19
Jacob	Mount	2020	1765	18
Parker	Maks	2021	1648	14
Dustin	Smith	1997	1492	11
Dustin	Smith	1998	1476	11
Al	Capello	1983	1413	12
Travante	Stallworth	2007	1340	10
Travante	Stallworth	2008	1339	14
Parker	Maks	2022	1261	13
Vic	Ortiz	1968	1100	14
Theron	Westerchil	2016	1024	9
Roland	Breaux	1965	997	4
Billy	Salim	1963	964	10
Billy	Salim	1964	960	9
Martin	Driscoll	2001	924	7
Justin	Goins	2004	871	11
Clint	Batteford	1985	884	8
Andre	Middlebrooks	1994	835	6
Jason	Green	1995	834	5
Corey	Davis	1993	809	2
Justin	Goins	2002	794	4

Bill Salim

Jacob Mount

First Name	Last Name	Year		
Al	Capello	1984	778	10
Clint	Battleford	1986	772	6
Justin	Goins	2003	755	9
Bobby	Stephens	1977	615	7

SINGLE GAME PASSING LEADERS

First Name	Last Name	Year	Opponent	Yards
Zack	Squyres	2010	Sulphur	402 (6 TDS)
Chris	Vargas	2017	St. Louis	369
Zack	Squyres	2009	Washington-Marion	358
Zack	Squyres	2009	Huntington-Shreveport	333
Zack	Squyres	2010	Huntington-Shreveport	332
Chris	Vargas	2017	Rayne	318
Zack	Squyres	2011	Peabody	314
Dustin	Smith	1997	Washington-Marion	298
Jacob	Mount	2020	Jennings	294
Zack	Squyres	2011	ASH	290
Zack	Squyres	2009	Tioga	289
Zack	Squyres	2010	W Monroe	280
Zack	Squyres	2011	Washington-Marion	269
Justin	Goins	2004	Natchitoches-Central	265
Jacob	Mount	2018	St. Louis	269
Jacob	Mount	2020	Elysian Fields	262
Marlon	Watts	2021	Jennings	251
Dustin	Smith	1997	Eunice	249
Zack	Squyres	2010	DeRidder	249
Zack	Squyres	2009	Grant	246
Jacob	Mount	2019	Northwood	244
Jacob	Mount	2019	Jennings	236
Zack	Squyres	2010	Grant	236
Dustin	Smith	1998	Crowley	236
Jacob	Mount	2018	Grant	233
Travante	Stallworth	2008	Natchitoches-Central	230
Jacob	Mount	2019	Washington-Marion	230
Parker	Maks	2021	Bolton	230
Jacob	Mount	2020	Pineville	229
Zack	Squyres	2011	Grant	228
Dustin	Smith	1998	Evangel	227
Jacob	Mount	2020	Peabody	225
Chris	Vargas	2017	Grant	225
Zack	Squyres	2011	Tioga	225

Travante Stallworth

Parker Maks

First Name	Last Name	Year	Opponent	Yards
Zack	Squyres	2010	Peabody	225
Dustin	Smith	1998	Bolton	222
Zack	Squyres	2010	Washington-Marion	221
Parker	Maks	2021	Pineville	220
Jacob	Mount	2018	Pineville	220
T.J.	Moore	1982	Westlake	220
Chris	Vargas	2017	DeRidder	218
Parker	Maks	2021	Peabody	215
Al	Capello	1983	Washington-Marion	216
Martin	Driscoll	1999	Abbeville	212
Parker	Maks	2022	LaGrange	211
Jacob	Mount	2019	DeRidder	210
Travante	Stallworth	2007	DeRidder	209
Zack	Squyres	2009	ASH	209
Jacob	Mount	2020	Northwood	204
Dustin	Smith	1997	DeRidder	203
Chris	Vargas	2017	Washington-Marion	201
Parker	Maks	2022	Iowa (2)	198
Zack	Squyres	2010	ASH	196
Roland	Breaux	1965	Tioga	195
Zack	Squyres	2010	Sam	194
Billy	Salim	1963	Westlake	192
Zack	Squyres	2009	DeRidder	192
Travante	Stallworth	2007	Peabody	191
Billy	Salim	1964	Jena	191
Zack	Squyres	2009	Sam Houston	185
Zack	Squyres	2010	Tioga	185
Al	Capello	1983	Bolton	183
Martin	Driscoll	2000	Sam Houston	182
Zack	Squyres	2009	Neville	175

Alan Capello

Roland Breauxux

CAREER RECEIVING LEADERS

First Name	Last Name	Years	Receptions	Yards	Average	TDs
Levander	Liggins	2008-10	118	2294	19.4	31
Caleb	Gallashaw	2018-21	105	1206	11.5	11
Clinton	Thurman	2009-11	88	1866	21.2	17
Khrystian	Hoffpauir	2018-20	75	1261	17.67	14
Darius	Sawyer	2018-19	75	1200	16	11
Andrew	Croker	2015-17	68	1335	19.63	14
Marcus	Thurman	1994-96	64	929	14.5	9
Percy	Burns	1982-84	63	1242	19.7	12
Duwon	Tolbert	2016-18	61	1207	19.8	13
Allen	Muse	2005-07	61	816	13.4	4
Noah	Allain	2017-19	52	828	15.9	14
Keith	Zinger	2000-02	48	894	18.2	5

First Name	Last Name	Year	Receptions	Yards	Average	TDs
Jeron	Hamm	2007-09	48	861	17.9	10
DeMond	McNeely	1996-98	43	766	17.8	6
Keith	Smith	1996-98	41	794	19.4	6
Demetrius	Mark	2006-08	38	623	16.4	7
Bernardo	Henry	2003-05	36	769	21.3	10
Kemhari	Pruitt	2020-21	31	637	20.35	6
Davion	Grubb	2021	27	633	23.4	7
D'Ante	Gallashaw	2017-2019	25	309	12.3	0
Robert	Bush	2007-09	24	644	26.8	7

SINGLE SEASON RECEIVING LEADERS

First Name	Last Name	Year	Receptions	Yards	Average	TDs
Clinton	Thurman	2011	57	1343	21.2	11
Levander	Liggins	2010	57	1209	18.7	17
Allen	Muse	2007	53	721	27.1	4
Darius	Sawyer	2019	47	743	15.8	9
Andrew	Croker	2017	42	800	19.04	9
Marcus	Thurman	1996	41	572	17.2	6
Khrystian	Hoffpauir	2020	40	585	14.62	8
Jeron	Hamm	2009	40	748	13.6	8
DeJuan	Taylor	2007	40	408	17.4	3
Demetrius	Mark	2008	35	494	15.3	4
Mike	Fuller	1992	34	444	19.8	3
Caleb	Gallashaw	2019	33	457	13.8	2
Duwon	Tolbert	2018	33	685	20.8	7
Levander	Liggins	2009	32	550	17.8	7
Anthony	Ford	1994	32	393	14.1	3
Kemhari	Pruitt	2021	31	637	20.35	6
Izaiah	Farley	2022	31	360	11.1	7
Caleb	Gallashaw	2021	31	328	14.1	3
Jeval	Chancy	2010	31	475	17.9	4
Caleb	Gallashaw	2020	30	462	15.2	5
Jimmy	Skinner	1964	30	560	18.6	7
Levander	Liggins	2008	30	535	17.1	7
Marshawn	Graham	2022	30	518	17.2	2
Makenzie	Jackson	2017	30	509	16.9	4
Clinton	Thurman	2010	30	513	21	5
Darius	Sawyer	2018	28	515	18.3	8
Lemarcus	Thurman	1996	28	414	14.8	5
Diontay	Thurman	2010	28	397	17.9	4
Khrystian	Hoffpauir	2019	27	450	16.7	6
Davion	Grubb	2021	27	633	23.4	7
Duwon	Tolbert	2017	27	514	19	6
Andre	Middlebrooks	1993	27	380	15.7	1
Kobe	Joiner	2017	26	416	16	3
Sam	Scott	1998	26	467	25.1	3
Andrew	Croker	2016	25	467	18.6	5

Noah	Allain	2019	25	343	13.6	7
Noah	Allain	2018	24	463	29.3	7
Percy	Burns	1983	24	505	14.1	3
Demetrius	Payton	1986	24	377	20.3	4
Keith	Zinger	2002	23	322	14	2
Calvin	Dixon	1983	23	400	15.3	5
Robert	Bush	2009	23	624	14	7
Marcus	Thurman	1995	23	336	14.5	3
Justin	Brown	2000	22	436	33.1	4
Percy	Burns	1982	21	395	12.3	4
Anthony	Gill	1992	19	237	12.5	
Andrew	Robinson	1983	18	451	13.1	4
George	Fisher	1954	18	392	21.7	
Keith	Smith	1998	18	365	19.5	4
Derek	Williams	2001	18	351	21.8	4
Percy	Burns	1984	18	342	19	5
Richard	Schwartz	1963	16	480	30	6
Jimmy	Funderburk	1965	16	381	23.3	4
Marquis	Williams	2004	16	349	19	4
Ju'liun	Colbert	2022	16	212	13.2	2
Marshawn	Graham	2020	15	271	17.1	3
Earnest	Bess	1980	14	114	8.1	1
Bernardo	Henry	2004	13	430	10.2	6
Ray	Macias	1974	13	168	9.3	3

Jeron Hamm, UL Monroe
5 x NFL Teams

Darius Sawyer
Ave Marie Univ

Alan Muse,
McNeese State

Bernardo Henry,
Arkansas State

The Defenders and The 100 Tackles Club

      This section is devoted to statistics of great Wampus Cat defenders. In an ideal world, statistics would be available for each year, with total tackles, assists, sacks, tackles for loss, interceptions and passes defended. As with offensive statistics, sadly, there is little continuity over time and information is both inconsistent and scarce. In conducting research for this section, we found a good number of years where tacklers, sack leaders and interception leaders were identified. We found a number of years where there were a few numbers (for example, just tacklers, or just interception leaders) available. For some years, nothing was discovered. We put out an all-call on social media and did our best; some years involved going through every box score or coach score card that appeared in the paper. Some coaches---Jerry Foshee, Jack Andre and Danny Smith were maybe the best---disseminating statistics for defenders in the paper every week. These days, LHS's coaching squad compiles the stats and disseminate weekly to the publicly.

      In the chart below, you will see defensive leaders, broken out by year. The top two tacklers (total tackles) and interception leader are identified. If you see a year where no stats are identified, it's because no stats could be found. When you see years that have players but no stats, the rule of thumb was to identify the mostly likely tackling or interception leader, based on All-District status and or multiple news accounts of the athlete in the media as a defensive leader. Often times, coaches or media would report a player led the team in tackles, or a player made All-District, and no stats were available. Oddly enough, some of those years are in recent history. As this book is the second version of Wampus Cat History Book, rest assured that future books will include stats uncovered in the ensuing research. For now, this is the best we have. We're also including some pictures of great defenders, one for each year.

      Without further ado, here are the greatest Wampus Cat defenders, from a statistical perspective and a collection of pictures of some of the best Cats ever to play defense.

Season	Athlete	Total Tackles	Solos	Assists	Tackle For Loss	Sacks	Interceptions
2022	Stefan James	91	45	46	1		2
	Frank Ford	82	30	52	3		
	Evan Combs	46	19	27	3		3
2021	Caden Bealer	116	41	75	14	1	
	Frank Ford	112	39	73	6		
	Derek Beebee	25	6	19			3
2020	Frank Ford	66	29	37	7	2	
	Christian Sage	58	18	40	7	3	
	Chris Tyler	32	15	17	6		3
2019	Chris Davis	94	26	68	3	1	
	Quan Williams	88	37	51	2		2
	Darius Allen	52	30	22	2		2
2018	Matt Pajinag	114	43	71	3		
	Talyn Adams	78	28	50	5	2	
	Tyler Brady	37	16	21	2		2
2017	Matt Pajinag	95	28	67	10	1	
	Sabian Matu	67	16	51	2		
	Mackenzie Jackson	26	12	14	2.5		3
	Jordan Dowden	55	12	43			3
2016	Jaelyn Edwards	102	32	70	1		
	Sabian Matu	75	19	56	1	1	
	Derek Hurt	48	11	37	1		2
	Mackenzie Jackson	58	21	37			2
2015	Jaelyn Edwards	78	31	47			
	Sabian Matu	50	19	31			
	Andrew Croker	38	18	20			1
2014	Corey Jones						
	Solomon Cross						
	Davion Clemons						
2013	Elbert Marbury						
2012	Roger Luafalemana	110	73	37	24	13	
	Elbert Marbury						
	Solomon Cross						
	Devail Lewis						
2011	Jeremiah Cross	102				2	
	Dalton Harville						
	Mason DeLapp						
	Deontay Thurman						
2010	Daniel Winnfield	102				7	
2009	Ellis Edwards						
	Daniel Phillips						
	Daniel Winnfield						
	Keedrick Mitchell						
2008	Rob Tunnifu-Sauvao						

Year	Player					
	Demetrius Woods					
	Devin Moran					3
2007	David Detz	121	40	71	12	
	Michael Harris	64	34	30	13	5
	DeAndre Atwater					3
2006	Damien Smith	63			4	1
	Michael Harris	74			5	
	Cornelius Jackson					
2005	Frank Larry	105				
	Wes Tunnifu-Sauvao					
	David Detz					
2004	Wes Tunnifu-Sauvao		37			
	Daryl Joiner					4
	Tommy Neubert					
2003	Josh Quayhagen	109				3
	Wes Harvey					
	Justin Harvey					
2001	Dante Williams					
	Roderick Lawhorn					
2002	Cordell Upshaw	61	53	8	3	5
	Chris White	53	48	5	3	
2000	Justin Brown					
	Roderick Lawhorn					
	Lorenzo Garner					
1999	Chris Cobb					
	Justin Brown					
1998	Chris Cobb	80			6	
	Keith Smith	125			1	1
	Kenny Jones	144			3	
1997	Andre Thurman	112	22	90		3
	Robbie Carter	95	5	90	12	3
	Wes Bailey	90	7	83	6	1
1996	Clement Robinson	79	12	67		2
	Mike Lewis	66	14	52		
	Andre Thurman	42	7	36		3
1995	Greg Rone	195	22	162	15	7	2
	Cedric Clemons	123	8	117	8	10	
	Robert Robinson	65	10	55	4	5	3
1994	Greg Rone	146	89	57	28	15
	Antoinel Goza	44			12	8
	Shermaine Jones	41				3
1993	Alton Harris	162	84	74	8	
	Willie McNutt	100	42	58	17	6
	Tyrone Sims	27				5
1992	Derrick Smart					
	Jonathan Payne					
	Tyrone Sims					

Year	Player					
1991	Kavika Pittman	81	16	65	16	2
	Antoine Shaw					
1990	Tyrone Smith					
	John Brown	56	32	24		2
1989	Anthony Johnson					
	Dwayne Johnson					
1988	Hubert Grant					
	Corey Tompkins					
	Kevin Smith					6
1987	Corey Lucas	204	48	156	8	2
	Stan Watley	46			3	4
1986	Robert Jenkins	98	52	46	11	5
	Mike Smith	131	77	54		
	Stacy Cooper	79	38	41		3
1985	Robert Jenkins	81	40	40		
	Mike Smith	74			9	
	Tony Rush					2
1984	Steve Gunn	180	105	75		
	Sam Hoecker	140	85	55	4	
	Craig Pierce					3
1983	Steve Gunn	145	85	60	3	
	Dexter Gatewood	100	55	45	6	
	Chris Robertson					6
1982	Jimbo Shapkoff	96			2	
	Melvin Maxwell	95			7	
	Chris Robertson					3
1981	Steve Gunn	100	47	53		
	Robert Pynes	88	35	53		
	Melvin Maxwell	88	42	46		
	Chris Robertson					2
1980	Mark Smith	107				
	Michael Deans					
	Earnest Bess					4
1979	Stacy Williams					
	Mark Smith					
	Robert Gaines	36	19	17		3
1978	Stacy Williams					
	Tony Jones					
	Robert Gaines					4
1977	Richard Bastedo		51			
	Joe Mastracchio		50			
	Terry Haynes					5
	Rod Symons					5
1976	Tommy Driscoll		33			
	Ricky West		31			
	Eddie Herndon					2

Year	Name			
1975	Jr Stevens III		51	
	Sam Fertitta		35	
	Greg Stracener			2
1974	Ralph Ortiz			
	Hubert Knight		35	
	Lionel Ceasarez			4
1973	Hubert Knight			
	Larry Wilson			4
1972	Charles Hanks			
	Johnny Mapu			
	Larry Dean			2
1971	Jimmy Mapu			
	Charles Hanks			
	Pat Lynch			2
1970	Sam Burnley			
	Jimmy Mapu			
	Jerry Haynes			4
1969	Jimmy Anderson	98		
	Jackson Mapu	90		
	Steve Hays			3
1968	Larry Carr			
	Elroy Treme			6
1967	Darwin Davis			
	John Driscoll			
	Jimmy Funderburk			4
1966	Jimmy Auvil			
	Dickie Bailes			
1965	Ronnie Morrow			5
1963	RJ Fertitta			2

100 Tackles Club

Below is a list of Wampus Cats who achieved over 100 or more tackles in a single season

Season	Athlete	Total Tackles	Solos	Assists	Tackle For Loss	Sacks	Interceptions
1987	Corey Lucas	204	48	156		8	2
1995	Greg Rone	195	22	162	15	7	2
1984	Steve Gunn	180	105	75			
1993	Alton Harris	162	84	74	8		
1994	Greg Rone	146	89	57	28	15	
1983	Steve Gunn	145	85	60		3	
1998	Kenny Jones	144			3		
1984	Sam Hoecker	140	85	55		4	
1995	Sedric Clemons	136	18	118			
1986	Mike Smith	131	77	54			
1998	Keith Smith	125			1		1
2007	David Detz	121	40	71	12		
2021	Caden Bealer	116	41	75	14		
2018	Matt Pajinag	114	43	71	3		
2021	Frank Ford	112	39	73	6		
1997	Andre Thurman	112	22	90			3
2012	Roger Luafalemana	110	73	37	24	13	
2003	Josh Quayhagen	109					3
2022	Stefan James	108	57	51	1		2
1980	Mark Smith	107					
2005	Frank Larry	105					
2016	Jaelyn Edwards	102	32	70	1		
2011	Jeremiah Cross	102				2	
2010	Daniel Winnfield	102				7	
1993	Willie McNutt	100	42	58	17	6	
1983	Dexter Gatewood	100	55	45		6	
1981	Steve Gunn	100	47	53			

Wampus Cat Defensive Stars

Kemp Tucker 1938   Robert Ferguson 1940

Frank Haynie 1945   Billy Blackburn 1946   Buddy Conley 1947   Red Smith 1949

Ted Paris 1951   Mitch Nicholas 1952   Wallace McRae 1953   Jerry Skinner 1954

Lewis Reid Brown 1955   Bobby Arthur 1956   JC Welch 1957   Doug Marhsall 1958

John Simonelli 1959   Jim Scogin 1960   Johnny Wood 1961   Roy Trahan 1962

RJ Fertitta 1963   Dwayne Palmer 1964

Ron Morrow 1965 Dickie Bailes 1966 Jimmy Funderburk, 1967

Elroy Treme 1968 Jackson Mapu 1969 Jimmy Mapu 1970 Charles Hanks 1971

Johnny Mapu 1972 Hubert Knight 1973 Ralph Ortiz 1974 Butch Stevens 1975

   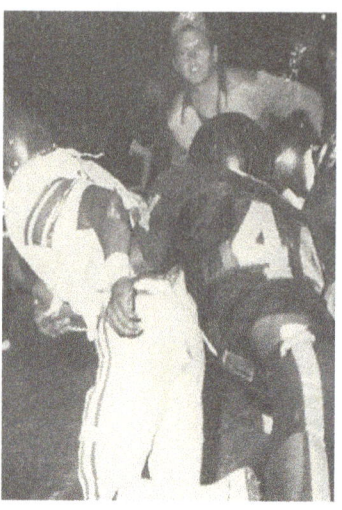

Tommy Driscoll 1976   Terry Haynes 1977   Stacy Williams 1978   Robert Gaines 1979

Mark Smith /Michael Deans 1980   Jimbo Shapkoff 1981   Melvin Maxwell 1982   Steve Gunn 1983

Sam Hoecker 1984   Robert Jenkins 1985

Mike Smith 1986 Corey Lucas 1987 Kevin Smith 1988

Anthony Johnson 1989 John Brown 1990 Kavika Pittman 1991 Derrick Smart 1992

Alton Harris 1993 Greg Rone 1994 Cedric Clemons 1995 Clement Robinson 1996

Robbie Carter 1997   Kenny Jones 1998   Chris Cobb 1999   Justin Brown 2000

Roderick Lawhorn 2001   Cordell Upshaw 2002   Josh Quayhagen 2003   Wes Tunnufi-Sauvo, 2004

Frank Larry 2005   Damien Smith 2006   David Detz & Michael Harris 2007

Devin Moran 2008   Ellis Edwards. 2009   Daniel Winnfield 2010   Jeremiah Cross 2011

Roger Luafalemana 2012   Elbert Marbury 2013   Solomon Cross 2014   Jaelyn Edward 2015

Sabian Matu 2016   Makenzie Jackson 2017   Matt Pajinag 2018   Chris Davis 2019

Frank Ford 2020   Caden Bealer 2021   Stefan James 2022

ALL-TIME RESULTS OF THE LEESVILLE HIGH SCHOOL FOOTBALL TEAM

In the first edition of this book, it was noted that many things were left to document in terms of the history of Wampus Cat Football. The first version was a narrative history with available stats. One of the deficiencies recognized and one of the goals for the ensuing versions of the book was a list of all scores and results of LHS football from years gone by.

Very pleased to announce that in this 2023 version, we have a section dedicated to all-time results. In short, in the 2 years since the first version of the book, we ve pieced together ALL-TIME results for Wampus Cat football. Every game (non-jamboree) and every score that is discoverable is included in this book. Great results are available all the way back to 1929, with a good number of results and final scores are chronicled as far back as 1910. Starting with the recently-concluded 2022 season, you'll find the results from every game, including playoff contests for the LHS football program. Also provided is a representative photograph from each season---selected at the editorial discretion of the author. Someday, hope to have every box score, but that effort will take a few more years to piece together. Here you go EVERY SCORE in EVERY YEAR of Leesville Wampus Cat Football.

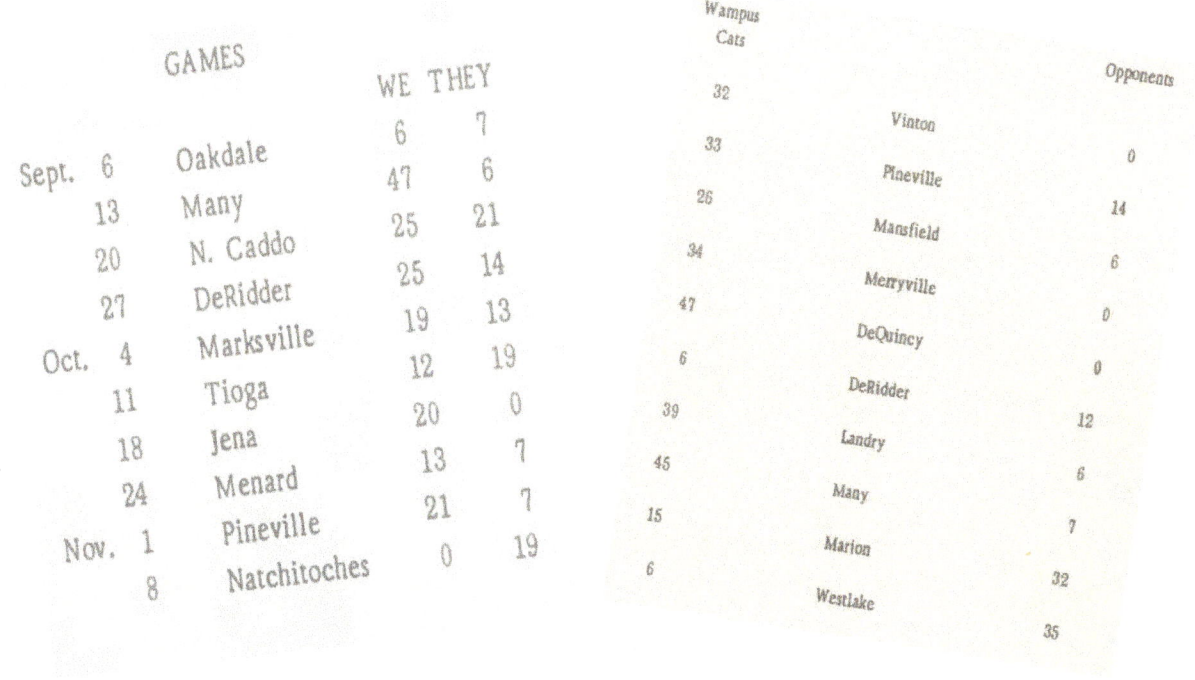

GAMES		WE	THEY
Sept. 6	Oakdale	6	7
13	Many	47	6
20	N. Caddo	25	21
27	DeRidder	25	14
Oct. 4	Marksville	19	13
11	Tioga	12	19
18	Jena	20	0
24	Menard	13	7
Nov. 1	Pineville	21	7
8	Natchitoches	0	19

1968 Results

Wampus Cats		Opponents
32	Vinton	0
33	Pineville	14
26	Mansfield	6
34	Merryville	0
47	DeQuincy	0
6	DeRidder	12
39	Landry	6
45	Many	7
15	Marion	32
6	Westlake	35

1954 Results

Every Score, Every Year

Opponent	Score	Season	Remarks
Jennings	W 25-7	2022	
Jena	W 21-14	2022	
Iowa	W 30-14	2022	
Catholic-New Ibera	W 26-0	2022	
Opelousas	L 56-20	2022	
Washington-Marion	W 41-18	2022	
DeRidder	W 42-15	2022	
LaGrange	W 56-6	2022	
Eunice	L 38-33	2022	
Rayne	W 47-6	2022	
Pearl River	W 42-14	2022	Playoff 1st Round
Jennings	W 21-7	2022	Playoff 2nd Round
Iowa	L 31-14	2022	Quarterfinal
Jennings	W 35-14	2021	
Captain Shreve	L 54-0	2021	
LaGrange	W 50-14	2021	
Pineville	L 35-32	2021	
Minden	W 49-36	2021	
Bolton	W 42-6	2021	
DeRidder	W 49-41	2021	
Peabody	W 54-0	2021	
Tioga	W 34-7	2021	
Assumption	W 41-32	2021	Playoff 1st Round
Westgate	L 16-7	2021	Playoff 2nd Round
Neville	L 29-7	2020	
Pineville	W 42-24	2020	
Elysian FieldsTX	W 55-38	2020	
Tioga	L 33-20	2020	
Jennings	L 56-41	2020	
Bolton	W 63-25	2020	
Peabody	W 42-12	2020	
Northwood	W 28-27	2020	Playoff 1st Round
Minden	L 21-14 (OT)	2020	Playoff 2nd Round

Jennings	W 48-41 (OT)	2019	
Lake Charles College Prep	W 54-40	2019	
Washington-Marion	W 48-12	2019	
Pineville	W 20-14	2019	
DeQuincy	W 43-21	2019	
Tioga	L 37-35	2019	
DeRidder	L 24-21	2019	
Bolton	W 47-20	2019	
Northwood	L 42-20	2019	
Peabody	L 45-28	2019	
Pearl River	W 47-21	2019	Playoff 1st Round
Lakeshore	L 41-14	2019	Playoff 2nd Round
Washington-Marion	W 38-18	2018	
South Beauregard	W 13-0	2018	
Westlake	W 35-7	2018	
Pineville	W 38-35	2018	
Rayne	W 41-26	2018	
Buckeye	W 41-14	2018	
Grant	W 42-8	2018	
DeRidder	W 26-7	2018	
Tioga	W 33-23	2018	
St. Louis Catholic	W 47-34	2018	
Woodlawn (Shreve)	W 49-28	2018	Playoff 1st round
Assumption	W 27-14	2018	Playoff
St. Martinville	W 53-49	2018	Quarterfinal
Warren Easton	L 54-14	2018	Semi-Final
Washington-Marion	W 33-2	2017	
South Beauregard	W 6-0	2017	
Westlake	W 18-14	2017	
Pineville	W 61-48	2017	
Rayne	L 28-18	2017	
Buckeye	W 42-7	2017	
Grant	W 63-30	2017	
DeRidder	W 27-0	2017	
Tioga	W 42-13	2017	
St. Louis Catholic	W 56-34	2017	
Franklinton	W 38-20	2017	Playoff 1st Round
Rayne	L 28-7	2017	Playoff 2nd Round

Westlake	W 42-7	2016	
South Beauregard	L 23-20	2016	
ASH	L 54-21	2016	
Pineville	W 41-21	2016	
Iowa	L 41-27	2016	
Washington-Marion	W 47-14	2016	
Rayne	L 26-13	2016	
LaGrange	W 21-14	2016	
Crowley	W 21-19	2016	
DeRidder	W 42-28	2016	
Beau Chene	W 40-7	2016	Playoff 1st Round
Edna Karr	L 55-0	2016	Playoff 2nd Round

Westlake	W 41-24	2015	
South Beauregard	L 43-41 (OT)	2015	
ASH	W 49-39	2015	
Pineville	W 41-20	2015	
Iowa	L 34-27	2015	
Washington-Marion	L 19-14	2015	
Rayne	L 20-14	2015	
LaGrange	L 49-14	2015	
Crowley	L 49-28	2015	
DeRidder	L 56-20	2015	

Buckeye	L 27-21	2014	
Many	L 33-7	2014	
Menard	W 41-10	2014	
Winnfield	W 34-21	2014	
Pineville	L 22-17	2014	
DeRidder	W 21-6	2014	
Grant	W 55-0	2014	
Tioga	W 41-12	2014	
Bolton	W 65-27	2014	
Peabody	L 76-56	2014	
Rayne	L 36-22	2014	Playoff 1st Round

Buckeye	L 15-6	2013	
Many	L 34-7	2013	
Menard	L 17-14	2013	
Winnfield	L 27-0	2013	
Pineville	L 37-7	2013	
DeRidder	L 36-7	2013	
Grant	W 35-28	2013	
Tioga	W 26-14	2013	
Bolton	L 48-28	2013	
Peabody	L 20-7	2013	

DeRidder	L 49-0	2012	
Sam Houston	L 24-7	2012	
Pineville	L 31-7	2012	
Sulphur	L 36-0	2012	
Washington-Marion	L 34-0	2012	
Bolton	L 35-31	2012	
Peabody	L 48-7	2012	
ASH	L 38-14	2012	
Grant	W 42-20	2012	
Tioga	L 33-19	2012	

DeRidder	L 42-14	2011	
Sam Houston	L 33-14	2011	
Pineville	L 37-8	2011	
Sulphur	L 31-28	2011	
Washington-Marion	L 40-27	2011	
Bolton	W 36-20	2011	
Peabody	W 45-16	2011	
ASH	L 49-42	2011	
Grant	W 64-6	2011	
Tioga	W 63-42	2011	

West Monroe	L 68-28	2010	
Sam Houston	L 42-37	2010	
Sulphur	W 45-40	2010	
Washington-Marion	W 35-28	2010	
DeRidder	W 24-17	2010	
Peabody	W 51-48	2010	
ASH	W 69-48	2010	
Grant	W 50-14	2010	
Tioga	W 50-20	2010	
Grant	W 49-28	2010	
DeRidder	W 34-20	2010	Playoff 1st Round
Franklinton	L 55-14	2010	Playoff 2nd Round

West Monroe	L 71-13	2009	
Sam Houston	L 46-27	2009	
Sulphur	L 51-27	2009	
Washington-Marion	W 40-18	2009	
DeRidder	L 37-18	2009	
Peabody	L 20-18	2009	
ASH	L 26-12	2009	
Grant	W 40-20	2009	
Tioga	W 40-19	2009	
Huntington	W 37-34	2009	
Neville	L 63-21	2009	Playoff 1st Round

West Monroe	L 28-7	2008	
Sam Houston	W 41-26	2008	
NCHS	W 62-0	2008	
LaGrange	W 54-24	2008	
DeRidder	W 68-29	2008	
Grant	W 49-0	2008	
Abbeville	W 27-25	2008	
Peabody	W 22-6	2008	
ASH	W 35-27	2008	
Tioga	W 42-29	2008	
St. Michael	W 28-7	2008	Playoff 1st Round
Zachary	L 21-19	2008	Playoff 2nd Round

Jennings	L 27-7	2007	
Sam Houston	L 29-12	2007	
NCHS	W 20-6	2007	
LaGrange	L 17-13	2007	
DeRidder	W 43-13	2007	
Grant	W 42-8	2007	
Abbeville	L 7-6	2007	
Peabody	W 33-14	2007	
Tioga	W 41-23	2007	
ASH	W 42-27	2007	
Vandebilt Catholic	L 35-6	2007	Playoff 1st Round

Carroll	W 41-33	2006	
Sam Houston	L 35-2	2006	
Redemptorist	L 26-9	2006	
Marksville	W 49-0	2006	
DeRidder	W 33-7	2006	
Pineville	L 28-7	2006	
ASH	L 28-13	2006	
Tioga	W 43-7	2006	
LaGrange	W 28-22	2006	
Peabody	W 47-19	2006	
Breaux Bridge	L 21-14	2006	Playoff 1st Round

Carroll	L 28-7	2005	
Sam Houston	L 28-6	2005	
Redemptorist	L 40-0	2005	
Marksville	L 28-8	2005	
Pineville	L 35-14	2005	
ASH	L 48-20	2005	
Tioga	W 21-14	2005	
LaGrange	W 31-14	2005	
Peabody	W 28-16	2005	

NCHS	W 40-28	2004	
Sam Houston	W 26-20	2004	
LaGrange	L 35-6	2004	
Eunice	W 13-6	2004	
DeRidder	W 46-7	2004	
Pineville	W 35-7	2004	
Peabody	W 44-21	2004	
Tioga	W 42-12	2004	
ASH	W 19-12	2004	
Bolton	W 46-0	2004	
Opelousas	L 34-28	2004	Playoff 1st Round

NCHS	L 48-20	2003	
Sam Houston	L 17-7	2003	
Lagrange	L 36-7	2003	
Eunice	L 33-7	2003	
Deridder	W 21-14	2003	
Pineville	W 20-17	2003	
Peabody	W 14-17	2003	
Tioga	L 33-13	2003	
ASH	L 45-22	2003	
Bolton	W 44-16	2003	

LaGrange	W 27-21	2002	
Pineville	W 20-10	2002	
Bolton	W 34-20	2002	
Many	W 30-13	2002	
ASH	W 21-7	2002	
Eunice	L 38-7	2002	
DeRidder	W 14-6	2002	
Washington-Marion	L 28-13	2002	
St. Louis	W 30-13	2002	
Sam Houston	L 14-7	2002	
John Curtis	L 28-0	2002	Playoff 1st Round

LaGrange	L 19-12	2001	
Pineville	W 28-10	2001	
Bolton	W 27-15	2001	
Many	L 26-18	2001	
ASH	W 28-0	2001	
Eunice	L 20-14	2001	
DeRidder	W 14-3	2001	
Washington-Marion	L 27-14	2001	
Sam Houseton	W 25-13	2001	
St. Louis	W 13-3	2001	
Neville	L 48-0	2001	Playoff 1st Round

LaGrange	L 35-0	2000	
St. Thomas More	L 35-21	2000	
Bolton	L 0-17	2000	
Tioga	W 47-0	2000	
ASH	W 28-15	2000	
Eunice	L 26-0	2000	
DeRidder	W 40-0	2000	
Washington-Marion	W 14-35	2000	
Sam Houston	L 34-32	2000	
Crowley	W 42-21	2000	
Walker	W 20-7	2000	Playoff 1st Round
Woodlawn	W 24-18	2000	Playoff 2nd Round
Assumption	L 35-14	2000	Playoff Quarterfinal

LaGrange	L 48-6	99	
St Thomas More	L 35-19	99	
Bolton	W 28-14	99	
Tioga	W 7-6	99	
ASH	L 23-14	99	
Eunice	L 3-0	99	
DeRidder	W 30-8	99	
Washington-Marion	L 51-24	99	
Sam Houston	L 35-7	99	
Crowley	W 38-14	99	
Abbeville	L 26-20	99	Playoff 1st Round

Evangel	L 37-20	98	
Peabody	W 28-6	98	
Sulphur	L 61-13	98	
Tioga	L 28-13	98	
Bolton	L 21-17	98	
DeRidder	W 36-24	98	
Crowley	L 32-22	98	
ASH	L 48-24	98	
Sam Houston	W 22-19	98	
Eunce	L 19-7	98	
Tioga	L 26-7	98	Playoff 1st Round

Evangel	L 24-14	97
Peabody	W 26-6	97
Sulphur	L 30-7	97
Tioga	W 20-13	97
Bolton	W 34-12	97
DeRidder	L 14-12	97
Crowley	L 33-13	97
ASH	W 14-12	97

Sam Houston	L 20-13	97	
Eunice	L 31-22	97	
ASH	W 21-7	96	
Peabody	W 52-7	96	
Sulphur	L 21-13	96	
Woodlawn (SHV	W 35-18	96	
Marksville	W 16-0	96	
Eunice	L 49-21	96	
Washington-Marion	W 36-20	96	
Sam Houston	W 13-7	96	
Crowley	L 53-0	96	
DeRidder	L 25-7	96	
Northwood	W 21-20	96	Playoff 1st Round
Wossman	L 34-21	96	Playoff 2nd Round
ASH	W 44-12	95	
Peabody	W 42-0	95	
Sulphur	L 20-14	95	
Woodlawn (SHV)	W 39-0	95	
Eunice	W 37-0	95	
Washington-Marion	W 44-14	95	
Sam Houston	W 25-0	95	
Crowley	W 44-28	95	
DeRidder	W 15-0	95	
Opelousas	W 31-0	95	Playoff 1st Round
Carroll	W 30-28	95	Playoff 2nd Round
DeRidder	W 29-0	95	State Quarter-Finals
Breaux Bridge	W 28-13	95	State Semi-Finals
Salmen	L 38-7	95	State Finals
ASH	W 34-7	94	
NCHS	L 36-13	94	
Peabody	L 12-7	94	
BTW	W 41-12	94	
Mansfield	W 39-26	94	
Washington-Marion	W 16-6	94	
DeRidder	W 28-0	94	
Sam Houston	W 37-35	94	
Crowley	L 23-20	94	
Grant	W 55-0	94	
Haughton	W 34-7	94	Playoff 1st Round
Wossman	L 8-6	94	Playoff 2nd Round

91

ASH	L 44-41	93	
NCHS	L 23-13	93	
Peabody	W 32-6	93	
BTW	W 19-12	93	
Mansfield	L 36-14	93	
Washington-Marion	W 41-14	93	
Leesville	W 24-14	93	
Crowley	W 29-6	93	
Grant	W 34-0	93	
DeRidder	L 24-14	93	
Pineville	W 39-7	93	Playoff 1st Round
Abbeville	L 25-7	93	Playoff 2nd Round
DeRidder	W 13-12	92	
Southwood	L 27-0	92	
Peabody	L 28-20	92	
Washington-Marion	W 27-22	92	
Mansfield	L 21-18	92	
Sulphur	L 34-3	92	
Barbe	L 48-6	92	
Lagrange	L 17-13	92	
NCHS	L 30-16	92	
DeRidder	L 26-12	91	
Southwood	L 26-22	91	
Peabody	L 20-14 (OT)	91	
Washington-Marion	L 31-7	91	
Mansfield	L 12-0	91	
Sulphur	L 17-7	91	
Barbe	L 20-0	91	
LaGrange	L 14-0	91	
NCHS	L 17-3	91	
Southwood	L 28-0	90	
Carencro	L 24-20	90	
NCHS	L 30-3	90	
Bastrop	W 28-0	90	
Ouachita	L 31-20	90	
LaGrange	L 36-20	90	
Parkway	L 12-7	90	
Sulphur	W 18-16	90	
DeRidder	W 15-0	90	
Barbe	L 34-14	90	

Carencro	W 34-17	89
Southwood	L 21-14	89
Bastrop	W 25-17	89
NCHS	L 35-21	89
Ouachita	L 42-6	89
Parkway	W 20-0	89
LaGrange	L 27-19	89
Sulphur	W 14-9	89
DeRidder	L 14-7	89
Barbe	L 14-3	89

Peabody	W 41-0	88
ASH	W 27-7	88
Lake Charles Boston	W 40-0	88
NCHS	L 21-14	88
Bastrop	W 6-3	88
Barbe	L 14-10	88
DeRidder	L 17-16	88
Pineville	W 34-13	88
Sulphur	W 44-24	88
LaGrange	L 34-10	88

Peabody	W 13-6	87	
ASH	W 33-14	87	
LC-Boston	W 28-0	87	
NCHS	W 24-0	87	
Bastrop	W 37-27	87	
Barbe	L 21-7	87	
DeRidder	W 23-14	87	
Pineville	W 26-0	87	
Sulphur	W 28-21	87	
LaGrange	W 28-25	87	
New Iberia	W 47-46	87	Playoff 1st Round
St. Amant	W 26-10	87	Playoff 2nd Round
Ruston	L 26-21	87	State Quarter Finals

Peabody	W 17-0	86
Tioga	W 28-7	86
NCHS	W 21-7	86

Pineville	W 24-0	86	
DeRidder	W 45-14	86	
Sulphur	W 24-21	86	
Barbe	W 29-14	86	
ASH	L 19-13	86	
Lagrange	W 17-12	86	
Carencro	W 15-8	86	Playoff 1st Round
Broadmoor	W 8-7	86	Playoff 2nd Round
Ruston	L 18-9	86	State Quarter Finals
Peabody	W 33-6	85	
Tioga	W 39-0	85	
NCHS	W 42-0	85	
Pinevill	W 42-14	85	
DeRidder	W 36-0	85	
Sulphur	W 13-11	85	
ASH	W 30-7	85	
Barbe	L 31-28	85	
LaGrange	W 23-20 (OT)	85	
Huntington	W 8-7	85	Playoff 1st Round
West Monroe	W 49-14	85	Playoff 2nd Round
St. Martinville	L 14-8	85	State Quarter Finals
Many	W 44-2	84	
Menard	W 56-12	84	
Bolton	W 52-16	84	
St. Louis	W 34-13	84	
Westlake	W 29-21	84	
Washington-Marion	L 28-21	84	
DeRidder	L 14-12	84	
Jennings	W 16-14	84	
Sam Houston	W 54-20	84	
Rayne	L 20-12	84	Playoff 1st Round
Many	W 38-6	83	
Menard	W 12-0	83	
Bolton	W 20-14	83	
St. Louis	W 33-8	83	
Westlake	L 9-0	83	
Washington-Marion	L 19-16	83	
DeRidder	W 37-26	83	
Jennings	W 22-16	83	
Sam Houston	W 25-7	83	
Abbeville	W 24-9	83	First playoff win in program history
Wossman	L 32-0	83	Playoff 2nd Round

St. Mary	W 24-9	82
Grant	W 28-8	82
Menard	W 13-12	82
Westlake	L 28-21	82
L Jennings	L 17-10	82
Sam Houston	W 34-13	82
Washington-Martion	L 28-14	82
Oakdale	W 42-6	82
Many	W 32-19	82
DeRidder	L 37-12	82

St.Mary	W 24-0	81
Grant	W 45-0	81
Menard	W 26-8	81
Westlake	L 20-13	81
Jennings	L 30-0	81
DeRidder	W 21-7	81
Sam Houston	L 29-28	81
Washingto	W 19-9	81
Oakdale	W 21-6	81
Many	W 48-6	81

Many	W 33-7	80
DeRidder	W 26-15	80
Welsh	L 7-0	80
Washington	L 22-0	80
Westlake	L 7-0	80
Sam Houston	W 12-7	80
Oakdale	W 13-6	80
Opelousas	L 28-9	80
Jennings	L 22-14	80
Eunice	L 6-0	80

Many	L 14-0	79
DeRidder	L 22-14	79
Welsh	W 15-12	79
Washington	L 29-6	79
Westlake	L 3-0	79
Sam Houston	L 32-0	79
Oakdale	W 35-6	79
Opelousas	L 18-6	79
Jennings	L 12-6 (OT)	79
Eunice	L 13-6	79

Many	W 26-16	78
DeRidder	L 23-6	78
Welsh	W 24-20	78
Eunice	W 12-0	78
Washington	L 31-7	78
Sam Houston	L 30-6	78
Westlake	W 20-6	78
Jennings	L 10-6	78
Marksville	W 27-8	78
Oakdale	L 21-14	78

Many	W 18-0	77
DeRidder	L 6-0	77
Welsh	W 39-12	77
Eunice	W 14-13	77
Jennings	L 21-7	77
Sam Houston	L 15-13	77
Westlake	L 18-7	77
Washington	W 15-14	77
Marksville	W 7-6	77
Oakdale	W 9-7	77

DeRidder	L 42-6	76
NCHS	L 20-12	76
ASH	L 27-14	76
Jennings	L 17-0	76
Rayne	L 18-6	76
Eunice	L 9-7	76
Oakdale	W 18-6	76
Washington	T 0-0	76
Many	W 12-6	76
Westlake	L 14-7	76

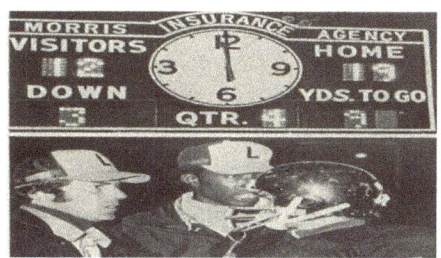

BROKE 20 GAME LOSING STREAK

DeRidder	L 50-0	75
NCHS	L 8-0	75
ASH	L 13-6	75
Jennings	L 28-6	75
Rayne	L 28-0	75
Eunice	L 10-0	75
Oakdale	L 42-6	75
Washington	L 22-0	75
Many	L 14-10	75
Westlake	L 27-6	75

DeRidder	L 28-6	74
NCHS	L 18-14	74
DeQuincy	W 6-2	74
Westlake	W 6-0	74
Jennings	W 14-13	74
Eunice	L 7-6	74
Rayne	L 24-6	74
Many	L 6-0	74
Washington	L 13-6	74

DeRidder	T 6-6	73
NCHS	L 28-14	73
DeQuincy	W 20-6	73
Westlake	W 14-6	73
Jennings	L 13-6	73
Eunice	L 22-16	73
Rayne	L 22-15	73
Many	L 24-18	73
Washington	L 35-14	73

DeRidder	W 2-0	72	Forfeit, Illegal player
Winnfield	L 35-10	72	
Menard	W 21-14	72	
Oakdale	W 40-6	72	
Pineville	W 7-7	72	
Jena	W 20-12	72	
Peabody	L 6-0	72	
Tioga	W 12-7	72	
Many	W 13-0	72	
NCHS	L 26-0	72	

DeRidder	L 21-6	71
Winnfield	L 54-0	71
Menard	W 18-0	71
Oakdale	L 24-0	71
Pineville	W 20-13	71
Jena	W 13-6	71
Peabody	L 33-8	71
Tioga	L 7-6	71
Many	L 24-12	71
NCHS	L 28-20	71

Northwood	L 24-12	70
Winnfield	L 33-13	70
Menard	L 22-8	70
Oakdale	W 28-0	70
Pineville	L 13-6	70
Jena	W 36-7	70
Peabody	T 6-6	70
Tioga	L 21-6	70
Coushatta	T 12-12	70
Natchitoches	L 34-0	70

Oakdale	W 25-6	69
Many	W 40-0	69
North Caddo	T 14-14	69
DeRidder	W 25-0	69
Marksville	W 38-14	69
Tioga	W 20-7	69
Jena	W 20-10	69
Menard	L 7-6	69
Pineville	W 19-8	69
Natchitoches	L 22-14	69

Oakdale	L 7-6	68
Many	W 47-6	68
North Caddo	W 25-21	68
DeRidder	W 25-14	68
Marksville	W 19-13	68
Tioga	L 19-12	68
Jena	W 12-0	68
Menard	W 13-7	68
Pineville	W 21-7	68
Natchitoches	L 19-0	68

Oakdale	W 26-8	67
Ville Platte	W 20-18	67
Jena	W 13-7	67
Northside	T 14-14	67
DeRidder	W 21-0	67
Tioga	W 14-7	67
Westlake	L 21-14	67
Menard	L 22-7	67
Pineville	L 20-7	67
Natchitoches	L 27-0	67

Oakdale	W 12-0	66
Ville Platte	L 6-0	66
Jena	L 33-0	66
Northside	T 0-0	66
DeRidder	W 21-0	66
Tioga	W 21-6	66
Westlake	T 14-14	66
Menard	L 19-14	66
Pineville	W 16-7	66
Natchitoches	L 20-7	66

Oakdale	L 12-0	65
Coushatta	W 13-0	65
Ferriday	W 14-13	65
Marion	W 39-7	65
Tioga	L 8-7	65
Jena	L 20-13	65
Menard	L 19-7	65
Many	W 13-7	65
Natchitoches	L 20-0	65
DeRidder	L 13-0	65

Oakdale	L 26-12	64	
Coushatta	L 20-13	64	
Ferriday	W 33-6	64	
Marion	W 33-13	64	
Tioga	W 41-12	64	
Jena	W 27-0	64	
Menard	L 31-6	64	
Many	T 12-12	64	
Natchitoches	T 20-20	64	
DeRidder	L 40-13	64	
Eunice	L 26-6	64	Playoff 1st Round

Oakdale	L 26-6	63	
Minden	L 19-39	63	
Westlake	W 34-7	63	
Pineville	W 21-19	63	
Marion	W 27-13	63	
Tioga	W 46-0	63	
Jena	W 33-7	63	
Menard	W 36-6	63	
Many	W 26-0	63	
Natchitoches	W 19-0	63	
DeRidder	W 28-6	63	
DeRidder	L 34-19	63	Playoff 1st Round

Oakdale	T 0-0	62
Minden	W 20-13	62
Westlake	W 13-7	62
Pineville	L 37-13	62
Marion	W 20-6	62
Jena	W 13-0	62
Menard	W 13-7	62
Many	W 28-6	62
Natchitoches	W 14-13	62
DeRidder	L 12-0	62

Oakdale	L 20-19	61
Many	W 21-0	61
Bunkie	W 33-0	61
Pineville	L 25-13	61
DeQuincy	L 14-0	61
Menard	L 34-13	61
Jena	W 19-0	61
Coushatta	L 20-19	61
Natchitoches	W 25-0	61
DeRidder	L 41-7	61

Oakdale	W 13-0	60
Many	W 34-0	60
Bunkie	L 25-0	60
Pineville	L 26-6	60
DeQuincy	W 40-0	60
Menard	L 13-6	60
Jena	L 12-7	60
Coushatta	W 40-13	60
Natchitoches	L 35-13	60
DeRidder	L 14-13	60

Pineville	L 20-7	59
Oakdale	T 7-7	59
Ferriday	L 20-0	59
DeQuincy	L 13-0	59
Pineville	L 30-7	59
Menard	W 19-7	59
Jena	W 18-13	59
Vinton	W 19-12	59
Many	W 13-0	59
Natchitoches	L 41-7	59
DeRidder	L 7-6	59
Oakdale	L 19-7	59	Lions Bowl

Lions Bowl

Bolton	W 13-0	58
Oakdale	W 20-0	58
Vinton	W 28-6	58
Dequincy	W 20-13	58
Menard	W 39-26	58
Westlake	W 49-13	58
Marion	W 21-18	58
Many	W 45-7	58
Natchitcohes	L 13-12	58
DeRidder	L 12-0	58

Pineville	L 28-21	57
Oakdale	W 21-13	57
Lake Charles	L 46-20	57
Menard	W 34-28	57
Westlake	W 26-13	57
Vinton	W 33-28	57
Many	W 40-14	57
Marion	L 45-14	57
DeRidder	W 33-6	57
DeQuincy	W 27-13	57
Landry	L 49-14	57

North Caddo	L 19-6	56
Natchitoches	L 20-6	56
Merryville	L 19-13	56
Pineville	L 39-6	56
Dequincy	L 46-27	56
Westlake	L 28-6	56
Vinton	L 34-6	56
Menard	L 28-7	56
Marion	L 28-13	56
Many	W 33-0	56
DeRidder	L 34-7	56

Bossier	L 32-6	55
Merryville	W 6-0	55
North Caddo	L 6-0	55
Natchitoches	L 19-13	55
Dequincy	L 63-6	55
Vinton	L 27-0	55
Westlake	L 27-7	55
Marion	L 24-7	55
Many	L 24-14	55
DeRidder	L 32-6	55

Vinton	W 32-0	54
Pineville	W 33-14	54
Mansfield	W 24-6	54
Merryville	W 34-0	54
DeQuincy	W 47-0	54
DeRidder	L 12-6	54
Landry	W 39-6	54
Many	W 45-7	54
Marion	L 32-15	54
Westlake	L 35-6	54

Oakdale	W 13-0	53
Pineville	W 7-6	53
Mansfield	W 25-18	53
Merryville	L 24-6	53
St. Augistine	W 20-7	53
Dequincy	W 26-6	53
DeRidder	L 18-7	53
Landry	W 39-6	53
Many	W 33-12	53
Marion	L 18-12	53
Westlake	L 40-7	53

Sacred Heart	W 25-6	52
Pineville	W 33-8	52
Merryville	W 26-14	52
Mansfield	L 27-12	52
Natchitoches	L 13-6	52
DeQuincy	W 22-0	52
Ville Platte	W 34-6	52
DeRidder	L 39-0	52
Landry	W 12-7	52
Many	W 33-0	52
Menard	W 19-6	52
Oakdale	L 27-6	52

Hardwood Bowl

Sacred Heart	W 13-6	51
Ville Platte	W 13-6	51
Landry	W 13-0	51
Merryville	W 25-14	51
Natchitoches	L 24-12	51
DeQuincy	W 26-18	51

DeRidder	L 28-7	51	
Bunkie	L 43-0	51	
Many	W 37-7	51	
Menard	W 23-0	51	
Oberlin	W 27-0	51	
Oakdale	L 7-0	51	Hardwood Bowl
Sacred Heart	L 25-6	50	
Ville Platte	L 20-6	50	
Landry	L 13-0	50	
Merryville	L 7-0	50	
Natchitoches	L 20-7	50	
DeQuincy	L 34-0	50	
Oakdale	L 19-0	50	
DeRidder	L 32-0	50	
Bunkie	L 12-7	50	
Many	W 20-12	50	
Menard	L 6-0	50	
Sacret Heart	L 14-12	49	
Vivian	L 32-7	49	
Winnfield	W 13-6	49	
Natchitoches	L 6-0	49	
Dequincy	L 40-6	49	
Crowley	L 26-22	49	
Oakdale	L 20-9	49	
DeRidder	L 29-19	49	
Menard	W 21-12	49	
Ville Platte	L 6-0	48	
Menard	L 9-0	48	
Winnfield	L 28-7	48	
Many	W 45-0	48	
Vivian	L 13-0	48	
Merryville	W	48	Win reported in media; no score
Natchitoches	L 38-19	48	
DeRidder	L 20-6	48	
Dequincy	L 59-7	48	
Oakdale	L 34-0	48	
American Foundational High School Mexico City	W 30-7	48	

Port Arthur	L 32-0	47	
Winnfield	L 19-0	47	
Menard	L 40-0	47	
Merryville	L 26-6	47	
Natchitoches	L 35-18	47	
Dequincy	L 58-0	47	
DeRidder	L 25-0	47	
Many	W 13-12	47	
Landry	L 15-6	47	
Westlake	L 32-0	47	
Ville Platte	L 27-6	47	
Winnfield	L 32-0	46	
Menard	L 26-0	46	
Many	L 7-0	46	
Port Arthur	L 32=0	46	
DeQuincy	L 43-0	46	
DeRidder	L 53=0	46	
Jennings	L 50-6	46	
Merryville	W 28-7	46	
Westlake	W 48-6	46	
Ville Platte	T 0-0	46	
Menard	L 34-6	45	
DeRidder	L 61-7	45	
Many	W	45	Win reported in media; no score
St. Marys	W	45	Win reported in media; no score
Jennings	L 47-6	45	
DeQuincy	L 21-0	45	
DeRidder	L 21-7	45	
St. Marys	W	45	Win reported in media; no score
All Stars	L	43	Loss reported in media; no score
Ville Platte	W 19-0	43	
DeRidder	L 13-7	43	
Ville Platte	W 26-0	43	
Opelousas	L 25-0	43	
Newton	W 7-6	43	
DeQuincy	L	43	Loss reported in media; no score
DeRidder	W 7-6	43	
Unknown	T 0-0	43	

Ville Platte	L 26-0	42	
Eunice	L	42	Loss reported in media; no score
DeRidder	L 13-7	42	
DeQuincy	L 48-6	42	

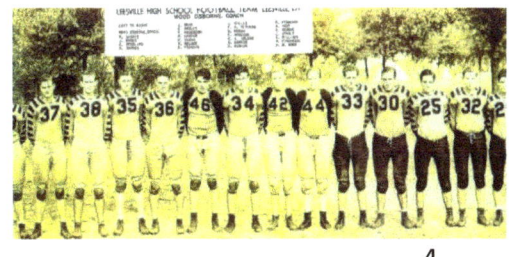

Ville Platte	L 26-7	41	
DeRidder	L 14-6	41	
Jennings	L 73-0	41	
Port Arthur	L 19-0	40	
Pelican	W 12-0	40	
Many	W 6-0	40	
Sulphur	L 7-6	40	
Oakdale	L 1-0	40	Forfeit, mid-game
St. Mary's	W 6-0	40	
Port Arthur	L 7-6	40	
DeRidder	L 39-0	40	
Crowley	L 28-0	40	
Natchitoches	L 19-6	40	
Merryville	W 25-0	40	

Port Arthur	L 13-6	39	
Oakdale	L 40-0	39	
Lake Charles	L (no score available)	39	
American Foundation School Mexico City	W	39	
Clarks	L	39	Loss reported in media; no score
DeRidder	L 33-0	39	
Natchitoches	L	39	Loss reported in media; no score
Port Arthur	T 6-6	38	
Fair Park	L 14-6	38	
American Foundation School Mexico C	W 12-6	38	
Menard	W 26-0	38	
Crowley	W 7-0	38	
St. Anthony	W 14-0	38	
Clarks	L 24=6	38	
DeRidder	W 49-0	38	
Winnfield	W 39-0	38	
Natchitoches	W 12-0	38	

Menard	W 20-0	37	
St. Anthony	W 20-12	37	
Jennings	L 26-0	37	
American Foundation School Mexico City	W 12-0	37	
Hemphill	W 30-0	37	
Glenmora	W 38-0	37	
Port Arthur	W 39-6	37	
DeRidder	T 7-7	37	
Natchitoches	W 21-0	37	
Boyce	W 19-0	36	
Winnfield	W 7-0	36	
Oakdale	W 19-13	36	
Hemphill	W	36	Win reported in media; no score
American Foundation School Mexico	CANCELLED--Virus	36	
Merryville	W	36	Win reported in media; no score
DeRidder	W 7-0	36	
Glenmora	L 19-0	36	
Natchitoches	L 12-6	36	
Hemphill	W 36-7	35	
Winnfield	W 7-0	35	
LA Normal	L 7-6	35	
American Foundation High School Mexico City	W 6-0	35	
DeQuincy	W	35	Win reported in media; no score
Oakdale	Unkonwn	35	
Jennings	L 19-0	35	
DeRidder	L 13-0	35	
Sulphur	T 0-0	35	
Natchitoches	Unknown	35	Thanksgiving Day Game
Merryville	W 38-0	34	
Lake Charles	L 19-0	34	
Jennings	L 33-0	34	
Oakdale	W 19-13	34	
DeQuincy	W 40-6	34	
DeRidder	W 25-13	34	
Sulphur	W 26-3	34	
Bossier	L 13-6	34	

Bossier	L 25-0	33
DeRidder	L 13-0	33
DeRidder	T 19-19	32

Oakdale	Unknown	31
Natchitoches	W 24-12	31
Normal Freshmen	L 38-0	31
Beaumont	Unknown	31
Pelican	W 66-0	31
Louisiana College	L 14-6	31
Sulphur	W 13-0	31
DeRidder	W 7-6	32
Merryville	W 33-0	30
Pelican	W 33-6	30
Natichitoches	W 19-6	30
Sulphur	W 14-12	30
Winnfield	L 32-12	30
Oakdale	W 19-0	30
DeRidder	L 13-0	30
Mansfield	W 26-0	30
Sulphur	L 12-0	30
Lake Charles	L 84-0	30

Merryville	T 0-0	29	
DeRidder	L 13-0	29	
Natichtoches	W 7-6	29	
Landry	W 18-0	29	
Oakdale	W 20-6	29	
Jasper	L 27-9	29	
St. Anthony	L 29-0	29	
Coushatta	W	29	Win reported in media; no score
Merryville	W 19-14	29	
Mansfield	L 9-0	22	
DeRidder	L 53-0	22	

DeRidder	L 19-7	21
DeRidder	T 6-6	20
Glenmora	L 6-0	19
Glenmora	T 0-0	17
Florien	W 30-0	15
Florien	L 13-12	15
DeRidder	L 6-0	15
DeRidder	L 24-0	13
Oakdale	W 22-0	12
Hornbeck	W 21-0	11
DeRidder	L 35-0	10

First Football Team
1910-1911

HISTORY OF THE HOOPER TROPHY

With Contributions from Brian Trahan and Daniel Green

The DeRidder-Leesville football rivalry has been known as the Hooper Trophy Series since the 1962 season, and has been a fierce rivalry since 1910. .

In the early 1960s, Leesville resident L.S. "Buck" Hooper, a graduate of Leesville High School, and his wife, Agnes Lewis Hooper, a graduate of DeRidder High School, donated a trophy for the football rivalry. The Hoopers decided the school winning the most games for every 10 seasons, or the first team to win six games, would take permanent possession of the trophy for its school. The winning team each year gets temporary possession of the trophy.

Leesville won Hooper Trophy I for the seasons from 1962 to 1972. DeRidder claimed the Hooper II for the years 1973 to 1979. Leesville captured Hooper Trophy III for the 1980 to 1987 seasons. DeRidder then won the Hooper Trophy IV series, six games to four. Leesville won Hooper V (2003) and VI (2014).

After the death of "Buck" Hooper, the two principals at that time — Bob McLamore of DeRidder High School and Richard Reese of Leesville High School — decided to continue the Hooper Trophy, with the two schools buying the trophy.

According to all available information, DeRidder leads the all-time series over Leesville 54-43-4. During the Hooper Trophy Series, the rivalry leans in Leesville's favor at 33-24-1. Leesville leads Hooper VII 6-2. Three games played since 1962 have not counted in the Hooper Trophy standings, a bi-district playoff game in 1963 when DeRidder defeated Leesville 34-19 and a regional playoff game in 1995 when Leesville defeated DeRidder 29-0, and a Leesville 34-20 win over the Dragons in the 2010 playoffs.

Some interesting points in the series: There is no valid documentation of Leesville beating DeRidder prior to 1931. The series began in 1910 and DeRidder won all but one contests with a lone game ending in a tie. The longest winning streak in the series is 10 games; Leesville won all games between 1998 – 2008 (no game was played in 2005 due to Hurricane Rita). DeRidder did not lose a game to Leesville for the entire decade of the 1970s; the Dragons won nine games and tied the Cats once. The most lop-sided score in a game was 1945, when DeRidder won 61-7. The most points scored in a game was 2008, when the Cats put 68 points on the board.

1968 Hooper Trophy

- Leesville won Hooper I which spanned from 1962 – 72
- DeRidder captured Hooper II, which included the years 1973 - 79
- Leesville won Hooper III, which spanned the years 1980 – 87
- DeRidder won Hooper IV, which ran from 1988 – 1997
- Leesville won Hooper V, which included 1998 – 2003
- Leesville won Hooper VI, spanning the years 2004 - 2014

DeRidder vs. Leesville
All Time Scores

DeRidder Leads Series 56 – 42 – 4
Leesville Won Hooper Trophy I, III, V and VI
DeRidder Won Hooper Trophy II and IV

1910: DeRidder 35, Leesville 0
1913: DeRidder 24, Leesville 0
1915: DeRidder 6, Leesville 0
1920: Tie, DeRidder 6, Leesville 6
1921: DeRidder 19, Leesville 7
1921: DeRidder 49, Leesville 0
1922: DeRidder 53, Leesville 0
1929: DeRidder 13, Leesville 0
1930: DeRidder 13, Leesville 0; at Leesville
1931: Leesville 7, DeRidder 6; at DeRidder
1932: Tie, DeRidder 19, Leesville 19
1933: DeRidder 13, Leesville 0; at DeRidder
1934: Leesville 25, DeRidder 13
1935: DeRidder 25, Leesville 0
1936: Leesville 7, DeRidder 0; at Leesville
1937: Tie, DeRidder 7, Leesville 7; at DeRidder
1938: Leesville 49, DeRidder 0; at Leesville
1939: DeRidder 33, Leesville 0; at DeRidder
1940: DeRidder 39, Leesville 0; at Leesville
1941: DeRidder 14, Leesville 6
1942: Score not found; 6 Nov 1942
1943: DeRidder 13, Leesville 7; at DeRidder
1943: Leesville 7, DeRidder 6
1945: DeRidder 61, Leesville 7
1945: DeRidder 27, Leesville 7
1946: DeRidder 53, Leesville 0; at DeRidder
1947: DeRidder 25, Leesville 0; at Leesville
1948: DeRidder 20, Leesville 6; at DeRidder
1949: DeRidder 20, Leesville 19; at Leesville
1950: DeRidder 7, Leesville 6; at Leesville
1951: DeRidder 28, Leesville 7; at DeRidder
1952: DeRidder 39, Leesville 0; at DeRidder
1953: Leesville 18, DeRidder 7; at Leesville
1954: DeRidder 12, Leesville 6; at DeRidder
1955: DeRidder 32, Leesville 6; at Leesville
1956: DeRidder 34, Leesville 7; at DeRidder

DEFEATS DE RIDDER.

Leesville, La., Nov. 13 (Special).—For the first time in years, some say as far back as 1914, Leesville high school team, coached by Wood Osborne, Monday defeated DeRidder eleven. The score was 25 to 13. All of the scoring was done in the first half. Fertita scored for Leesville on passes in the first and second quarters and Roy Jones scored once on a blocked punt and Anderson tallied through the line. Herrington recovered a loose ball behind the goal line for one of DeRidder's touchdowns after Fidler had fumbled and Beard scored on a pass. Leesville made 17 first downs and DeRidder four.

1

Leesville 49, DeRidder 0

On Armistice Day came the highlight of the football season, the traditional game with DeRidder played this year on Gilbert Field. It was in this game that the "Dragons" lost their scales. It all started when Sepeda, on a well-directed spinner, on the third play of the game brought the ball to DeRidder's one-foot line. When the game ended, the "Cats" had dragged the "Dragons" all over the field for a good clean "skunking."

1   8

On Armistice Day came the highlight of the football season, the traditional game with DeRidder played this year on Gilbert Field. It was in this game that the Dragons lost their scales. It all started when Sepeda on a well-directed spinner, on the third play of the game brought the ball to DeRidder's one foot line. When the game ended, the Cats had dragged the Dragons all over the field for a good clean skunking.

Here is an account of this years game:

Dick Berry, after throwing a 21 yard pass to Fisher, went over for a T.D. from the one yard line. Coburn's kick was blocked and the score stood Leesville 6, DeRidder 0.

At the first of the second quarter, a heartbreaker was witnessed. Sonny Byrd raced 90 yards for a T.D. only to have it nullified by a clipping penalty.

DeRidder scored in the third quarter with a pass from Frank Roe to Leo Bass. The Dragons' kick was good leaving the score 7-6.

Leesville made their last two scores in the last quarter when helped by 25 yards in penalties went to the 3 yard line. Dawin Smart went over for the tally. Coburns kick was no good. The score was then 12-7.

The last score came when the Dragons lost the ball on the Cats 21 yard line. Leesville assisted by 35 yards of penalties went to the 13 yard line. Dawin Smart carried the ball over from there. Berry's pass to Fisher for the extra point was no good. When the game ended Leesville was well on the way to another touchdown.

If the sportsmanship in the future is like this year, we should have little trouble in downing the Dragons for many years to come.

1   5

1957: Leesville 33, DeRidder 6; at Leesville
1958: DeRidder 14, Leesville 0; at DeRidder
1959: DeRidder 7, Leesville 6; at Leesville
1960: DeRidder 13, Leesville 12; at DeRidder
1961: DeRidder 47, Leesville 7; at Leesville
1962: DeRidder 12, Leesville 0; at DeRidder --- Hooper Trophy Begins
1963: Leesville 28, DeRidder 6; at Leesville
1963: DeRidder 34, Leesville 19; at Leesville (Playoff Game)

1964: DeRidder 39, Leesville 13; at DeRidder
1965: DeRidder 13, Leesville 0; at Leesville
1966: Leesville 21, DeRidder 7; at Leesville
1967: Leesville 21, DeRidder 0; at DeRidder
1968: Leesville 26, DeRidder 20; at Leesville
1969: Leesville 25, DeRidder 0; at DeRidder
1971: DeRidder 21, Leesville 6; at Leesville
1972: DeRidder 14, Leesville 0; at DeRidder   Leesville Wins Hooper I
  DHS forfeit of game---ineligible player (official score recorded as 2-0)
1973: tie, DeRidder 6, Leesville 6; at Leesville

1974: DeRidder 28, Leesville 6; at DeRidder
1975: DeRidder 50, Leesville 0; at Leesville
1976: DeRidder 42, Leesville 6; at DeRidder
1977: DeRidder 6, Leesville 0, OT; at Leesville
1978: DeRidder 23, Leesville 6; at DeRidder

1979: DeRidder 22, Leesville 14; at Leesville   DeRidder Wins Hooper II
1980: Leesville 26, DeRidder 15; at DeRidder
1981: Leesville 21, DeRidder 7; at Leesville
1982: DeRidder 37, Leesville 12; at DeRidder
1983: Leesville 37, DeRidder 26; at Leesville
1984: DeRidder 14, Leesville 12; at DeRidder
1985: Leesville 36, DeRidder 0; at Leesville
1986: Leesville 45, DeRidder 14; at DeRidder

1987: Leesville 23, DeRidder 14; at DeRidder   Leesville Wins Hooper III
1988: DeRidder 17, Leesville 16; at Leesville
1989: DeRidder 14, Leesville 7; at DeRidder
1990: Leesville 15, DeRidder 0; at Leesville
1991: DeRidder 26, Leesville 12; at DeRidder
1992: Leesville 13, DeRidder 12; at Leesville
1993: DeRidder 24, Leesville 14; at DeRidder
1994: Leesville 28, DeRidder 0; at Leesville
1995: Leesville 15, DeRidder 6; at DeRidder
1995: Leesville 29, DeRidder 0; at DeRidder (Playoff Game)

1996: DeRidder 25, Leesville 7; at Leesville
1997: DeRidder 14, Leesville 12; at Leesville   DeRidder Wins Hooper IV
1998: Leesville 36, DeRidder 34, OT; at DeRidder
1999: Leesville 30, DeRidder 8; at DeRidder
2000: Leesville 40, DeRidder 0; at Leesville
2001: Leesville 14, DeRidder 3; at DeRidder
2002: Leesville 14, DeRidder 6; at Leesville
2003: Leesville 21, DeRidder 14; at Leesville
Leesville Wins Hooper V
2004: Leesville 46, DeRidder 7; at DeRidder
2005: Did Not play due to Hurricane Rita
2006: Leesville 33, DeRidder 7; at DeRidder
2007: Leesville 43, DeRidder 13; at Leesville
2008: Leesville 68, DeRidder 29; at DeRidder
2009: DeRidder 37, Leesville 18; at Leesville
2010: Leesville 24, DeRidder 17; at DeRidder
2010: Leesville 34, DeRidder 20; at Leesville (Playoff Game)

1999
Sam Scott

2011: DeRidder 42, Leesville 14; at Leesville
2012: DeRidder 49, Leesville 0; at DeRidder
2013: DeRidder 36, Leesville 7; at Leesville
2014: Leesville 21, Deridder 6, at DeRidder
   Leesville Wins Hooper VI
2015: DeRidder 56, Leesville 20, at Leesville
2016: Leesville 42, DeRidder 28, at DeRidder
2017: Leesville 27, DeRidder 0, at DeRidder
2018: Leesville 26, DeRidder 7, at Leesville
2019: DeRidder 24, Leesville 21, at DeRidder
2020: No Game—COVID
2021: Leesville 49, DeRidder 41, at Leesville
2022: Leesville 42, DeRidder 15, at Leesville
Leesville Leads Hooper VII 5-2

2006

2017

2016 Hooper Trophy

FIRST TEAM ALL STATE AWARD WINNERS

1951 Tackle  Ted Paris

1958 Back  Robert Pynes

1984 Running Back  Charles Buckley

1984 Linebacker  Steve Gunn

1985 Running Back  Eddie Fuller

1986 Tackle  Brian Estep

FIRST TEAM ALL STATE AWARD WINNERS

1986 Lineman  Robert Jenkins

1987 Tackle  Raymond Smoot

1987 Running Back  Vincent Fuller

1988 Offensive Lineman Kevin Mawae

1988 Punter  Chip Clark

1994 Guard  Andrew Mageo

1994/1995 Running Back  Cecil Collins

FIRST TEAM ALL STATE AWARD WINNERS

1995 Tackle  Dennis Fetting

1995 Linebacker  Greg Rone

1998 Defensive Back  Keith Smith

2000 Athlete 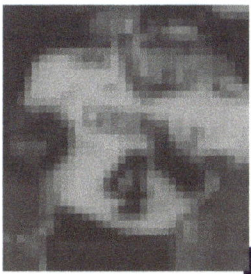 Justin Brown

2001/2002 Tight End Keith (Alleger) Zinger

2007 Athlete  Travante Stallworth

2008 Running Back  Michael Ford

FIRST TEAM ALL STATE AWARD WINNERS

2008 Defensive Back — Devin Moran

2010 Return Specialist — Levander Liggins

2011 Wide Receiver — Clinton Thurman

2018 Offensive Tackle — Matthew Anderson

2022 Running Back — Xavier Ford

WAMPUS CATS ON THE AIR

One of the great joys of Wampus Cat football has always been being in the stands, primarily at home, and also on the road. The Cats have always had a loyal following, some years more than others, but there's always a core group that will travel to games or drive over to Gilbert Field or Wampus Cat Stadium to see a game. For those who couldn't make the games, however, the Cats have had long standing radio broadcasts that have been a fixture for the Wampus Cat family.

In 1961, a group of high schoolers from Leesville undertook the initial efforts to share the game with those who couldn't make the event in person. Jim Hawthorne, Hanley Sanders, Len "Stevie" Stevens, and Nick Pollacia, Jr were the cadre who initiated the tradition of transmitting Wampus Cat games over the air. Hawthorne and Sanders were the film team; as the story goes, the two would take a heavy-duty tape recorder (aka "reel to reel") to the game and record the action. The next morning, the two, along with Len Stevens and Nick Pollacia would work diligently at the station to record a broadcast that would be played at the local AM station, KLLA.

The time as make-shift broadcasters would influence the men significantly. Len Stevens would go on to become a fixture at KLFY in Lafayette. Nick Pollacia would become so intrigued that he would one

Nick Pollacia

Len Stevens

Jim Hawthorne

125

day buy the AM facility (KLLA) and stand up an FM station (KJAE). Jim Hawthorne would become a hall of fame broadcaster for the LSU Tigers, retiring in 2017.

In the late 1970s, a new FM station, KVVP, would also begin broadcasting Wampus Cat games. For a period of time, both stations were transmitting the games, and there were back and forth negotiations between school officials, the radio stations, and the Vernon Parish School Board regarding who would be the primary broadcasters. Eventually, KVVP would settle into a "game of the week" paradigm and would rotate their game schedule between Leesville and the other Vernon Parish schools that play football (Pickering and Rosepine). KJAE has exclusively been a Wampus Cat broadcast agent on the air, first on AM, then on FM bands, occasionally on Saturdays but mostly live on Friday nights.

For a brief period in the mid 1990s, Wampus Cat games were broadcast over the television airwaves. Cablevision of Leesville, with long time radio broadcaster Rick Barnickle would record, play and re-play Wampus Cat games during one of the most exciting times of LHS football history. Barnickle teamed with 1950s Wampus Cat star John Coburn to broadcast the contests. A number of the games are digitized and saved for viewing on Youtube at the following links

- youtube.com/watch?v=RVtqJYho8k4
- youtube.com/watch?v=pBh9k9UQzBc

On the KVVP team, Barnickle was the primary broadcaster on and off over a 40 year period and was joined by a number of former players and local celebrities, including Jimmy Funderburk, Joe Pope, "B-1 Boomer" Boone and Huell Haymon. The KJAE team has seen a number of squads move in and out, with Pollacia as a primary broadcaster for many years, along with former Wampus Cat greats Bobby Craft and George Smith. In time, the broadcast teams would include the likes of Clay Tillman, Mike Anderson, Harles Smart, Sam Fertitta, Jeff Skidmore, Scott Grady, and Charles Owen. At this writing KJAE broadcasts all Wampus Cat games over the air (FM 93.5) and streaming over the internet.

KJAE/KLLA Owner, Penny Scogin

Rick Barnickle

Hantey Sanders

Jeff Skidmore, Andrew Croker & Sam Fertitta

Coach Causey & Scott Grady

Harles Smart, Sam Fertitta and Jeff Skidmore

Clay Tillman

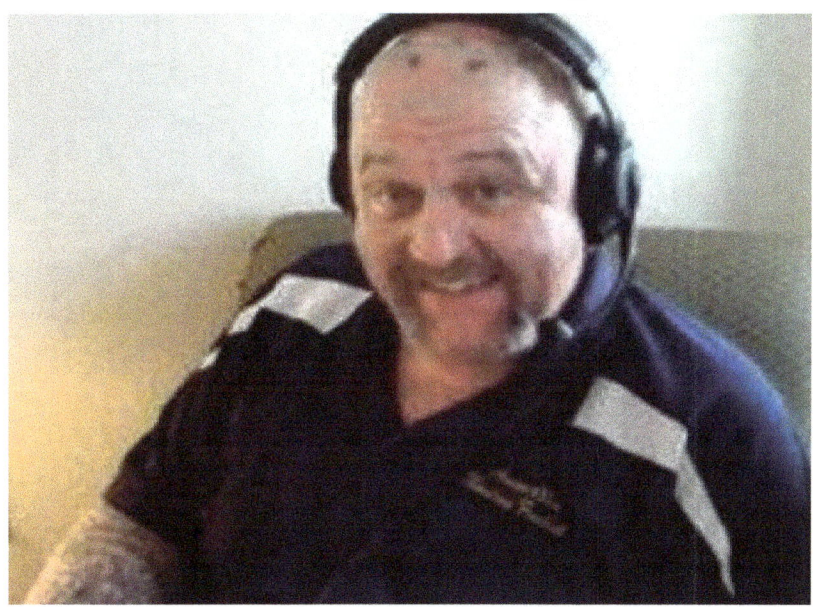
B-1 Boomer

THE OLD TIMERS GAME

From 1972 – 1975, the Junior Class at Leesville High School held an "Old Timers' Football Game" at Wampus Cat Stadium. This "game" was used as a fund raiser for the Junior Class and all four games were big successes in terms of participation and fund raising.

The concept was an intra-squad game between former Cat players. The teams were arranged by odd and even years of graduation. For example, those who graduated in 1960, 62, 64, etc were on one team; those who graduated in 1961, 63, 65, etc were on the other team. Practices were held and uniform and full pads were issued and used. The only requirement for "players" was to bring their own cleats and have been out of high school for at least three years. A roster from the 1974 game and some of photos that appeared in the Leesville Leader are included in these pages. Special thanks to the Leader for allowing access to their historical files for this effort.

The games were always held at the conclusion of the LHS football season in early to mid- November. The reason(s) as to why the game ceased is the subject of some speculation. Regardless, the fans of Leesville got to see their favorite players from years and decades gone compete again on the gridiron.

Everyone was in on this play. The light uniformed players are No. 39 Chris Smith and No. 23 Danny Rowzee at the right. Others include No. 32 Bill Barton, No. 81 Jimmy Funderburk, No. 60 Doug Marshall and No. 72 Dickie Bailes.

131

EVEN YEARS

NO.	NAME	POS.	WEIGHT	CLASS
10	Donnie Gill	WB	165	68
11	Sam Piranio	QB	170	50
17	Harles Smart	QB	170	54
22	Darwin Davis	LB	210	68
23	Robert Nock	DB	175	60
24	*Bill Beavers	FB	235	50
25	Mitch Nicholas	E	180	54
28	Robert Schwartz	HB	165	60
30	Julian Stevens	HB	190	56
32	Bill Barton	DB	180	64
33	Jackson Mapv	DB	195	70
38	Guy Stone	DB	125	50
00	Bill Prassell	G	135	66
50	Alan Nickerson	G	275	66
51	Pat Garner	E	180	60
52	Nelson M'Manus	C	185	54
53	Thad Bailes	T	205	68
60	Doug Marshall	T	230	60
61	Johnny Beltz	G	170	64
62	Roger Johnson	G	180	56
63	*R. J. Fertitta	G	225	64
65	Ray Mayo	G	200	60
64	John Driscoll	G	190	70
70	Joe Woods	T	190	62
75	Billy Marshall	T	235	68
80	Richard Schwartz	E	180	64
81	*Jimmy Funderburk	HB	165	68
82	Bobby Craft	E	210	68
83	Don Davis	E	185	66
85	Jackie Self	E	190	64
86	Doug Goldsby	E	190	70

*Captains

Coaches: Rickey French
Richard Schwartz

Colors: Black Pants
Black Jerseys

ODD YEARS

NO.	NAME	POS.	WEIGHT	CLASS
8	Vic Ortiz	QB	180	69
*10	Carl Morrow	G	175	65
11	Louis Magee	TB	170	63
12	Tony Ortiz	CB	150	69
14	Allan Fertitta	B	175	67
21	Ronnie Morrow	HB	160	67
22	Don Jackson	HB	165	65
23	Danny Rowzee	HB	180	59
24	James Armas	E	150	69
27	Jackie Edwards	E	165	65
*28	Billy Lewis	LB	180	59
48	Burk Richardson	T	220	59
51	Angelo Simonall	DE	185	69
62	Phil Lewis	G	165	61
64	Paul Albritten	G	200	63
66	Joe Ewing	G	185	69
70	Bryan Smith	T	190	65
71	Jimmy Auvil	T	275	67
72	Wayne Cavenaugh	T	225	67
75	Larry Jeane	T	275	65
76	Allison Beilas	T	225	57
77	Bobby McCain	T	205	69
78	Gary Trama	T	200	65
79	Emerson Singletary	G	190	53
*80	Larry Laurant	DE	210	69
81	Eddie Boone	E	180	63
83	Aubrey Temple	E	200	65

*Captains

Coaches: Rolf Kuhlow
         Carl Morrow

Colors: Black Pants
       Gold Jerseys

THE RICH HISTORY OF LEESVILLE HIGH SCHOOL

Hopefully, this book on the history of Wampus Cat football will inspire others to craft histories of other aspects of the Old School on the Hill. The school in Vernon Parish has been both an incubation center and a launching pad for many great citizens in our State and country. LHS has also been the home of many great organizations, events and served as a focal point for the entire community.

Graduates of Leesville High School have achieved positions of esteem and acclaim in State and Federal government. Suzette Kuhlow Kent (1986 graduate) served as the Chief Information officer of the United States in the late 2010s; two other Wampus Cats, 1986 graduate Jon Howerton and 1984 graduate Ronald Clark remain on active duty as general officers in the United States Army. Cindy Haygood, class of 85, is a general officer in the Louisiana National Guard.

1978 graduate David Smith, a career Army officer (and former Wampus Cat player), twice appeared on the cover of LIFE magazine, most prominently in the middle of Operation DESERT STORM. 1951 graduate Guy Stone was the recipient of the Navy Cross for gallantry in the Vietnam War. 1980 graduate Sam Cox recently retired as a Lieutenant General from the United States Air Force.

Two LHS grads have served as US Congressmen (Jim McCrery, Class of 67 & Claude Leach, Class of 1951). Carolyn Leach Huntoon (Class of 1958) was selected as the first female Director of NASA's Johnson Space Center in Houston.

Garland Riddle, Class of 67 is an Emmy-nominated costume designer who had a 30+ year in the television and movie business. Larrie King, Class of 2001, is a professor of Art & Design at Kent State. 1972 graduate Tony McDonald led a US contingent to the Havana Arts Biennial in Cuba in 2015 and was one of the first US citizens to engage the Cubans in an official art consortium. 1941 graduate Ted Castillo went on to a Hall of Fame career as a sports writer in Baton Rouge and still comes back for LHS Homecomings.

Academically, LHS remains consistently ranked high in the State of Louisiana. LHS has produced graduates of all US service academies and has sent students to colleges throughout the

LTC (ret) David Smith

world. Countless National Merit Scholarships have come forth from their years in the black and gold and millions of dollars of scholarships for college and technical training have been awarded to our students through the decades.

Wampus Cat athletes have achieved great things in all other sports, including basketball, baseball, softball, soccer, track and field, cross country, swimming, powerlifting, and others. Without question, the presence of the Wampus Cat Marching Band, cheerleaders, majorettes, dance line, flag lines, JRTOC and other auxiliary organizations make Leesville High School a special place.

So much history could be written on all these topics, and this author hopes others will endeavor to document what has taken place. Not mentioning or deep-diving into these topics is not meant to disparage nor take away from the other wonderful things that have taken place at Leesville High School.

LtGen (ret) Sam Cox

LTG Ronald Clark

BG Cindy Haygood

BG Jon Howerton

Cong Jim McCrery

Cong Buddy Leach

Carolyn Leach Huntoon

Guy Stone, SEAL & Navy Cross Recipient

Tony McDonald

FOR THE LOVE OF BOX SCORES

Long before the days of social media & Internet, football fans found scores & details from a great little element of news media called box scores. A box score was and still is a review of scores, stats and performers in games. They still exist, but most are found in digital media, and are instantly accessed. In decades gone by, they were found in newspapers in the ensuing days after a game.

Over time, box scores change in their format and are framed by the media outlets that carry them. Box scores tell stories without saying very much. In the following pages, a representative box score from every year of Wampus Cat football that could be found is provided. Box scores did not exist for every game the Cats played. The author of this book found what he could, and tried to provide a box score for a momentous game from each year. No agenda is present with these box scores---simply providing for readers as a trip down memory lane.

2019: LHSAA First Round Playoff Game

SCORE BY QUARTERS
Leesville | 7 | 21 | 6 | 13 | 47
Pearl River | 3 | 0 | 6 | 12 | 21

SCORING SUMMARY
First quarter
Leesville – Jacob Mount 4 run (Caden Catron kick), 7-0, 9:00
Pearl River – Brayden Bond 25 field goal, 7-3, 4:28
Second quarter
Leesville – Noah Allain 12 pass from Mount (Catron kick), 14-3, 9:15
Leesville – Caleb Gallashaw 6 run (Catron kick), 21-3, 6:15
Leesville – Darius Sawyer 5 pass from Mount (Catron kick), 28-3, 1:25
Third quarter
Pearl River – Corey Warren 10 run (kick failed), 28-9, 10:40
Leesville – Sawyer 24 pass from Mount (kick blocked), 34-9, 4:18
Fourth quarter
Pearl River – Blain Bourgeois 21 pass from Christian Kosinski (pass failed), 34-15, 11:53
Leesville – Caleb Gallashaw 18 run (Catron kick), 41-15, 9:07
Leesville – D'Ante Gallashaw 8 run (run failed), 47-15, 6:20
Pearl River – Warren 20 run (run failed), 47-21, 4:50

2018 Quarterfinal: Leesville vs. St. Martinville

LEESVILLE 53, SMSH 49

Leesville	7 14 12 20	— 53
St. Martinville	7 21 7 14	— 49

FIRST QUARTER
LEE – Caleb Gallashaw 5 run (Ben Ward kick)
SMSH – Travien Benjamin 9 run (Matthew Landry kick)

SECOND QUARTER
LEE – Caleb Gallashaw 5 run (Ben Ward kick)
SMSH – Benjamin 1 run (Landry kick)
LEE – Jacob Mount 1 run (Ward kick)
SMSH – Benjamin 15 run (Landry kick)
SMSH – D'Aaron Marshall 6 pass from Markavon Williams (Landry kick)

THIRD QUARTER
LEE – Caleb Gallashaw 3 run (Ward kick)
SMSH – Benjamin 10 run (Landry kick)
LEE – Caleb Gallashaw 5 run (Kick failed)

FOURTH QUARTER
LEE – Duwon Tolbert 27 pass from Mount (Conversion failed)
SMSH – Benjamin 8 pass from Williams (Landry kick)
LEE – D'Ante Gallashaw 41 run (Conversion failed)
SMSH – Benjamin 10 run (Landry kick)
LEES – D'Ante Gallashaw 10 run (Ward kick)
LEE – Noah Allain 22 pass from Mount (Ward kick)

Caden Wheeler hands off to Cory MCcoy

2017 Leesville Vs. Pineville

yards (1,138) and first downs (58).

LINE SCORE
Leesville 18 16 20 7 — 61
Pineville 0 9 12 27 — 48

FIRST QUARTER
L — Andrew Croker 4 run (kick blocked)
L — Croker 10 run (pass fail)
L — Croker 3 run (run fail)

SECOND QUARTER
L — Kobe Joiner 17 pass from Andrew Vargas (Croker run)
P — John Joseph 92 kickoff return (Parker Lee kick)

P — Safety
L — Joiner 35 pass from Vargas (D'ante Gallashaw run)

THIRD QUARTER
L — Gallashaw 55 run (Xavier Reyes kick)
P — Ben West 19 pass from Cam Bates (kick blocked)
L — Croker 15 pass from Vargas (kick blocked)
P — Bates 11 run (kick blocked)
L — Gallashaw recovers fumble in end zone (Reyes kick)

FOURTH QUARTER
P — Joseph 38 pass from Bates (Lee kick)
L — Darius Allen 9 (Reyes kick)
P — Bates 6 run (blocked)
P — Joseph 22 from Bates (Lee kick)
P — Joseph 38 from Bates (Lee kick)

STANDOUTS
Leesville — And Croker (15 carries, yards, 3 TDs; 2 catche yards, TD); Chris Va (14/19, 217 yards, 3 T D'ante Gallashaw (10 ries, 110 yards, TD); K Joiner (3 catches, yards, 2 TDs).

2016 First Round Playoff Game

Leesville 40, Beau Chene 7

Leesville 7 10 7 16 – 40
Beau Chene 0 7 0 0 – 7

Scoring summary
LHS Cory McCoy 20 pass from Theron Westerchil (Jacob Adams kick).
LHS Jaelyn Edward 2 run (Adams kick).
BCHS Deontrae Eaglin 26 pass from Dar Duplechain (kick good)
LHS FG Adams 24
LHS McCoy 49 run (Adams kick
LHS Safety Xavier McCoy blocked punt out of endzone
LHS Andrew Croker 63 punt return (Adams kick)
LHS Talyn Adams 4 run (Jacob Adams kick)

Individual statistics
Rushing: LEESVILLE Cory McCoy 9-145, DaQuan Davis 14-67, Theron Westerchil 4-20, Andrew Croker 1-16, Talyn Adams 1-4, Jaelyn Edwards 1-2 BEAU CHENE Dar Duplechain 15-73, Deontrae Eaglin 13-55, Jy'Lon Henry 10-32 Markaylin Milburn 5-23
Passing: LEESVILLE Theron Westerchil 5-11-0–66. BEAU CHENE. Dar Duplechain 10-22-3–142.
Receiving: LEESVILLE Cory McCoy 3-30, DaQuan Davis 2-36 BEAU CHENE. Deontrae Eaglin 4-46, Markeille Richard 2-80, Jy'Lon Henry 2-10, Jhaleb Citizen 2-6

2015 LHS Vs Westlake

Leesville 41, Westlake 24

Westlake.. ...3 7 7 7—24
Leesville.......14 14 0 13—41

Scoring summary
WHS. FG Johnathan Peshoff 37.
LHS: Cory McCoy 21 run (Jacob Adams kick).
LHS: Jaelyn Edwards 33 interception return (Adams kick).
LHS: Caden Wheeler 2 run (Adams kick).
LHS McCoy 54 run (Adams kick).
WHS. Brayden Winn 13 pass from Hunter Racca (Peshoff kick).
WHS Racca 2 run (Peshoff kick).
LHS. McCoy 92 run (Adams kick).
LHS DaQuan Davis 32 run (kick failed).
WHS. Michael Boudreaux 5 run (Peshoff kick).

Individual statistics
Rushing: WESTLAKE — Daniel Eaglin 8-78, Michael Boudreaux 13-46, Joseph January 3-42, Brevin Ned 1-2, Hunter Racca 11-(-27). LEESVILLE — Cory McCoy 20-230, Caden Wheeler 7-93, DaQuan Davis 4-83, Cody Williams 6-24.
Passing: WESTLAKE — Hunter Racca 10-24-1—123. LEESVILLE — Caden Wheeler 1-5-1—26.
Receiving: WESTLAKE — Joseph January 6-67, Gabe Buxton 1-28, Brayden Winn 1-13, Daniel Eaglin 1-9, Cade Witherwax 1-6. LEESVILLE — Cory McCoy 1-26.

LHS Vs Tioga, 2014

LEESVILLE 41, TIOGA 12

Leesville	21	0	13	7	— 41
Tioga	0	0	12	0	— 12

SCORING SUMMARY

First Quarter
L—Moses Tolbert 12 pass from Caden Wheeler (Jacob Adams kick)
L—Cory McCoy 3 run (Adams kick)
L—Wheeler 6 run (Adams kick)

Third Quarter
L—Tolbert 1 run (Adams kick)
T—Hayden Weltz 39 pass from Logan Dubois (kick fail)
L—Tolbert 73 run (kick fail)
T—Markez Thomas 4 pass from Dubois (pass fail)

Fourth Quarter
L—Tywaan Brown 13 run (Adams kick)

TEAM STATISTICS

	LHS	THS
First downs	17	13
Rushes-yds	51-365	23-65
Passes (C-A-I)	6-9-0	15-36-3
Passing yds	77	209
Total offense	442	274
Fumbles-lost	3-1	4-1
Punts-avg	4-37	4-32
Penalties-yds	13-105	10-83

INDIVIDUAL STATISTICS

RUSHING: Leesville, Moses Tolbert 19-194, Cory McCoy 18-126, Caden Wheeler 6-25, Tywaan Brown 6-14, Amone Tolbert 2-6, Dontrell Lewis 1-4; Tioga, Tre Allen 11-48, Daniel Hayes 7-15, Kenny Neal 2-3.
PASSING: Leesville, Caden Wheeler 6-9-0—77; Tioga, Logan Dubois 15-36-3—209.
RECEIVING: Leesville, Moses Tolbert 3-41, E.J. Ane 2-36, Matthew Hoecker 1-0; Tioga, Hayden Weltz 6-135, Zack Hornsby 4-44, Brady McGehee 2-17, Markez Thomas 2-11, Daniel Hayes 1-1.

LHS Vs Grant, 2013

LEESVILLE 35, GRANT 28 (OT)

L	7	6	0	15	7	— 35
G	6	14	7	0	0	— 28

First Quarter
G—Nathan Odom 8 run (Danilo Solar kick)
G—Odom 51 run (Solar kick)
L—Cory McCoy 23 run (Jonathon Price kick)

Second Quarter
L—Solomon Cross 27 blocked punt return (kick fail)
G—Odom 53 run (Solar kick)

Third Quarter
G—Jay Jones 39 run (Solar kick)

Fourth Quarter
L—Julian Rodriguez 29 fumble return (Price kick)
L—Moses Tolbert 16 pass from Caden Wheeler (Tolbert run)

Overtime
L—Tolbert 10 run (Price kick)

	L	G
First downs	11	12
Rushes-yds	123	231
Passes (C-A-I)	6-13-1	4-5-0
Passing yds	86	47
Total offense	209	278
Fumbles-lost	2-2	2-1
Punts-avg	3-36.33	5-22.4
Penalties-yds	4-30	6-60

INDIVIDUAL STATISTICS

RUSHING — Leesville, Quentin Coleman 10-51, Cory McCoy 6-29, Moses Tolbert 10-25; Grant, Nathan Odom 22-138, Chase Cannon 13-63, Terrell Boyd 8-23.
PASSING — Leesville, Caden Wheeler 6-12-1—86; Grant, Brennan Flory 4-5-0 57.
RECEIVING — Leesville, Moses Tolbert 2-32, Quentin Coleman 1-23, Cory McCoy 1-12, Jesse St. Clergy 1-10; Grant, Jay Jones 1-39, DeAngelo Williams 2-18.

LHS Vs Bolton, 2012

Tioga 33, Leesville 19

Leesville	0	7	12	0	— 19
Tioga	0	7	14	12	— 33

Scoring Summary

Second Quarter
T - Dontrell Johnson 10-yard blocked punt (Robert Silva kick)
L - Kory Jones 1 run (Aaron Heinen kick)

Third Quarter
T - Derrick Sampson 62 run (Silva kick)
L - Jones 1 run (kick block)
T - Sampson 16 run (Silva kick)
L - Devon Perkins 21 run (Pass fail)

Fourth Quarter
T - Sampson 7 run (Silva kick)
T - Safety
T - Silva 42 field goal

	L	T
First Downs	11	11
Rush-Att-Yards	34-176	54-265
Passing	130	0
Total Offense	306	265
Passes (C-A-I)	9-22-0	0-2-0
Punts-Average	1-40	1-24.25
Fumbles-Lost	3-0	3-1
Penalties-Yards	7-50	9-60

INDIVIDUAL STATISTICS

RUSHING — Leesville, Denell Lewis 15-142, Perkins 6-34-1TD; Tioga, Sampson 26-1TD, Jackson 15-92, Darius Logan 3-27.
PASSING — Leesville, Jones 9-22-0-130; Tioga, Zack McLaren 0-2-0-0.
RECEIVING — Leesville, Darrell McQueen 4-44, Tony Smith 3-38, Lewis 1-34; Tioga, None.

LHS Vs. Sam Houston 2011

Sam Houston 33, Leesville 14

Sam Houston	6	15	0	12	— 33
Leesville	0	7	0	7	— 14

STATISTICS

	SH	LEE
First downs	12	14
Rushes-yards	39-197	36-97
Passing yards	135	133
Total yards	332	230
Passes	4-5-0	13-26-1
Punts-avg	5-25.0	4-31.0
Fumbles-lost	5-1	2-1
Penalties	9-81	7-53

SCORING

Sam Houston: Collin Kober 66 pass from Cliff Reid (kick blocked).
Leesville: Derrick Blackshire fumble recovery in endzone (Colton Honeycutt kick).
Sam Houston: Matt Hollingsworth 2 run (Tanner Stewart pass from Reid).
Sam Houston: Kober 54 pass from Kelsey Richard (Evan Morris kick).
Sam Houston: Eric Peterson 10 run (kick failed).
Sam Houston: Richard 25 run (kick failed).
Leesville: Marshall Smith 81 kickoff return (Honeycutt kick).

INDIVIDUAL LEADERS

Rushing — Sam Houston - Cliff Reid 10-93, Matt Hollingsworth 12-35, Kelsey Richard 3-24, Eric Peterson 4-21, Matt Mixon 4-11, Tyrell Jones 4-10, Joey Bailey 1-2, Chris Hubert 1-1. Leesville - Derrick Blackshire 18-75, Juwon Simon 4-23, Kingsley Matthews 8-12, Dewayne Richard 1-2, Zack Squyres 5-(-15).
Passing — Sam Houston - Cliff Reid 3-4-0—81, Kelsey Richard 1-1-0—54. Leesville - Dewayne Richard 9-16-1—107, Zack Squyres 4-10-0—26.
Receiving — Sam Houston - Collin Kober 4-135. Leesville - Clinton Thurman 9-110, Kole Smith 2-19, Derrick Blackshire 2-4.

LHS Vs. Peabody, 2010

Leesville 51, Peabody 48

Peabody	13	13	8	14	- 48
Leesville	0	30	7	14	51

Scoring Summary

Peabody: Jalen Richard 4 run (Bennie Lucas kick)
Peabody: Richard 3 run (kick failed)
Peabody: Richard 25 run (Lucas kick)
Leesville: Levander Liggins 47 pass from Zack Squyres (Clinton Thurman run)
Leesville: Liggins 35 pass from Squyres (Colton Honeycutt kick)
Peabody: Richard 84 run (kick failed)
Leesville: Liggins 4 run (Honeycutt kick)
Leesville: Diontay Thurman 11 run (Clinton Thurman run)
Peabody: Richard 2 run (Richard run)
Leesville: Diontay Thurman 4 run (Honeycutt kick)
Leesville: Liggins 7 run (Honeycutt kick)
Peabody: Richard 5 run (pass failed)
Peabody: Richard 3 run (Richard run)
Leesville: Liggins 7 run (Honeycutt kick)

Team Statistics

	PHS	LHS
First downs	18	20
Rushes-yds	54-415	32-241
Passing yds	23	259
Total yards	438	500
Passes	4-10-0	16-31-0
Punts-avg	4-26.8	2-29.0
Fumbles lost	0-0	5-5
Penalties	9-65	7-65

Individual statistics

Rushing: Peabody, Jalen Richard 38-286, Keverick Tanner 6-59, Jaquavriante Wright 8-53, Martavius Rhone 1-18, Gus Snowden 1-(-1). Leesville, Levander Liggins 11-148, Diontay Thurman 10-82, Clinton Thurman 1-8, Joe Horlacher 1-4, Zack Squyres 9-(-1).
Passing: Peabody, Keverick Tanner 4-10-0—23, Leesville, Zack Squyres 15-20-0—225, Levander Liggins 1-2-0—34.
Receiving: Peabody, Arkendrous Duncan 1-30, Jaquavriante Wright 1-(-3), Jalen Richard 2-(-4). Leesville, Levander Liggins 6-117, Clinton Thurman 4-74, Jeval Chancy 3-37, Diontay Thurman 3-31.

Marshall Smith

Levander Liggins

LHS Vs. Wash-Marion, 2009

Leesville 40, W-Marion 18

Leesville	19	7	14	0	— 40
W-MHS	6	6	0	6	— 18

SCORING SUMMARY

Leesville: Levander Liggins 67 pass from Zack Squyres (kick failed)
W-MHS: Dwight Barker 1 run (run failed)
Leesville: Robert Bush 72 pass from Squyres (Allen Perry kick)
Leesville: Jeron Hamm 6 pass from Squyres (kick failed)
W-MHS: Desmond Richard 4 run (run failed)
Leesville: Hamm 27 pass from Squyres (Perry kick)
Leesville: Liggins 1 pass from Squyres (Perry kick)
Leesville: Bush 46 pass from Squyres
W-MHS: Gerrick Harmon 4 run (run failed)

LHS Vs. St. Michael, Playoff Game 2008

Leesville 28, St. Michael 7

St. Michael	0	7	0	0 — 7
Leesville	14	0	7	7 — 28

Leesville-Stallworth 1 run (Perry kick)
Leesville-Stallworth 9 run (Perry kick)
SM-Meyers 7 run (Fletcher kick)
Leesville-Ford 5 run (Perry kick)
Leesville-Stallworth 6 run (Perry kick)

	SM	Leesville
First downs	9	17
Rush-Att/yards	30-175	51-254
Passing	51	175
Total Offense	226	429
Passes (C-A-I)	7-12-1	10-14-0
Punts	4-37.5	1-28
Fumbles-Lost	1-1	1-0
Penalties-Yards	3-15	5-40

INDIVIDUAL STATISTICS

RUSHING—SM, Meyers 20-154. Leesville, Ford 34-206, Stallworth 14-65.
PASSING—SM, Meyers 7-12-1-51. Leesville, Stallworth 10-14-0-175.
RECEIVING—SM, Williams 2-21. Leesville, Mark 4-44, Hamm 2-42, Ford 3-51, Liggins 1-38.

LHS Vs. DeRidder 2007

Leesville 43, DeRidder 13

DeRidder	0	0	6	7 — 13
Leesville	16	12	6	13 — 43

LHS — Allen Muse 39 pass from Travante Stallworth (Kick blocked)
LHS— Stallworth 23 run (Pass failed)
LHS — Devin Moran 65 run (Pass failed)
LHS — Stallworth 1 run (Run failed)
LHS — Stallworth 85 run (Kick failed)
DHS — Shadrick Taylor 5 run (Kick failed)
LHS — Demetrius Mark 18 pass from Stallworth (Tashun Burnett kick)
DHS — Tevon Steward 1 run (Sam Durham kick)
LHS — David Detz 60 fumble return. (No PAT attempt)

	DHS	LHS
First downs	13	20
Rush yards	171	309
Passing	42	209
Total Offense	213	518
Passes (C-A-I)	8-15-2	10-15-1
Punts	5-30.4	1-36
Fumbles-Lost	3-2	3-1
Penalties-Yards	9-55	9-61

INDIVIDUAL STATISTICS

RUSHING—DeRidder, Shadrick Taylor 14-76, Stephen Richmond 3-29, Tevon Steward 5-27, Vance Worthen 1-23, Clinton Wills 4-13, Danny Williams 5-10, Samuel Peterson 1-6, Ronald Acker 1-3, John Schlag 8-(-15). Leesville, Devin Moran 19-158, Travante Stallworth 12-134, DeJuan Taylor 2-15, Chris Brown 2-6, Eddie McTear 3-(-4).

LHS Vs. DeRidder 2006

Leesville 33, DeRidder 7

Leesville	0	12	14	7 — 33
DeRidder	0	0	0	7 — 7

LHS—Michael Ford 2 run (kick failed).
LHS—Josh Cryer 26 run (kick failed).
LHS—Justin Ford 12 run (kick good).
LHS—Cryer 1 run (kick good).
LHS—M. Ford 46 run (kick good).
DHS—Danny Williams 15 run (Casey Burk kick).

	LHS	DHS
First downs	14	11
Rush-Att/yards	35-272	41-105
Passing	55	13
Total Offense	327	118
Passes (C-A-I)	6-8-0	2-9-0
Punts	4-42.7	6-27.3
Fumbles-Lost	0-0	2-1
Penalties-Yards	6-65	5-30

INDIVIDUAL STATISTICS

RUSHING—DeRidder, Williams 20-55, Darius Bruce 11-31, Stuart Peterson 1-8, Vance Worthen 4-6, Hunter Bardin 5-4, Burks 1-(-10). Leesville, Michael Ford 7-111, Cryer 13-81, Tyson Ingram 4-7, Justin Ford 5-24, DJuan Taylor 2-20, Tyrell McTear 3-5, Norman Allen 1-(-6).
PASSING—DeRidder, Bardin 2-9-0-13. Leesville, Allen 6-7-0-55, Chris Brown 0-1-0-0.
RECEIVING—DeRidder, Tate O'Neal 1-6, Peterson 1-5. Leesville, Travante Stallworth 3-28, Allen Muse 1-14, Cryer 1-7, Taylor 1-6.

LHS Vs. Peabody 2005

Leesville 28, Peabody 16

Peabody	0	8	8	0 — 16
Leesville	6	15	7	0 — 28

LEES—Kenyon Martin 1 run. Kick failed.
LEES—Justin Ford 17 pass from Norman Allen. (Bernardo Henry pass from Allen.)
PB—Rayshaun Williams 29 pass from Latonio Pryear. Pryear run.
LEES— Ford 10 run. Scott Eves kick.
LEES— Ford 75 run. Eves kick.
PB— Pryear 1 run. Pryear run.

	LEES	PB
First Downs	10	12
Rushing	234	158
Passing	54	79
Total Offense	288	237
Passes	4-6-0	11-21-0
Fumbles	0-0	0-0
Punts	4-32.0	5-17.4
Penalties	3-25	14-117

Bernardo Henry

LHS Vs. ASH 2004

Leesville 19, ASH 12

Alexandria	0	0	7	5 — 12
Leesville	6	0	6	7 — 19

LV—Casey Vinson 1 run (run failed).
ASH—Chris Brown 70 run (Joe Marrazzo kick).
LV—Vinson 1 run (pass failed).
ASH— safety, Leesville punter stepped out of end zone.
ASH—22 Marrazzo FG.
LV—Vinson 1 run (Scott Eaves kick).

	ASH	LV
First downs	7	9
Rush-att/yards	36-226	40-180
Passing yards	0	32
Total Offense	226	212
Comp-Att-Int	1-10-2	3-12-0
Punts/avg	4-37	3-32.7
Fumbles-Lost	2-0	0-0
Penalties-Yards	6-36	10-55

INDIVIDUAL STATISTICS

RUSHING-ASH, Brown 29-233, William Slaughter 1-2, Chris McGhee 6-(-9). LV, Bernardo Henry 7-73, Edwin Ivory 8-60, Kenyon Martin 10-31, D.J. Holbrook 10-15, Vinson 4-5, Justin Ford 1-1.
PASSING-ASH, McGhee 1-8-2-0; Brown 0-1-0-0. LV, Holbrook 3-11-0-32; Ivory 0-1-0-0.
RECEIVING-LV, Martin 1-13, Henry 1-11, Ivory 1-8.

LHS vs. Bolton 2003

Leesville 44, Bolton 16

Leesville	13	12	6	13—44
Bolton	0	8	0	8—16

L—Quentiza Scott 24 run (Josh Quayhagen kick)
L—Bernard Henry 30 run (kick failed)
B—Justin Phillips 18 run (Phillips run)
L—Scott 2 run (kick failed)
L—Justin Goins 1 run (kick failed)
L—Kenyon Martin 62 run (kick failed)
L—Henry 24 pass from Goins (Quayhagen kick)
B—Phillips 28 run (Phillips run)
L—Cloth Mills 2 run (kick failed)

	LHS	BHS
First downs	8	10
Rush-att/yards	38-316	51-270
Passing yards	101	284
Total Offense	417	284
Comp-Att-Int	3-7-0	1-5-2
Punts/avg	1-33	2-25
Fumbles-Lost	0-0	0-0
Penalties-Yards	6-40	8-57

INDIVIDUAL STATISTICS
RUSHING—Leesville, Scott 9-89, Henry 6-74, Martin 5-76. Bolton, Phillips 32-205.
PASSING—Leesville, Goins 3-7-0-101. Bolton, James Webb 1-5-2-14.
RECEIVING—Leesville, Henry 2-71. Bolton, Phillips 1-14.

LHS Vs St Louis 2002

Leesville 30, St. Louis 13

St. Louis	0	0	0	13—13
Leesville	6	14	3	7—30

L: Jason Leacock 4 run (pass failed)
L: Michael Cephas 61 run (run failed)
L: Leacock 12 run (Leacock run)
L: FG Michael Coode 27
SL: Cody Chaisson 10 pass from Brady Flavin (Blake Thevenot kick)
SL: Brent Flavin 15 run (run failed)
L: Cephas 6 run (Coode kick)

	SL	Leesville
First Downs	20	14
Rushing Yards	113	319
Passing Yards	205	59
Passes	23-31-1	3-9-1
Punts	2-22	0
Fumbles-Lost	3-1	1-0
Penalties-yards	4-35	1-10

INDIVIDUAL LEADERS
RUSHING - St. Louis: Brent Flavin 24-95, Freddie Hannie 4-14, Asa Ange 7-9, Brady Flavin 5-4, Cody Chaisson 1-(minus 9). Leesville: Jason Leacock 13-132, Michael Cephas 4-77, Derek Williams 1-36, Bernardo Henry 2-26, Chris Nash 6-20, Justin Goins 4-15.
PASSING - St. Louis: Brady Flavin 23-31-1-205. Leesville: Goins 3-9-1-59.
RECEIVING - SL Louis: Chaisson 16-165, Hannie 3-24, Brent Flavin 3-8, Matt Harudel 1-8. Leesville: Williams 1-32, Daniel Dotson 1-21, Nash 1-6.

LHS Vs. Bolton 2001

Leesville 27, Bolton 15

Bolton	0	7	0	8—15
Leesville	0	13	14	0—27

B—Trent Woodlawn 91 run (Don Grafton kick)
L—Martin Driscoll 2 run (Ryan Conner kick)
L—Derek Williams 68 pass from Driscol (kick blocked)
L—Driscoll 1 run (run failed)
L—Chris Nash 5 run (Marcus Johnson pass from Driscol)
B—Woodlawn 67 run (Blair Phillips run)

	BHS	LHS
First downs	9	16
Rushes-yards	34-271	47-205
Passing	30	130
Total Offense	301	335
Comp-Att-Int	2-7-0	6-16-1
Punts-Avg	2-40.5	3-32
Fumbles-Lost	3-2	0-0
Penalties-Yards	9-60	4-30

INDIVIDUAL STATISTICS
RUSHING—Bolton, Woodlawn 13-162, Phillips 13-47, Jabari Woods 6-37. Leesville, Nash 14-94, Roderick Lawhorn 14-57 m Michael Cephas 5-31, Driscoll 7-11.
PASSING—Bolton, Woods 2-7-0—30. Leesville, Driscoll 5-14-1—115, Derek Skidmore 1-7-0-15.
RECEIVING—Bolton, Carvetrick Swafford 1-18, Kevin Sylvan 1-12. Leesville, Williams 2-75, Daniel Dotson 3-20, Andre Woods 1-27, Nash 1-8.

LHS Vs. Woodlawn (BR); Playoff Game

L'ville 24, W'lawn 18 (2 OT)

LHS Vs. Bolton 1999

Leesville 28, Bolton 14

Leesville	14	0	7	7—28
Bolton	7	7	0	0—14

Leesville— Ashley Deans 9 run (Jason Whitfield kick)
Bolton—Kedric Varra 9 run (Marc Chaudoir kick)
Leesville—Deans 1 run (Whitfield kick)
Bolton—Varra 1 run (Chaudoir kick)
Leesville— Gijon Robinson 17 pass from Martin Driscol (Whitfield kick)
Leesville—Justin Brown 1 run (Whitfield kick)

	Leesville	Bolton
First downs	11	8
Rushes-yards	44-265	31-135
Passing	77	50
Total Yards	342	185
Comp-Att-Int	6-8-0	4-11-0
Punts	1-28	4-38.5
Fumbles-Lost	4-3	4-2
Penalties-Yards	9-54	10-56

INDIVIDUAL STATISTICS
RUSHING—Leesville, Sam Scott 15-90, Justin Brown 7-59, Kenny Jones 7-45, Derrick Beebe 6-33, Arliss Williamson 4-21, martin Driscoll 1-(-2). Bolton, Kedric Varra 13-83, Jabari Woods 11-29, Antonio Logan 6-17, Chris Brooks 1-6.
PASSING—Leesville, Sam Scott 4-5-0-38, Martin Driscol 2-3-0-39. Bolton, Jabari Woods 4-11-0-50.
RECEIVING—Leesville, Tim Johnson 1-18, Mark Dowden 1-27, Gijonn Robinson 2-39, Justin Brown 2(-7). Bolton, Kedric Varra 2-27, Trent Woodland 1-21, Antonio Logan 1-2.

LHS Vs. Eunice 1998

Eunice 19, Leesville 6

Leesville	0	6	0	—	6
Eunice	0	7	0	12	— 19

Second Quarter
Eun: Derek Allison 21 run (Josh Moreau kick)
Third Quarter
LEE: Deshun McNeely 5 run (kick failed)
Fourth Quarter
Eun: Spencer Aucoin 5 run (kick failed)
Eun: Aundraay Hudson 15 run (pass failed)

	Lee	Eun
First Downs	12	17
Rushes-Yards	39-174	50-270
Passing	62	8
Comp-Att-Int	6-14-2	1-4-0
Punts-Avg	1-35	3-31
Fumbles-Lost	2-2	2-1
Penalties-Yards	5-45	4-45

INDIVIDUAL STATISTICS
RUSHING—Lee:Deshun McNeely 25-118, 1 td; Kenny Jones 6-48; Dustin Smith 7-5.Eun: Aundraay Hudson 23-139, 1 td; Spencer Aucoin 14-64, 1 td; Derek Allison 12-59 1 td; James Skinner 1-8.
PASSING—Lee:Dustin Smith 8-14-2 62 yds.Eun: Aundraay Hudson 0-3-0; Carl Abbott 1-1-0 8 yds.
RECEIVING—Lee: Sam Scott 2-28; Demond McNeely 2-21; Keith Smith 2-13.Eun:Aundraay Hudson 1-8.
Next: Eunice (7-3,3-1) 4-4A Co-champs, will host wildcard; Leesville (3-7,2-2)

SMSH 49 BCHS 6

LHS Vs. Evangel 1997

Evangel 39, Leesville 14

Evangel   6 12 21 0 — 39
Leesville   7 7 0 0 — 14

EV-Brock Berlin 1 run (kick failed)
LV-Clennon Turner 85 interception return (Stan Catron kick)
LV-Dustin Smith 1 run (Catron kick)
EV-Richard Smith 24 pass from B. Berlin (run failed)
EV-Smith 50 pass from B. Berlin (run failed)
EV-Smith 20 pass from B. Berlin (Brad Cobb kick)
EV-Phillip Geiggar 22 interception return (Cobb kick)
EV-Corey Berlin 2 pass from B. Berlin (Cobb kick)

	EV	LV
First downs	24	2
Rushes-yards	28-130	22-13
Passing	386	125
Comp-Att-Int	24-33-1	7-15-1
Punts-Avg.	1-37	7-38
Fumbles-Lost	0-0	1-0
Penalties-Yards	11-107	5-34

INDIVIDUAL STATISTICS
RUSHING-Evangel, Neimi Rodgers 6-66, Jelani Lewis 6-47, Cobb 6-41. Leesville, Deshun McNeely 13-12.
PASSING-Evangel, Brock Berlin 24-33-1 386. Leesville, Dustin Smith 6-13-1 119.
RECEIVING-Evangel, Smith 8-185, Lewis 8-66, Corey Belln 6-60. Leesville, Keith Smith 3-123.

LHS Vs. Northwood, Playoff 1996

Leesville 21, N'wood S-P 20

Leesville   0 0 7 14 — 21
Northwood   0 7 13 0 — 20

NW — Greg Linnear 8 run (Luke Oliver kick)
NW — Linnear 86 run (Oliver kick)
L — Deshun McNeely 8 run (Stan Catron kick)
NW — Montgomery 50 pass from Beach (kick failed)
L — Xavier Burrell 8 run (Catron kick)
L — Burrell 2 run (Catron kick)

	L	NW
First downs	16	10
Rushes-yards	42-224	27-242
Passing	145	145
C-A-I	10-15-1	4-8-1
Punts	1-37	2-14
Fumbles-Lost	2-1	2-1
Penalties-Yards	1-15	9-70

INDIVIDUAL STATISTICS
RUSHING-Leesville, Burrell 30-175, McNeely 5-28, D. Smith 5-17. Northwood, Linnear 10-197, Montgomery 5-59.
PASSING-Leesville, D. Smith 10-15-1 145. Northwood, Beach 4-8-1 145.
RECEIVING-Leesville, LaMarcus Thurman 6-81, Keith Smith 2-30, Ronnie Robinson 1-30. Northwood, Linnear 1-24, Montgomery 2-90.

Xavier Burrell (4) scored two fourth-quarter touchdowns against Northwood as Leesville advanced in the Class 4A state playoffs for the fourth straight season.

LHS Vs. Breaux Bridge Semi-Final 1995

L'ville 28, B. Bridge 13

Breaux Bridge   0 7 0 6 — 13
Leesville   0 7 7 14 — 28

BB-Nick Frederick 15 pass from Guy Wiltz (Jamie Castille kick)
LV-Cecil Collins 56 run (Josh Dill kick)
LV-Collins 42 run (Dill kick)
LV-Collins 9 run (Dill kick)
BB-Castille 12 pass from Wiltz (kick failed)
LV-Vernon Lee 27 interception return (Dill kick)

	BB	LV
First downs	6	17
Rushes-yards	22-44	44-335
Passing	88	6
C-A-I	6-17-1	1-4-1
Punts	6-34	1-40
Fumbles-Lost	0-0	1-1
Penalties-Yards	4-35	2-10

INDIVIDUAL STATISTICS
RUSHING-Beau Bridge, Dominick Davis 12-28. Leesville, Collins 37-294, Greg Rone 5-33.
PASSING-Beau Bridge, Wiltz 6-17-1 88. Leesville, Jason Green 1-4-1 6.
RECEIVING-Beau Bridge, Castille 3-31, Frederick 3-29. Leesville, Collins 1-6.

LHS Vs. Haughton, Playoff 1994

YARDSTICK

Team	HHS	LHS
First Downs	10	19
Rushing Yards	42	354
Passing Yards	125	99
Total Yards	167	453
Passes	10-27-3	5-10-1
Punts	4-43.0	3-34.0
Fumbles-Lost	2-0	4-2
Penalties	4-45	9-83

SCORE BY QUARTERS
Haughton   0 0 0 7 — 7
Leesville   7 14 0 13 — 34

SCORING SUMMARY
LHS — Cecil Collins 55 pass from Andre Middlebrooks (Josep Culic kick)
LHS — Collins 1 run (Culic kick)
LHS — Collins 6 run (Culic kick)
LHS — Collins 1 run (kick failed)
HHS — Bruce Backhaus 12 pass from Kennon Gaspard (Alex Jordan kick)
LHS — Collins 49 run (Culic kick)

INDIVIDUAL STATISTICS
Rushing — Haughton: Rodney Anderson 2-28 Lamont Poole 7-21, Victor Hart 7-15, Archie Salery 3-10, Kennon Gaspard 6-(-32). Leesville: Cecil Collins 28-230, Andre Middlebrooks 7-50, Matt Glasper 10-34, Andre Mageo 1-33, Bruce Billings 1-7.
Passing — Haughton: Kennon Gaspard 10-27-3—125. Leesville: Andre Middlebrooks 5-9-1—99, Jason Green 0-1-0—0.
Receiving — Haughton: Antonio Burks 5-106, Blair Backhaus 2-19, Gary Morrison 1-4, Archie Salery 1-(-4). Leesville: Anthony Ford 3-31, Cecil Collins 1-55, Lawrence Powell 1-13.

LHS Vs. Pineville, Playoff 1993

Leesville 39, Pineville 7

Pineville   0 0 0 7 — 7
Leesville   14 10 15 0 — 39

L—Cecil Collins 50 run (Ton Isaac kick)
L—Andre Middlebrooks 9 pass from Corey Davis (Isaac kick)
L—Isaac 27 FG
L—Collins 9 run (Isaac kick)
L—Collins 4 run (Isaac kick)
L—Davis 5 run (Ben Eugene pass from Isaac)
P—Jon Taylor 20 run (Andrew Taylor kick)

	P	L
First Downs	11	22
Rushes/Yds.	30-146	50-368
Yds. Passing	90	78
Passes (C-A-I)	4-16-0	6-8-1
Punts/Avg.	5-25	2-46
Fumbles/lost	4-2	3-2
Penalties/Yds.	6-56	8-60

LHS V. Wash-Marion 1992

Leesville 27, W.-Marion 22

```
W. Marion    6  0  8  8 — 22
Leesville   14  7  0  6 — 27
```
WM—Roy Francois 2 run (Kick failed)
L—Mike Fuller 92 kickoff return (Thomas Issac kick)
L—Fuller 57 pass from Andre Middlebrooks (Issac kick)
L—Heggie Reynolds 24 run (Issac kick)
WM—Arthur Charles 1 run (Jarvis Daigle from Mike Selders)
L—Cecil Collins 8 run (Kick failed)
WM—David Guillory 8 pass from Selders (Ronald Goodly from Selders)

	WM	L
First Downs	17	17
Rush Yds.	169	279
Yds. Passing	141	91
Passes (C-A-I)	12-29-1	5-8-0
Punts/Avg.	4-29	3-31
Fumbles/lost	3-0	3-2
Penalties/Yds.	11-85	9-100

LHS Vs. Sulphur 1991

Sulphur 17, Leesville 7

```
Leesville   0  7  0  0 —  7
Sulphur     7  0  0 10 — 17
```
S—Jeff Vercher 31 run (Michael Reeder kick)
L—Corey Davis 11 run (Thomas Issacc kick)
S—Vercher 2 run (Reeder kick)
S—Reeder 29 FG

	L	S
First Downs	6	16
Rushing Yds.	79	252
Yds. Passing	39	61
Passes (C-A-I)	6-12-0	5-10-2
Punts-Avg.	5-27	2-21
Fumbles/lost	1-0	0-0
Penalties/Yds.	5-43	7-55

LHS Vs. DeRidder 1900

Leesville 15, DeRidder 0

```
DeRidder   0  0  0  0 —  0
Leesville  0  3  6  6 — 15
```
L—FG Richard Brennan 24
L—John Brown 82 kickoff return (Kick failed)
L—Ellis Garner 4 run (Run failed)

	D	L
First downs	8	13
Rushes-Yds.	27-48	42-168
Yds. Passing	80	12
Passes (C-A-I)	8-15-0	1-7-1
Punts-Avg.	6-31	3-35
Fumbles/lost	2-1	2-0
Penalties/Yds.	5-30	4-26

Raymon Smoot (79)

Joe Williams (35)

Chris Davis with the ball

LHS Vs. Parkway 1989

Leesville 20, Parkway 0

```
Parkway    0  0  0  0 —  0
Leesville  0  0  6 14 — 20
```
L— Erwin Brown 55 run (kick failed)
L— Brown 1 run (Chip Clark kick)
L— Brown 44 run (Clark kick)

	P	L
First downs	9	12
Rushes-yards	110	296
Passing yards	69	14
Passes (A-C-I)	12-7-0	8-2-0
Punts-average	7-37	5-39
Fumbles-lost	3-2	1-0
Penalties-yards	8-70	14-100

LHS Vs. LC-Boston 1988

Leesville 40, LC Boston 0

```
LC-Boston  0  0  0  0 —  0
Leesville  0 26  0 14 — 40
```
L— Chip Clark 10 run (Jason Giuntini kick)
L— Erwin Brown 12 run (Guintini kick)
L— Eric Rhodes 10 pass from Clark (kick failed)
L— Joe Williams 1 run (kick failed)
L— Giuntini 27 pass from Rob Davis (Guintini kick)
L— Chris Barrow 1 run (Guintini kick)

	LCB	LV
First downs	11	18
Rushes-Yds.	41-143	44-340
Yds Passing	53	100
Passes (C-A-I)	3-9-1	5-8-0
Punts-Avg.	4-39.5	3-41.2
Fumbles/lost	3-2	3-0
Penalties/Yds.	4-40	8-85

LHS Vs. St. Amant, Playoff 1987

Leesville 26, St. Amant 10

```
St. Amant  3  0  7  0 — 10
Leesville  6  0  7 13 — 26
```
SA—Kirno Hickman 38 field goal
L—Vincent Fuller 33 run (kick failed)
SA—Ricky Deverteuil 1 run (Hickman kick)
L—Fuller 4 run (Jason Guintini kick)
L—Fuller 4 run (Guintini kick)
L—Stan Whatley 4 run (kick failed)

	SAmnt	Lsville
First downs	14	17
Rushing yards	153	33
Passing yards	105	30
Passes (A-C-I)	17-8-1	5-7-0
Punts	3-36.2	3-34
Fumbles-lost	4-2	0-0
Penalties-yards	5-45	6-60

INDIVIDUAL STATISTICS
RUSHING—St. Amant, Donny Willis 18-89. Leesville, Vincent Fuller 24-144, Joe Williams 13-177.
PASSING—St. Amant, Willis 8-17-1-105. Leesville, Stan Whatley 2-5-0-30.
RECEIVING— St. Amant, Percy Thombar 2-28, Connie Trobeau 3-36, Joe Miles 3-34. Leesville, Frank Ford 1-17, Joe Williams 1-13.

LHS Vs. Broadmoor, Playoff 1986

Leesville	0	0	0	8 —	8
Broadmoor	0	0	0	7 —	7

B — Alphonse Ambeau 64 pass from Buc Richardson (Richardson kick)

L — Richardson tackled in end zone safety

L — Vincent Fuller 2 run, (pass failed)

	L	B
First downs	18	13
Yards Rushing	208	120
Yards Passing	104	100
Passes (A-C-I)	12-6-2	10-4-0
Punts/Avg.	2-33	3-41
Fumbles/Lost	5-3	1-0
Penalties/Yards	5-49	2-6

Dester Gatewood

LHS Vs Abbefille Playoff 1983

Leesville	7	0	0	7 —	14
Abbeville	0	7	0	2 —	9

LHS — Calvin Dixon 9 pass from Al Capello (J.R. Dethorn kick)
AHS — Kelly Trahan 1 run (Bang Bui kick)
LHS — Mark Clay 5 run (Dixon from Capello)
AHS — John Boudreaux Safety On Capello
LHS — J.R. Dethorn 20 field goal
LHS — Capello 16 run (Kick failed)

	Leesville	Abbeville
First Downs	9	13
Yards Rushing	146	74
Yards Passing	94	28
Passes	10-14-1	2-13-3
Fumbles-Lost	2-0	3-1
Punts Avg	4-33	4-40
Penalties	7-50	6-75

LHS Vs. Huntington, Playoff 1985

Leesville 8, Huntington 7

Leesville	0	0	0	8 —	8
Huntington	0	7	0	0 —	7

Scoring Summary

H-Thomas McLemore, 8 pass from Joe Hughes (Hughes kick)

L-Rayford Clayton, 5 run (Eddie Fuller run)

Statistics	Lees	Hunt
First Downs	10	8
Rushing Yards	219	172
Passing Yards	4	27
Passes (A-C-I)	5-1-1	7-4-1
Punts-Average	5-41.5	5-32.2
Fumbles-Lost	3-0	3-0
Penalties-Yds	3-30	7-45

INDIVIDUAL STATISTICS

RUSHING—Leesville: Eddie Fuller 25-127, Rayford Clayton 19-81, Clint Battleford 5-11. Huntington: Mark Washington 15-90, Jackie Hunt 8-36, Joe Hughes 10-46.

PASSING—Leesville: Battleford 5-1-1, 4 yards. Huntington: Hughes 7-4-1, 27 yards.

RECEIVING—Leesville: Fuller 1-4. Huntington: Thomas McLemore 1-8, Hunt 3-19.

LHS Vs. Oakdale 1982

Oakdale	0 0 6 0 — 6
Leesville	7 14 13 7 — 41

Scoring:

L-T.J. Moore 27 run. Daniel Aboutboul kick.

L-Melvin Maxwell 6 pass from Mark Clay. Aboutboul kick.

L-Moore 3 run. Aboutboul kick.

L-Moore 52 run. Pass failed.

L-Mark Clay 52 run. Pass failed.

O-Mark Williams 10 run. Pass failed.

L-Al East 63 run. Aboutboul kick.

L-Andrew Robinson 37 pass from Moore. Aboutboul kick.

	O	L
First Downs	8	18
Rushing	195	441
Passing	0	147
Passes	5-0-2	10-5-0
Punts	5-32	0
Fumbles	1-0	1-0
Penalties	3-25	4-35

LHS Vs. Menard 1984

Leesville	0	14	21	21 —	56
Menard	15	6	0	0 —	21

M — Chris Hooter 88 kickoff return (Matt Raxdale kick)

M — Hooter 10 run (Steve Smith pass from Adam Carnahan)

L — Charles Buckley 9 run (Tony Marsh pass from Al Capello)

M — Smith 73 run (kick failed)

L — Jeff Steele 95 kickoff return (pass failed)

L — Buckley 56 run (Jeff Mitchum kick)

L — Tony Daniels 6 run (Mitchum kick)

L — Steele 1 run (Mitchum kick)

L — Steele 3 run (Mitchum kick)

L — Buckley 10 run (Mitchum kick)

L — Rayford Clayton 5 run (Mitchum kick)

	L	M
First downs	20	12
Yards Rushing	425	236
Yards Passing	138	0
Passes (A-C-I)	13-7-0	8-0-1
Punts/Avg.	1-40	3-45.3
Fumbles/lost	3-3	4-4
Penalties/Yards	10-85	5-25

LHS Vs. Washington 1981 (#1 team)

Washington	0 3 0 6 — 9
Leesville	0 7 6 6 — 19

Scoring:

W-Kenneth Broussard 18-field goal.

L-Matt Miller 18-pass from T.J. Moore. Dana Gatewood kick.

L-Miller 14-pass from Moore. Kick failed.

L-Oscar Joiner 96-run. Kick failed.

W-Keith Lewis 10-pass from Carl Issac. Kick failed.

	W	L
First Downs	24	8
Rushing	315	141
Passing	63	123
Passes	21-6-3	13-5-1
Punts	3-36	6-41.7
Fumbles	3-3	4-2
Penalties	11-140	12-110

LHS Vs. DeRidder 1980

Score By Quarters:
Leesville 0 14 12 0 — 26
DeRidder 0 7 0 8 — 15

Scoring:
L—Charles Owens 7-pass from Eddie Barber. Tom Peavy kick.
L—Ernest Bess 2-run. Tom Peavy kick.
D—Ted Harris 2-run. Tom Peavy kick.
L—Oscar Joiner 77-punt return. Run failed.
L—Oscar Joiner 87-run. Run failed.
D—Andy Sander 7-pass from Ted Harris. Sanders pass from Harris.

Yardstick
(Leesville-DeRidder) First Downs: 9-18. Yds. Rushing: 246-133. Yds. Passing: 78-166. Passes (A-C-I): 5-4-1, 32-13-3. Punts-Avg.: 3-33.0, 3-35.0. Fumbles-Lost: 2-2, 1-1. Penalties-Yds.: 8-95, 4-30.

LHS Vs. Oakdale 1979

Leesville 6 8 7 14 — 35
Oakdale 0 0 6 6 — 6

Scoring:
L — Tony Jones 5-run (kick failed)
L — Charles Owens 11-run (Ernest Best to Rob Gaines)
O — Aswell Accliss 33-run (kick failed)
L — Best 8-run (James Johnson kick)
L — Matt Oliver 16-pass from Best (Johnson kick)
L — Jones 10-run (Johnson kick)

Yardstick
(Leesville-Oakdale) First downs, 12-13; yards rushing, 143-73; yards passing, 40-123; passes, 11-5-3, 15-6-0; punts, 1-31, 3-18; fumbles, 1-0, 6-2; penalties, 6-78, 7-64.

LHS Vs. Welsh 1978

Welsh 0 0 7 13 — 20
Leesville 6 12 6 0 — 24

Scoring:
L-Jim Tucker 27 run. (Kick failed).
L-Terry Holt 8 run. (Pass failed).
L-Holt 7 run. (Pass failed).
L-Scott Herrington 4 run. (Pass failed).
W-Dwayne VanNess 5 pass from John Gay. (Randy LaBauve kick).
W-VanNess 14 pass from Gay. (LaBauve kick).
W-VanNess 52 pass from Gay. (Pass failed).

LHS Vs. Welsh 1977

Score by quarters:
Leesville 7 7 18 7 — 39
Welsh 0 6 6 0 — 12

Scoring:
Leesville—Holt 2 run, (Payton kick)
Payton 9 run, (Payton kick)
Stephens 4 run, (kick failed)
Holt 12 run, (kick failed)
Clark 2 run, (Payton kick)

Yardstick
First Downs, L 14, W 4. Rushing, L 390, W 75. Passing, L 4-2-0, W 9-6-0. Punts, L 6-31, W 5-30.2. Fumbles, L 5-3, W 2-0. Penalties, L 6-60, W 3-35.

LHS Vs. Washington 1976

Washington 6 0 8 0 — 14
Leesville 0 7 0 8 — 15

Scoring:
W — Beloney 12 run (kick failed)
L — Gaines 4 pass from Stephens (Payton kick)
W — Churchill 4 run (Batchan pass from Reed)
L — Stephens 1 run (Holt run)

Yardstick:
First downs: L 14, W 9. Rushing: L 151, W 158. Passing: L 18-8-1, 94; W 17-5-3, 71. Punts: L 5-40, W 6-28. Fumbles: L 6-4, W 2-1. Penalties: L 2-10, W 7-56.

LHS Vs. Jenninngs 1975

JENNINGS JOLTS LEESVILLE
Score by Quarters:
Jennings 0 12 7 7 — 26
Leesville 0 0 0 6 — 6

Scoring Summary:
J—Chris Lehman, 7 pass from David Cormier (kick failed)
J—Bill Price, 3 run (run failed)
J—Price, 8 run (Chris Mott kick)
L—Terry Holt, 73 pass from Bobby Stephens (run failed)
J—Price, 3 run (Mott kick)

Terry Haynes & Richard Bastedo

LHS Vs. Jennings 1974

LEESVILLE BY ONE

Score by Quarters:
Jennings .... 7 0 0 6—13
Leesville .... 0 6 8 0—14

Scoring Summary:
J — Harlan Miller, 4 run (Glenn Green kick)
L — Freeman Mosley, 1 run (run failed)
L — Dennis Driscoll, 73 run (William Dowden run)
J — Gordon Fruge, 10 pass from Miller (run failed)

LHS Vs. Westlake 1973

WESTLAKE VS. LEESVILLE

	W	L
First Downs	9	16
Yards Rushing	54	325
Yards Passing	99	44
Passes (A-I-C)	15-8-1	5-2-1
Punts-Average	3-39	2-32
Fumbles-Lost	6-2	7-1
Penalties-Yards	6-50	16-140

Score by quarters:
Westlake 0 0 8 0—8
Leesville 7 0 0 7—14

Scoring:
L—Driscoll, 80 run (Richard kick).
W—Compton, 16 run (Crick run).
L—Johnson, 29 run (Richard kick).

LHS Vs. Jena 1972

Leesville vs. Jena

	J	L
First Downs	8	11
Yards Rushing	37	190
Yards Passing	73	0
Attempts	16	0
Completions	4	0
Had Intercepted	0	2
Punts	6	2
Average	25	36
Fumbles	4	5
Lost	2	3
Penalties	4	12
Yards Penalized	30	106

Score by quarters:
Jena   0 6 0 6—12
Leesville 7 0 0 13—20

Scoring:
L — Garner 3-run (Mapu kick)
J — Stewart 12-pass from McCartney (kick failed)
L — Driscoll 27-run (kick failed)
L Garner 6-run (Mapu kick)
J — Hodges 6-fumble recovery (pass failed)

Lorenzo Garner (32), Dennis Driscoll (11), Willie Buckley (24)

LHS Vs. Pineville 1971

STATISTICS

	P	L
First Downs	14	4
Yards Rushing	162	30
Yards Passing	43	0
Passes Attempted	14	4
Passes Completed	5	0
Had Intercepted	1	1
Punts	4	6
Punting Average	25	29
Fumbles Lost	3	2
Yards Penalized	35	20

Score by Quarters:
P — Funderburke, 25-yard run, kick failed.
P — Allgood, one-yard run, Hawthorne kick.
L — Jimmy Mapu, 80-yard kickoff return, Lewis run.
L — Jimmy Mapu, 80-yard kickoff return, Lewis run.
L — Johnny Mapu, 90-yard run with blocked fieldgoal, kick failed.
L — Lynch, 35-yard pass interception, kick failed.

LHS Vs. Oakdale 1970

Statistics

	O.	L.
First Downs	9	15
Yards Rushing	130	326
Yards Passing	54	69
Passes Attempted	8	7
Passes Completed	3	5
Had Intercepted	0	0
Punts	3	2
Average	15	41
Fumbles	1	1
Fumbles Lost	1	0
Yards Penalized	40	90

Score by quarters:
Oakdale   0 0 0 0—0
Leesville 0 7 7 14—28

Scoring:
L—Haynes 12-run (Mapu)
L—Haynes 11-run (Mapu)
L—Haynes 13-run (Mapu)
L—Carter 25-run (Mapu)

NOTE: 1970 was first season of football after LHS & Vernon High were merged into a single school

LHS Vs. DeRidder 1969

Score by quarters:
Leesville   0 0 13 12—25
DeRidder   0 0 0 0— 0

Scoring:

L-TD: Goldsby 70-kickoff return (Driscoll kick)

L-TD: Ashfield 1-run (kick failed)

L-TD: Hays 14-run (kick failed)

L-TD: Goldsby 20-pass from Wood (kick failed)

LHS Vs. North Caddo 1968

North Caddo ....0 14 7 0—21
Leesville .. ..6 19 0 0—25

Score Summary:

L — Larry Lavrent, 58 pass fro Vic Oritz (kick failed)

N — Ron Holt (70 pass from Tom Flores, (Hol tkick)

L — Jim Armes, 32 pass from Ortiz (Lanrent kick)

L — Ortiz, 3, run (kick failed)

L — Ortiz, 7 run (kick blocked)

N — Billy Allen, 7 pass from Flores (Holt kick)

N — Holt, 52 pass from Flores (Holt kick)

Jack Ashfield (34)

LHS Vs. Tioga 1967

Score by Quarters
Leesville ..... 7 7 0 0—14
Tioga   0 7 0 0— 7

Score Summary:

L — Donny Gill, 4 run, (Mike Dudley kick)

L — Darwin Davis, 6 run, (Dudley kick)

T — Buster Avery, 7 pass from Cecil Caldwell, (Sak Sellers kick)

LHS Vs. Tioga 1966

TIOGA vs LEESVILLE	T.	L.
First Downs	5	8
Net Yards Rushing	52	136
Net Yards Passing	34	45
Total Offense	86	181
Passes Attempted	13	9
Passes Completed	4	3
Interceptions by	3	1
Punts	5	5
Punting Average	26.4	44.6
Fumbles	4	2
Fumbles Lost	1	2
Yards Penalized	45	100

Score by Quarters:
Tioga   0 0 0 0— 0
Leesville   7 6 8 0—21

Long Runs:
Tioga — Colwell (49).
Leesville — Causey (16), Seamands (18, 13), Word (10, 14).

Scoring:
Leesville — Touchdowns Causey 5-run), Funderburk (47-pass interception), Seamands (4-run), safety.

LEESVILLE RUSHING

Name	Tries	Yards	Lost	Net	T.D.
Causey	16	65	1	64	1
Seamands	8	45	0	45	1
Word	3	24	2	22	0
Davis	1	5	0	5	0
Hindsman	3	4	0	4	0
Ortiz	5	5	2	3	0
Leach	1	1	0	1	0
Karamales	2	6	6	0	0
Gill	1	0	8	-8	0

PASSING

Name, School	Att.	Comp	H.I.	Yds.	T.D.
Colwell, Tioga	10	2	1	17	0
Prestridge, Tioga	3	2	0	17	0
Karamales, Leesville	8	3	2	45	0
Gill, Leesville	1	0	0	0	0

RECEIVING

Name, School	Rec.	Yards	T.D.
Morgan, Tioga	2	17	0
Axery, Tioga	2	17	0
Nash, Leesville	1	13	0
Hadnot, Leesville	1	4	0
Word, Leesville	1	28	0

PUNTING

Morgan, Tioga	5	132	1	26.4
Hadnot, Leesville	3	119	0	39.7
Karamales, Leesville	2	99	0	49.5

LHS Vs. Marion 1965

Leesville ....0 13 6 20—39
Marion   ....0 7 0 0— 7

L—Roland Breaux 2 run. Run failed.
L—Rodger Causey 38 run. Keith Carver run.
M—Terry Johnson 98 kickoff return. Robert Ellis kick.
L—Keith Carver 2 run. Run failed.
L—Keith Carver 4 run. Run failed.
L—Keith Carver 5 run. Carl Williams run.
L—Randy Martin 1 run. Jack Gross run.

STATISTICS
	Leesville	Marion
First downs	16	7
Rushing yardage	298	33
Passing yardage	33	42
Passes	4-8	4-14
Passes Intercepted by	3	1
Punts	3-35.0	3-23.3
Fumbles lost	0	3
Yards penalized	68	15

Ronnie Morrow

The Varsity

Team Managers 1965

LHS Vs. Ferriday 1964

```
Ferriday      0  0  0  6— 6
Leesville     6 14  7  6—33
L—Don Jackson 7 pass from Bill Salim.
  Run failed.
L—Keith Carver 12 run. Aubrey Temple
  pass from Bill Salim.
L—Danny Cathings 29 pass from Bill
  Salim. Keith Carver run.
L—Jimmy Skinner 34 pass from Bill
  Salim. Keith Carver run.
L—Jimmy Haymon 49 run. Run failed.
F—Jerry Ziegler recovered fumble in
  Leesville end zone. Pass failed.
                      Ferriday  Leesville
First downs ............. 10       14
Rushing yardage ......  210      153
Passing yardage ......    6      195
Passes ............... 1-7     13-18
Passes intercepted by ..  1        1
Fumbles lost ...........  3        2
Penalties ............... 15      10
```

LHS Vs. Tioga 1963

```
Leesville    13 20  7  6—46
Tioga         0  0  0  0— 0
L—Paul Nicholas, 51 run. Run failed.
L—Roy Trahan, 88 run. Mike Shokley
  run.
L—Paul Nicholas, 1 run. Mike Shokley
  run.
L—Paul Nicholas, 6 run. Mike Shokley
  run.
L—John Martinez, 4 pass from Billy
  Salim. Run failed.
L—Keith Carver, 3 run. Danny Catchings
  run.
L—Keith Carver, 1 run. Run failed.
         STATISTICS
                     Leesville  Tioga
First downs ............. 12      5
Rushing yardage ...... 489      11
Passing yardage ......   55     84
Passes ............... 3-4    9-27
Passes intercepted by .. 2       1
Punts ............... 1-27.0  3-34.4
Fumbles lost ............  0      1
Yards penalized ......   50      0
```

Mike Shockley

LHS Vs. Menard 1962

```
       Menard Vs. Leesville
                         M.    L.
First Downs ............ 11    17
Net Yards Rushing ..... 186   280
Net Yards Passing .....   0    29
Total Offense ......... 186   309
Passes Attempted ......   1     3
Passes Completed ......   0     1
Interceptions By ......   0     0
Punts .................   3     0
Punting Average ...... 24.0   0.0
Fumbles ...............   1     1
Fumbles Lost ..........   0     1
Yards Penalized .......  30    10
       Menard Rushing
Player          T.   Yds.  Avg.
Yoist            7    24    3.5
Mayeaux         12    55    4.6
Flynn           12    48    4.0
Crouch           9    31    3.4
Beavers          8    28    3.5
Totals          48   186    3.9
       Leesville Rushing
Player          T.   Yds.  Avg.
Magee           25   177    7.0
Trahan          13    45    3.4
Sumney          12    52    4.3
Montgomery       7     6    0.8
Totals          57   280    4.9
Score by quarters:
Menard    0  7  0  0— 7
Leesville 0  0  6  7—13
First Down Runs: Menard — May-
eaux (11). Leesville — Magee (40,
27, 11) Sumney (32).
Scoring: Menard — Touchdown:
Mayeaux (11-run). Extra Point —
Yoist (run).
Leesville — Touchdown: Magee
2 (2-run, 8-run) Extra Point —
Sumney (Run).
```

LHS Vs Bunkie 1961

```
Bunkie       0  0  6  0— 6
Leesville    7 14  6  6—33
BUNKIE SCORING: TD—James Knoll
(14 run).
LEESVILLE SCORING: TD — Louis
Magee (11 run), George Smith 3 (1 run,
4 run, 60 run), Bobby Croft (45 inter-
cepted pass). PAT— R. J. Fertitta 3
(kick).
         STATISTICS
                     Bunkie Leesville
First downs ...........   6     7
Rushing yardage ..... 133   177
Passing yardage .....   0    44
Passes attempted ....   3     4
Passes attempted ....   3     4
Passes completed ....   0     3
Passes intercepted by   0     0
Punts .............. 7-32  5-33
Fumbles lost .........   1     0
Yards penalized .....  65    30
```

LHS Vs Coushatta 1960

```
Coushatta    0  6  7  0—13
Leesville    7 20  6  7—40
Coushatta Scoring: TD—Ted Jackson (5
run), Stanley Dickson (3 run). PAT—Stan-
ley Dickson (run).
Leesville Scoring: TD—Jerry McLaren
(5 run), Ronnie Byrd 2 (20, 1 runs),
George Smith 2 (31, 17 runs), Sid Morris
(36 pass from Ronnie Byrd). PAT—
Ronnie Byrd 2 (runs), Sid Morris 2
(runs).
         STATISTICS
                     Coushatta Leesville
First downs ............. 14      18
Rushing yardage ...... 254      302
Passing yardage ......   0       40
Passes ............... 0-7      2-2
Passes intercepted by .. 0        0
Punts ................ 1-0        0
Fumbles lost ...........  2        0
Yards penalized ......   10       35
```

Ronnie Byrd   Roy Trahan

LHS Vs. Menard 1959

MENARD VS LEESVILLE

	M.	L.
First Downs	5	12
Net Yards Rushing	-4	167
Net Yards Passing	93	70
Passes Attempted	27	11
Passes Completed	12	5
Interceptions By	1	1
Punts	7	6
Punting Average	36.4	39.9
Fumbles	1	3
Yards Penalized	45	45

MENARD RUSHING

Player	T.	Yds.	Ave.
Boisvert	7	-12	-1.7
Tamburo	3	9	3.0
LaBorde	3	5	1.7
Totals	11	-4	-.3

LEESVILLE — RUSHING

Player	T.	Yds.	Ave.
R. Schwartz	20	57	2.9
Terry	23	69	3.0
Morris	5	16	3.2
Byrd	12	25	2.1
Totals	60	167	2.8

Score by quarters:

Menard	0	0	7	0	— 7
Leesville	0	6	7	6	— 19

First Down Runs: Leesville—Schwartz (10), Terry (10). Scoring: Menard—Touchdowns: D. Boisvert 1 (10-yard pass from Bobby Boisvert). Extra Points—Bobby Boisvert (run).

Leesville—Touchdown: Terry 2 (Runs of 3, 1 yards) Schwartz (2-yard run) Extra Points: Terry(run).

LHS Vs. Menard 1958

SUMMARY
Score By Quarters

Menard	7	0	0	20	—27
Leesville	6	19	14	0	—39

LEESVILLE: TD—Pynes 2 (4-yd. run; 43-yd run); Hall 2 (14-yd run, 2-yd run); Norris (2-yd run); Rowzee (36-yd pass from Norris). PAT—Norris (run); Rowzee (run).

MENARD: TD—Tamburo 2 (35-yd run, 60-yd pass from Boisvert); Chenevert 2 (30-yd pass from Boisvert, 40-yd pass from Boisvert). PAT—Mahfouz 3 (placement)

Statistics

Menard		Leesville
14	First downs	18
110	Rushing yardage	406
231	Passing yardage	55
9 of 17	Passes complete	2 of 5
0	Passes intercepted by	0
2 for 38	Punt average	1 for 29
2	Fumbles lost	3
30	Yards penalized	30

LHS Vs. Menard 1957

SUMMARY
Score By Quarters

Leesville	7	7	13	7	—34
Menard	7	6	0	14	—27

Leesville scoring: TD — Piranio (24-yd. run); Hall 2 (16, 19-yd. runs); Pynes (24-yd run); W. Morris (6-yd run. PAT — Hall 2 (runs); Welch (pass from Piranio); B. Lewis (run).

Menard scoring: TD — Deville 2 (1-yd. runs); Chenevert 2 (40, 46-yd. passes from Mahfouz. PAT — Watson (run); Sanders 2 (passes from Watson).

STATISTICS

Leesville		Menard
19	First downs	18
333	Rushing yardage	73
17	Passing yardage	214
1 of 4	Passes completed	10 of 15
2	Passes intercepted by	0
0 for 0	Punts, avg.	1 for 20
5	Fumbles lost	3
65	Yards penalized	30

INDIVIDUAL RUSHING

Leesville	Carries	Net Gain	Avg.
Pynes	14	126	9.0
Hall	10	84	8.4
Piranio	7	56	8.0
Rowzee	1	7	7.0
W. Morris	12	60	5.0

Menard	Carries	Net Gain	Avg.
Watson	21	75	3.6
Deville	11	35	3.2
Mahfouz	7	-18	-2.7

INDIVIDUAL PASSING

Leesville	Att	Com	Int	Yds
Piranio	4	1	0	17

Menard	Att	Com	Int	Yds
Mahfouz	15	10	2	214

PASS RECEPTION

Leesville	Catches	Yards	TD
W. Morris	1	17	0

Menard	Catches	Yards	TD
Chenevert	5	154	2
Deville	3	41	0
Sanders	2	19	0

LHS Vs. Menard 1956

SCORE BY QUARTERS

Menard	7	14	0	7	—28
Leesville	0	0	7	0	— 7

Menard scoring: TD — Bootsy Watson (55-yd. run); Joe Serio (4-yd. plunge); Butch Willis 2 (15-yd. run, 2-yd. plunge). PAT — Serio 4 (2 runs, 2 placements).

Leesville scoring: TD — Sam Piranio (5-yd. run); PAT — J. C. Welch (placement).

STATISTICS

Menard		Leesville
14	first downs	11
371	rushing yardage	149
22	passing yardage	61
2 of 6	passes completed	6 of 17
2	passes intercepted by	0
0 for 0	punts, avg.	3 for 51
1	fumbles lost	1
55	yards penalized	50

Individual Rushing

Menard	Carries	Gain	Avg.
Watson	6	141	23.5
Willis	11	101	9.2
Serio	13	101	7.6
Cosenza	1	3	3.0
Deville	1	11	11.0
Soprano	2	11	5.5
Veillon	1	3	3.0

Leesville	Carries	Gain	Avg.
Allen	7	44	6.3
Hall	11	49	4.5
Piranio	8	35	4.4
Grant	3	15	5.0
Morris	6	16	2.7

Wayne Morris (20); Sam Piranio on the block

LHS Vs. Bossier 1955

Score by quarters:
Leesville ... 0 6 0 0—6
Bossier ... 19 7 0 0—26
Scoring: Bossier TDs—Laughlin 2, Seaburn 2, Howard. PATs—Nattin, Mercer. Leesville TD—Harles Smart.

THE YARDSTICK

	Wampus Cats	Bearcats
First Downs	9	12
Yds Gn. Rush.	115	322
Yds. Lost Rush.	13	9
Net Yds. Rush.	102	313
Pass Attem.	11	6
Pass Com.	6	2
Yds. Gn Pass.	61	18
Yds Lost Pass.	0	0
Net Yds. Pass	61	18
Pass. Intercept. by	0	2
Total Yardage	163	331
Punts, Average	3-37	0-0
Blocked Punts		
Fumbles	2	3
Opp. Fumb. Rec.	2	2
Penalties, Yds.	5	20

LHS Vs. Mansfield 1954

SCORE BY QUARTERS

Mansfield ... 0 0 0 6—6
Leesville ... 0 7 6 13—26

Mansfield Scoring: TD — Joe Stout (2-yd run).

Leesville Scoring: TD — James Coburn 2 (60-yd run with recovered fumble, 2-yd run); George Fisher (24-yd pass from Harlis Smart); Julian Stevens (53-yd run). PAT—George Fisher 2 (placement.)

STATISTICS

	Leesville	Mansfield
First downs	12	8
Yards rushing	240	133
Yards passing	24	72
Passes attempted	11	15
Passes completed	1	7
Passes intercepted by	1	0
Punts	2	2
Punt average	34	30
Fumbles lost	0	1
Penalties	70	60

LHS Vs. Pineville 1953

	Leesville	Pineville
First Downs	3	13
Net yards rushing	174	157
Yards passing	0	29
Passes Attempted	3	13
Passes completed	0	2
No. of Punts	3	1
Punting average	38	50
Fumbles (rec. & lost)	3-0-3	5-3-2
Yards penalized	7-55	4-30

Score by quarters:

	1	2	3	4	
Leesville	0	0	7	0	—7
Pineville	0	6	0	0	—6

Scoring touchdowns: Pineville—Washington (15 yards around end). Leesville—Byrd (from one foot line). Extra point—Coburn 1.

LHS Vs. Pineville 1952

	Rebels	Cats
First downs	11	11
Net Yards Rushing	62	216
Passes Attempted	16	1
Passes Completed	3	1
Yds. Gained Passing	48	6
Passes Intercepted	0	2
Number of Punts	4	0
Punting Average	22.7	X
Fumbles	3	1
Fumbles Recovered	1	1
Penalties (Number)	1	10
Yds. Lost Penalties	5	70

Score by periods:
Pineville ... 0 0 0 8 - 8
Leesville ... 19 0 7 7 - 33

Scoring. Touchdowns: Leesville: Nichols 2 (48 yard punt runback and 5 yard run) Moses 2 (20 yard run and two yard run), Wright (20 yard end run). Pineville: Fowler (five yard buck). PAT — Leesville: Moses (end un) Moss 2 (Conversons. Pineville — Safety. Oficals: Referee — Barron. Umpire —McFee. Head Linesman Sills. Field Judge — Hubert.
LEESVILLE SUBS: K. Smart, Sliman, Tumminello, Wright, Dunham, Moss, Byrd, Fisher, James, Gregg, McManus, McClain, Mixon, Moore, Skinner, Stone.

LHS Vs. Natchitoches 1951

Score by quarters:
Natchitoches .... 6 0 12 6—24
Leesville .... 6 0 0 6—12

Teddy Berry

LHS Vs. Menard 1950

Score by quarters:
Menard ... 0 0 0 0—0
Leesville ... 0 0 0 0—0

Officials: Crenshaw, referee; Hunt, umpire; Burke, headlinesman; Bates, field judge.

Statistics

	Menard	L'ville
Net yards rushing	238	69
First downs	14	5
Passes attempted	11	10
Passes completed	1	0
Yards passing	6	0
Passes had intercepted	1	4
Penalties	1	3
Yards penalized	5	15
Fumbles lost	2	0
Times punted	6	9
Average yards punting	17	30

THE FIRST GOLDEN AGE

THE MID 1980s

The pictures in this section chronicle the first and arguably most successful sustained period of LHS football. The photos were provided by one of the stars of one of the best teams ever at LHS, quarterback Chris Davis. Some are repeats from elsewhere in the book, but are included in their entirety as commemoration for the great days of winning during the coaching tenures of Jack Andre and Brownie Parmlee.

Caught with the game's intensity written on their faces in LHS' sensational 47-46 victory over New Iberia in double overtime are, from left, 6' 2", 240 pound offensive lineman Andy Bellamy (52) and quarterback Stan Watley (8). (Commander Photo)

YARDSTICK

TEAM	DeR	LHS
First downs	15	14
Yds. rushing	193	249
Yds. passing	80	31
Total yards	273	280
Att-comp-int	10-5-1	8-2-0
Punts	2-3.0	1-37.0
Fumb., lost	2-0	0-0
Penalties	7-45	8-75

SCORE BY QUARTERS

DeRidder .... 7- 0- 7- 0— 14
Leesville .... 13- 0- 3- 7— 23

SCORING SUMMARY

LHS— Kevin Smith 64 kickoff return; Jason Giutini kick.
DHS— Scott Lowe 1 run; Tim Wilcox kick.
LHS— Vincent Fuller 31 run; kick failed.
DHS— Millard Bradford 2 run; Tim Wilcox kick.
LHS— Giutini 32 field goal.
LHS— Fuller 1 run; Giutini kick.

INDIVIDUAL STATS

RUSHING— DeRidder: Johnny Thibodeaux 5-12; Earl Hadnot 10-60; Derek Knighton 4-21; Scott Lowe 5- -3; Marcus Lee 17-68; Millard Bradford 8-35. Leesville: Chris Davis 6- -7; Vincent Fuller 29-178; Joe Williams 8-78.

PASSING— DeRidder: Scott Lowe 10-5-1-80. Leesville: Chris Davis 8-2-0-31.

RECEIVING— DeRidder: David Simmons 3-54; Maurice Groening 1-21; Charles Thomas 1-5. Leesville: Erwin Brown 1-11; Paul Clay 1-20.

Getting down

Left Tackle Raymond Smoot, number 79, has Tioga defender down while left guard Ronnie Lara, number 65, blocks out another Indian.

We're ready coach
Coach Brownie Parmley, seen here with quarterback Chris Davis, will make his debut as head coach of Leesville, Friday at Peabody. Kickoff is set for 7:

Getting the plan straight
...esville Head Coach Brownie Parmley talks to his charges during a timeout of the Lake Cha...

Leesville captures double OT victory

NEW IBERIA — Joe Williams plowed over from the 1 on fourth and goal to give Leesville a 47-46 double overtime victory over New Iberia in a rip-snorting first-round Class AAAAA slugfest Friday night.

The exhausting victory extended Leesville's record to 10-1 and sends the Wampus Cats into next week's regional playoff at Leesville against St. Amant.

New Iberia, powered by the two-touchdown, 262-yard rushing performance of Chris Fontenette, closed the season at 8-4.

Fontenette scored on runs of 27, 50 and 65 yards.

The Wampus Cats led by eight points, 34-26, and lined up for a field goal at the New Iberia 26 with 3½ minutes left to put the game out of reach.

The center snap was bad and New Iberia recovered at its 13. Quarterback Corey Sorrel started working his magic.

Sorrel completed four passes for 41 yards on the drive, including a 16-yard scoring toss to Mike Moity. Fontenette ran for a two-point conversion to tie the game.

Erwin Brown, who rambled for 147 yards and three touchdowns on 30 carries, scored Leesville's first touchdown in the first overtime.

Sorrel hit Moity for a 16-yard touchdown pass to cap New Iberia's first overtime drive.

The Wampus Cats blocked the Yellow Jackets' extra-point kick to force a second overtime.

Leesville 7 17 3 7 6 7—47
N.Iberia 14 6 0 14 6 6—46

NI—Corey Sorrel 5 run (Viradeth Rajaphe kick)
L—Vincent Fuller 2 run (Jason Guntini kick)
NI—Seth Porche 50 pass from Sorrel (Rajaphe kick)
NI—Chris Fontenette 27 run (kick failed)
L—Stan Whatley 12 run (Guntini kick)
L—Erwin Brown 11 run (Guntini kick)
L—FG Guntini 26
L—FG Guntini 25
L—Erwin Brown 29 run (Guntini kick)
NI—Fontenette 65 run (pass failed)
NI—Mike Moity 16 pass from Sorrel (Fontenette run)
L—Brown 1 run (kick blocked)
NI—Moity 16 pass from Sorrel (kick blocked)
NI—Sorrel 10 run (kick blocked)
L—Joe Williams 1 run (Guntini kick)

Just a little farther

Playoff tickets

Season ticket holders for Wampus Cat football will be able to purchase their tickets for Friday night's playoff game with St. Amant starting Wednesday at the High School office, Principal Richard Rosse announced Saturday.

Season ticket holders will be able to buy their seats Wednesday through noon Friday. At noon Friday, those seats held by season ticket holders will go on sale to the general public.

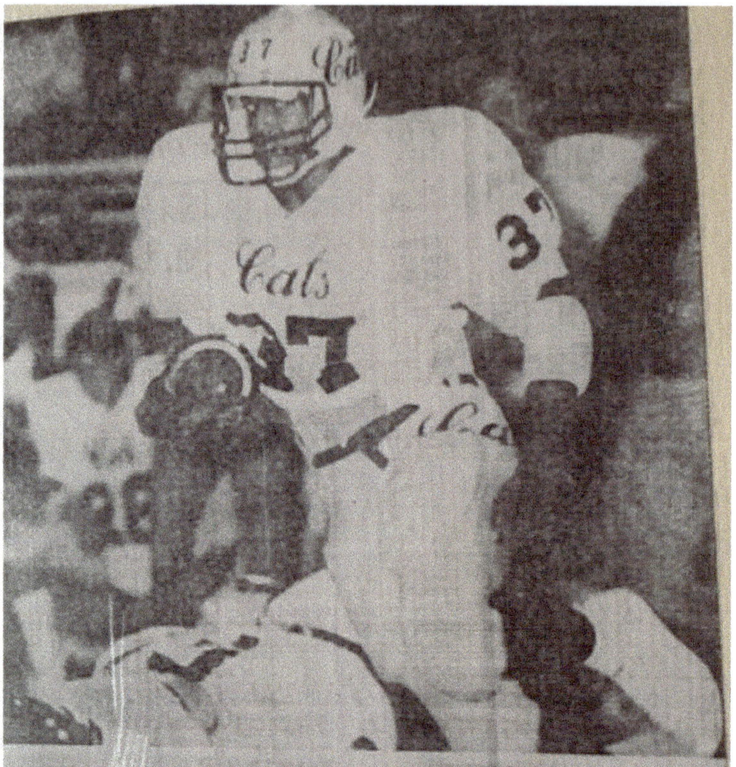

American Press Photo/Eric Marchand

Leesville running back Vincent Fuller (37) rushed for 193 yards and a touchdown in the Wampus Cats' 24-0 win over Natchitoches-Central

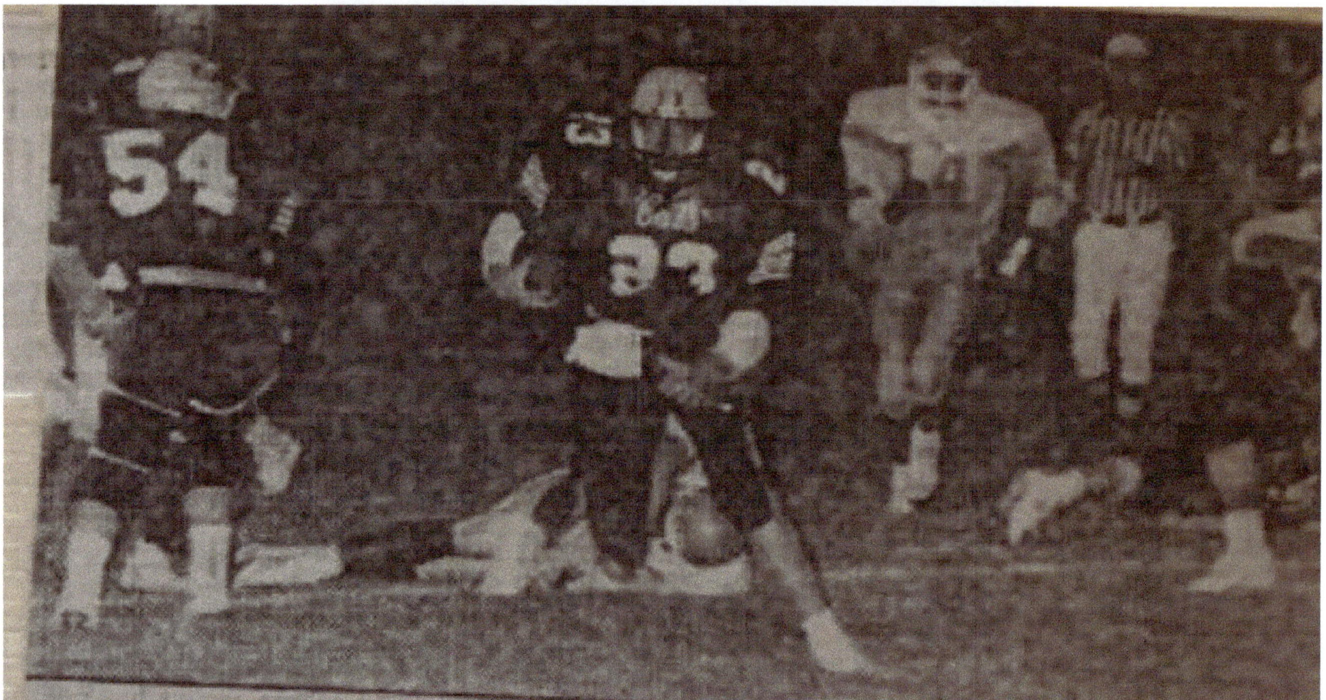

Breaking through

Leesville's Paul Clay hopes to breaking through plenty of holes against Barbe Friday night in Wampus Cat Stadium.

Crush!

In this shot we see the aftermath of a collision between the Wampuscats and Trojans. Up to now, the Wampuscats have really made the grade, and we're all hoping that the loss doesn't get them down and that they continue to play the game at their peak! The Wampuscats may have had their streak snapped, but they played the game to the hilt.

Ready for action
Starting defensive ends Dennis Mitchell, left, and Carl Wallace get ready for Peabody.

STATISTICS

Leesville		DeRidder
15	First Downs	14
392	Rushing Yardage	139
86	Passing Yardage	85
4-6-0	Passes	6-25-1
1-35	Punts	3-41
2-1	Fumbles, lost	0
11-121	Penalties, yards	2-25

SCORE BY QUARTERS

Leesville	14	7	7	17	—45
DeRidder	0	0	14	0	—14

L - Tony Rush 6 run. Jeff Mitcham kick.

L - Clint Batteford 3 run. Jeff Mitcham kick.

L - Demetrius Payton 27 pass from Clint Batteford. Jeff Mitcham kick.

L - Tony Rush 50 run. Jeff Mitcham kick.

D - Raymond Porter 12 run. Raymond Porter run.

D - Scott Nease 1 run. Pass failed.

L - Jeff Mitcham 21 field goal.

L - Vincent Fuller 6 run. Jeff Mitcham kick.

L - Anthony Burns 24 pass from Clint Batteford. Jeff Mitcham kick.

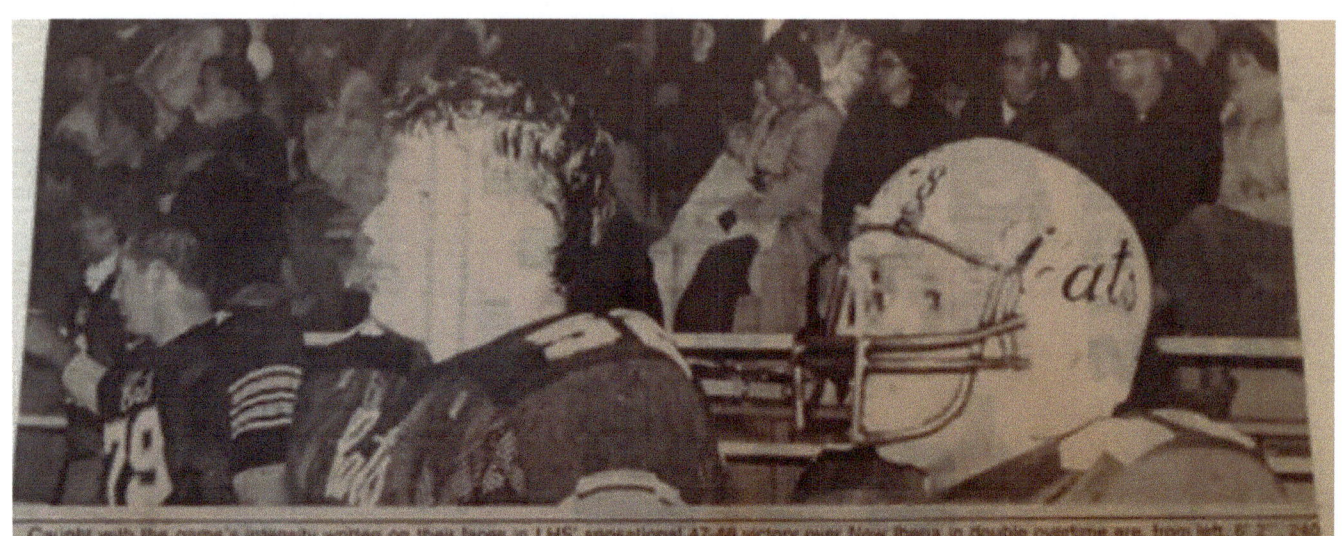

Caught with the game's intensity written on their faces in LHS' sensational 47-46 victory over New Iberia in double overtime are, from left, 6' 2", 240 pound offensive lineman Andy Bellamy (52) and quarterback Stan Watley (8). (Commander Photo)

Leader photo/

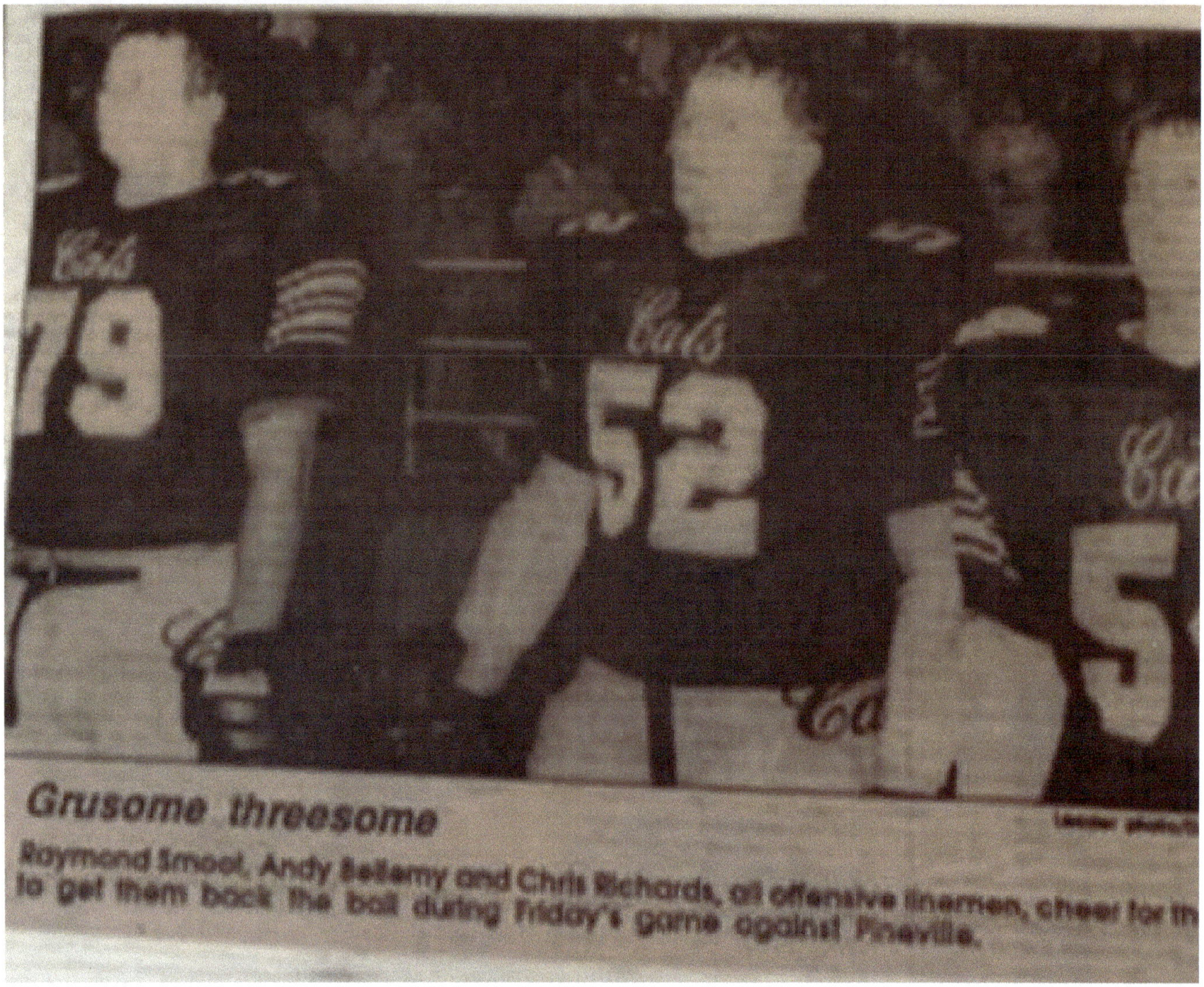

Grusome threesome

Raymond Smoot, Andy Bellamy and Chris Richards, all offensive linemen, cheer for th to get them back the ball during Friday's game against Pineville.

first team all-district honors

Roger Anderson

Anderson played center for the Cats at 5-11 and 200 pounds. The senior anchored the offensive line and was a strong, aggressive blocker who handled middle guards exceptionally well.

Ronnie Lara

Lara played right guard at 5-9 and 185 pounds. He was Leesville's best one-on-one blocker. The senior also excelled at trap blocking.

Jeff Mitcham

Mitcham kicked 36 out of 37 attempted extra points and made three field goals out of six attempts. His field goals were 36, 25 and 26 yards. Mitcham kicks accounted for 37 points. He booted the field goal in overtime against LaGrange which clinched the Division 5A championship.

Robert Jenkins

Jenkins is a junior, 6-4 and 250 pounds, who played defensive right tackle. He recorded 97 total tackles in 11 games. He was credited with 47 solo tackles and threw opposing ball carriers for losses 11 times. He was leader of the defensive front.

Earl Wallace

Wallace played left end at 6 feet and 200 pounds. A senior, he registered 75 total tackles and was credited with 25 solo tackles. He recorded six tackles for losses and is a fierce pass rusher.

Mike Smith

The Cats' left linebacker, Smith, at 5-10 and 185 pounds, recorded 74 total tackles, 40 of them unassisted. He threw ball carriers for losses six times. He has excellent speed so is a terrific pass rusher.

LHSAA STATE RUNNER UP SEASON

13 - 2

This section provides pictures from the 1995 State Runner Up Team. While some of these photos appear elsewhere in the book, I decided to create this special section out of appreciation for source of the pictures. Former Cat great Sig Milerski submitted these pictures and, because of the great success of the 1995 team, I thought they merited their own section, as a special commemoration to the superb achievements from that year.

Clemons stops Bondurant
Sedric Clemons (35) stops Dragon quarterback Jody Bondurant for a loss during the Wampus Cats Class 4A quarterfinal win Friday night. The Cats held DeRidder to only 146 total yards in the game, including 87 on the ground. The 29-0 shutout was the fifth of the season for Leesville as they head to this week's semifinal contest at home against the Breaux Bridge Tigers.

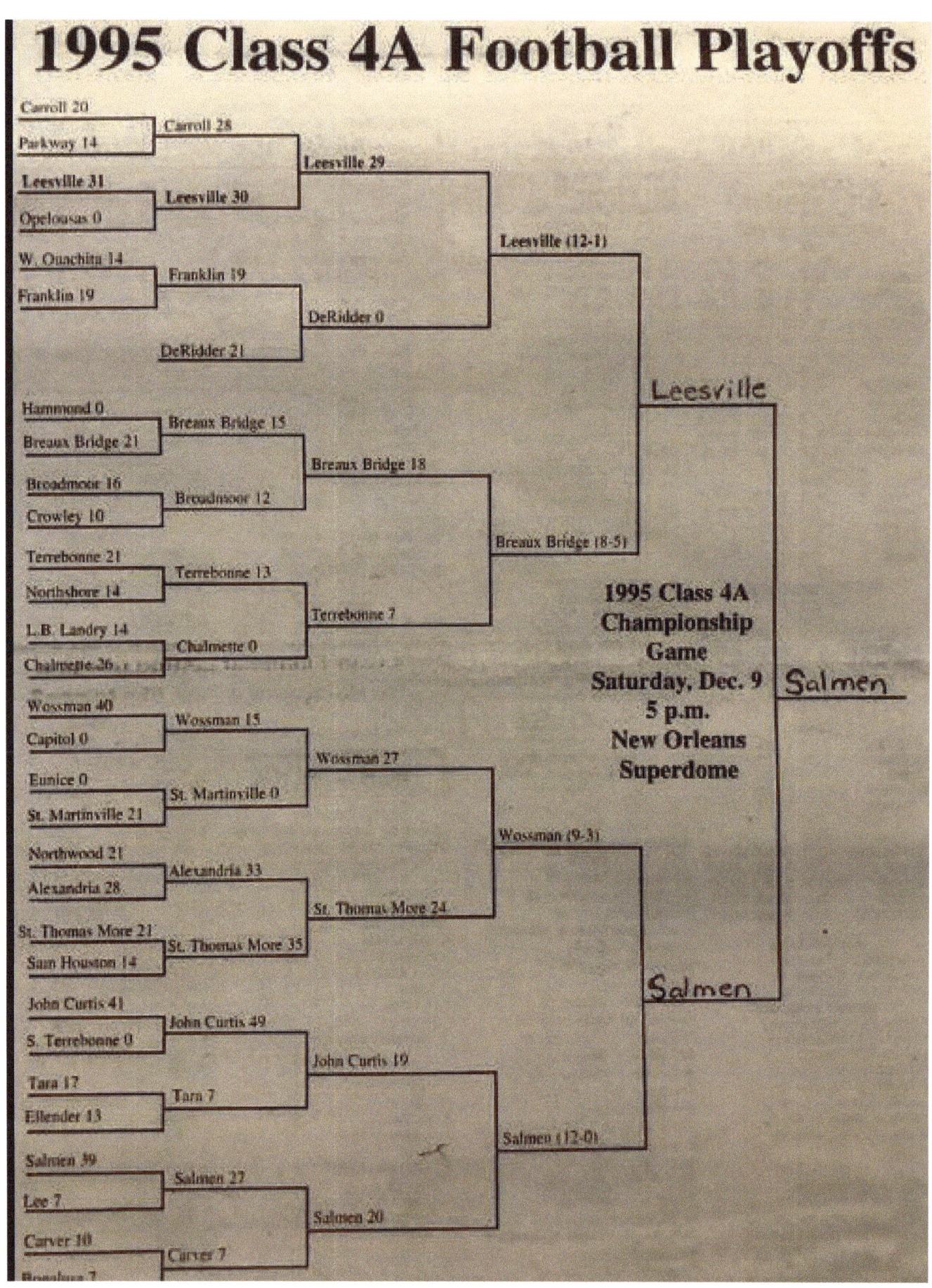

Leesville defenders Marcus Gill, 87, Sigi Milerski, 58, and Vernon Lee, 30, wrap up Sam Houston running back Pat Sullivan for no gain on Sullivan's only first-half carry.
JOHN DAVID PHELPS / STAFF PHOTOGRAPHER

1995 District 4-4A All-District Football Team

First Team Offense

Pos.	Player	School	Ht.	Wt.	Class
C	William Broussard	Crowley	6-0	225	Sr.
OL	David Dotson	Sam Houston	6-1	270	Sr.
OL	Denni Fetting	Leesville	5-10	225	Sr.
OL	Jessie Harmon	Crowley	6-3	280	Sr.
OL	William Brown	Eunice	6-0	190	Sr.
TE	Joey Domingeaux	Crowley	6-3	230	Jr.
WR	Jerry Dixon	Crowley	6-4	210	Sr.
WR	Dennis Nelson	Washington-Marion	5-10	175	Sr.
RB	Cecil Collins	Leesville	5-10	205	Sr.
RB	Bill Phillips	Crowley	5-10	195	Sr.
RB	Daniel Lavine	Sam Houston	5-11	190	Sr.
QB	Kevin Cormier	Crowley	6-1	205	Sr.
PK	Kevin Cormier	Crowley	6-1	205	Sr.
KR	Sy Price	Eunice	6-0	165	Sr.
KR	George Guidry	Washington-Marion	6-3	230	Sr.

Outstanding Offensive Player: Cecil Collins, Leesville.
Coach of the Year: Danny Smith, Leesville.

Second Team Offense

Center: Jason Hatchett (DeRidder).
Offensive Linemen: Eric Powell (Washington-Marion); Earl Scott (DeRidder); Jimmy Thorton (Sam Houston); Wesley Kibodeaux (Crowley).
Tight End: Trey Langley (Eunice).
Wide Receivers: Marcus Thurman (Leesville); Sy Price (Eunice).
Running Backs: Derrick Peters (DeRidder); Andre Allison (Eunice); Shaun Hooper (DeRidder).
Quarterback: Jason Green (Leesville).
Placekicker: Jabby Cormier (Eunice).

First Team Defense

Pos.	Player	School	Ht.	Wt.	Class
DL	David Havard	Sam Houston	6-0	230	Sr.
DL	Stacey Bradford	DeRidder	5-11	250	Sr.
DL	George Guidry	Washington-Marion	6-3	230	Sr.
DL	Trey Langley	Eunice	6-5	265	Sr.
LB	Greg Ross	Leesville	5-9	185	Sr.
LB	Ben Duhon	Sam Houston	6-1	210	Sr.
LB	Aaron Dean	Washington-Marion	6-1	180	Jr.
LB	Titus Latichison	DeRidder	6-0	210	
DB	Shermaine Jones	Leesville	5-10	175	
DB	Mike Fontenote	Sam Houston	5-11	170	
DB	Sy Price	Eunice	6-0	165	
DB	Dennis Nelson	Washington-Marion	5-10	170	
P	Kevin Cormier	Crowley	6-1	205	

Outstanding Defensive Player: Trey Langley, Eunice.

Second Team Defense

Defensive Linemen: Robbie Carter (Leesville); Ken Apcock (Crowley); Sigi Milerski (Leesville); Duke Johnson (Sam Houston); Harry Fra (Eunice).
Linebackers: Sedric Clemons (Leesville); Brandon Smith (Crowley); Franco Guillory (Eunice); Reggie Silas (DeRidder).
Defensive Backs: Mike Lewis (Leesville); Kevin Thomas (Crowley); Elliott Mitchell (Eunice); Melvecchio Guidry (Crowley); Terrell Latchison (DeRidder).
Punter: Brian Cock (Sam Houston).

Clemons stops Bondurant
Sedric Clemons (35) stops Dragon quarterback Jody Bondurant for a loss during the Wampus Cats Class 4A quarterfinal win Friday night. The Cats held DeRidder to only 146 total yards in the game, including 87 on the ground. The 29-0 shutout was the fifth of the season for Leesville as they head to this week's semifinal contest at home against the Breaux Bridge Tigers.

Buckner follows his blockers
Leesville fullback Ryan Buckner (44) follows his blockers on a run during the Wampus Cats 15- over the DeRidder Dragons Friday night. Leesville, ranked third in the state, completed their best son since 1987 with the win and improved to 9-1 on the season. The Cats will host a wild card tea the first round of the playoffs this Friday night.

Leesville 15, DeRidder 6

Team	LHS	DHS
First Downs	8	9
Rushing Yards	178	103
Passing Yards	56	31
Total Yards	234	134
Passes	2-5-2	2-6-1
Punts	3-26	2-25
Fumbles-Lost	1-0	2-2
Penalties	12-105	1-5

SCORE BY QUARTERS

Leesville	7	8	0	0	—15
DeRidder	0	0	0	0	— 6

SCORING SUMMARY

LHS — Cecil Collins 2 run (Josh Dill kick).
DHS — Chris Ashworth 7 run (pass failed).
LHS — Collins 4 run (Greg Rone run).

INDIVIDUAL STATISTICS

Rushing — **Leesville**: Cecil Collins 31-153; Ryan Buckner 5-30; Greg Rone 1-1; Jason Green 3-(-6). **DeRidder**: Jody Bondurant 4-46; Derrick Peters 6-28; Sheaun Hooper 11-23; Marvin Scott 1-5; Chris Ashworth 2-4; Ray Peters 3-4; Titus Latchison 1-0; Marion Woods 3-(-7).

Passing — **Leesville**: Jason Green 5-2-2—56. **DeRidder**: Jody Bondurant 1-1-0—16; Marion Woods 5-1-1—15.

Receiving — **Leesville**: Jerry Haynes 2-56. **DeRidder**: Ray Peters 2-31.

1995 Vernon Parish Football Leaders

Rushing	Att.	Yds.	Avg.	TD
Cecil Collins (Leesville)	396	3045	7.7	40
Marvin Hawkins (Pickering)	128	1133	8.9	11
Micah Douglas (Rosepine)	100	455	4.6	4
Sam Blocker (Pickering)	48	414	8.6	4
Mikey Young (Rosepine)	92	374	4.1	2
Ryan Buckner (Leesville)	66	351	5.3	2
Greg Rone (Leesville)	33	281	8.5	2
Neil Thompson (Rosepine)	53	191	3.6	2
Vann Morris (Pickering)	41	179	4.4	1
Kalem Richardson (Rosepine)	28	144	5.1	1

Passing	C	A	Pct.	Yds.	Int.	TD
Jason Green (Leesville)	50	122	41.0	834	5	5
Vann Morris (Pickering)	34	59	57.6	518	5	2
Mikey Young (Rosepine)	10	41	24.3	229	4	2
Brandon Rannakliev (RHS)	10	44	22.7	120	1	3

Receiving	Rec.	Yds.	Avg.	TD
Marcus Thurman (Leesville)	20	336	16.8	3
Jerry Haynes (Leesville)	13	159	12.2	0
Daniel Roberts (Pickering)	13	237	18.2	3
Xavier Burrell (Leesville)	10	222	22.2	1
Marcus Fontenot (Pickering)	9	74	8.2	0
Jon Burnham (Rosepine)	7	168	24.0	2
Chad Christian (Pickering)	7	157	22.4	2

Scoring	TD	XP	FG	Pts.
Cecil Collins (Leesville)	43	5	0	268
Marvin Hawkins (Pickering)	11	0	0	66
Josh Dill (Leesville)	0	35	4	47
Micah Douglas (Rosepine)	6	2	0	40

Tackles	Solo	Assists	Total
Greg Rone (Leesville)	32	163	195
Sedric Clemons (Leesville)	18	118	136
Scotty Lawerence (Pickering)	64	54	118
Sam Briggs (Pickering)	57	54	111

Statistics are for all games in the 1995 season.

Jones, Milerski on the sack
Leesville's Shermaine Jones (25) and Sigi Milerski combine to stop DeRidder quarterback Jody Bondurant during the Wampus Cats 29-0 win over the Dragons Friday night. The win puts the third-ranked Wampus Cats into the Class 4A semifinals for the first time in school history. Leesville (12-1) will host Breaux Bridge in the semifinals Friday night.

Green with the handoff
Wampus Cat quarterback Jason Green gets ready to hand the ball off to Cecil Collins during Leesville's 29-0 quarterfinal win Friday night. Green attempted only two passes in the game as the running game took over for the Cats. Green's lone completion help set up the second touchdown of the night for Leesville.

Coach of the year

Leesville High School head football coach Danny Smith (left) was named the Vernon Parish coach of the year for the 1995 season. Smith guided the Wampus Cats to the outright District 4-4A title in 1995 with a 5-0 record. The Cats finished the regular season with a 9-1 record and advanced to the state championship game in New Orleans. It was the first-ever appearance for the Wampus Cats in a state championship game.

Rone to make the tackle
Leesville Wampus Cat linebacker Greg Rone (22) moves through traffic to make the tackle on DeRidder's Derrick Peters. The Leesville defense held the Dragons to only 134 yards of total offense and one score in the 15-6 win for the Hooper Trophy. The Wampus Cat defense also had a goal line stand following a turnover which was the key series of the game. The Cats will host a wild card team Friday night in the playoffs.

Leader photo/Krista Duhon

Cecil Collins

Denni Fetting

Shermaine Jones

Greg Rone

Smith congratulates the Wampus Cats
Leesville head football coach Danny Smith congratulates the Wampus Cat team following their 29-0 Class 4A quarterfinal win over DeRidder Friday night. Smith and the coaching staff returned to work Saturday as they begin preparing for the Breaux Bridge Tigers in the semifinals this Friday at 7:30 p.m. in Wampus Cat Stadium.

Honoring the Wampus Cats
A parade was given in honor of the Wampus Cats football team yesterday. Several area dignitaries and lots of fans of the team were on hand for the event. Pictured is Mayor Jim Shapkoff Jr. presenting Coach Danny Smith with a proclamation declaring December 12th as Wampus Cat Day.

TEAMS IN PICTURES

This section of the book contains team photos of Leesville High School football teams. The search for these photos took place in the hard copy and digital realm. Many photos were found in the digital archives of the Leesville Daily Leader through the collection at the Vernon Parish Library. There is a single picture of a team that was not "Wampus Cats." The mascot of the 1910 team is unknown, but we do know that the team played under the banner of Leesville High School.

A number of team photos are not available or are missing. It is assumed that team photos are taken each year, and often times are disseminated via programs at football games. As with so many other aspects of history, if no one is keeping the copies, the copies eventually go missing.

I have included what I could find, and this section is meant to chronicle and docu-ment the teams, good and bad who have suited up as Wampus Cats through the decades. If you're reading this book and are in possession of a team photo not included, please get it to me and I will include it in future editions.

1910 Team

The 1929 Leesville High Wampus Cat football team

Leesville High school field its first football team since 1921 in the Fall of 1929. This photograph of the 1929 Wampus Cats was provided to the Vernon Journal by Percy Cabra, a member of the team which compiled a won-loss record that year of 6-3. The team, composed of Juniors and Seniors defeated Sulphur, Jasper, Texas, which boasted a barefooted halfback who could really "streak" according to Cabra, Pelican, Natchitoches, Merryville and Oakdale. The Cats dropped decisions to DeRidder, Mansfield and St. Anthony of Beaumont, Texas. Members of the team included, front row, left to right, A.B. Cain, halfback; Ducky Cordeau, end; John K. Foster, quarterback; Fred Rowzee, captain and quarterback; George Bolton, halfback; Cecil Lowery, guard; Jack Colvin, halfback; and Martin Lipscomb, quarter; middle row, left to right, Jeff Hicks, tackle; John Stafford, guard; Perry G. Pye, center; Anthony Fertitta, tackle; Mitchell, guard; John Lee Bagents, guard; and Buddy Hadnot, fullback; back row, standing left to right, Mr. A.H. Nanney, Principal; Jimmy Nichols, halfback; Sam Fertitta, end; W. L. Dunlap, halfback; Hubert McInnis, tackle; unknown; unknown; Percy Cabra, end; George Fisher, fullback; J. C. Arnold, Athletic Director; and Bill Turner, Coach.

1929 Team

1932 Team

BACK ROW: Klyde McClure, Norris Bush, Peter Anderson, Ira Craft, Homer Robinson, Douglas Sartin, Ernest Franklin, Aubrey Bunch.
MIDDLE ROW: George Walker, manager, Kemp Tucker, Allen Wood, Howard Martin, Louis Moses, Darrell Smart, Howard Ford, Wood Osborne, Coach.
FRONT ROW: Pete Sliman, Clayton Lyons, John Sepeda, J. B. Dowden, Danny Ferguson, Malcolm Smart.

1938 Team

1939 Team

Back Row—Woody Osborne, Coach; Murph Hughes, Jack Droddy, Casson Crim, Jack Dickerson, Ernest Franklin, Howard Martin, Bill Carlock.
Middle Row—Tom Allen, Manager; Noble Tousha, Norris Bush, Paul Anderson, J. A. Withers, Teddy Castlin, Mgr.
Front Row—Bobby Pinchback, Jimmie Pynes, Robert Ferguson, Hansen Scobee.
Boys not appearing in this picture that did yeoman work for the Cats this year are Rudolph Weldon, end; Wild Bill Parker, Guard; Cyril Williams, Back; Norman Johnston, end, and Robert Earl Lewis, Back.

1940 Team

1947 Team

FOOTBALL

1951 Team

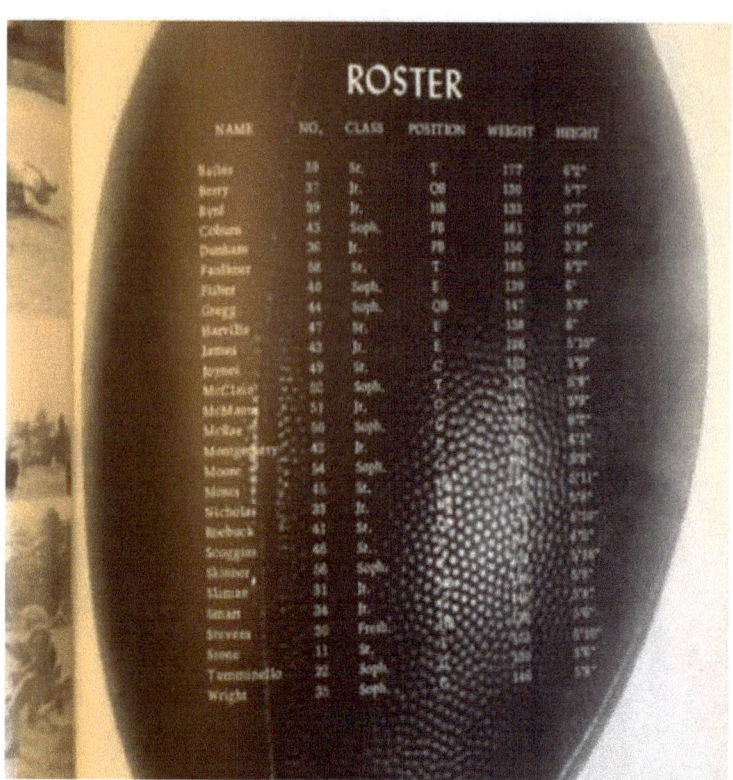

1952 Team

Leesville Wampus Cat Roster

NO.	NAME	WT.	NO.	NAME	WT.
32	Bucky Tuminello	125	33	Harlas Smart	135
30	Wallace McRae	182	35	James Wright	142
38	Bobby Smith	170	36	Harold Craft	150
44	Jerry Gregg	162	41	Oscar Smith	129
43	Harold Smart	144	42	Wayne Mayo	132
34	Jerry Skinner	190	43	Don James	135
40	George Fisher	167	45	Gerald Norris	145
37	Dick Berry	131	47	Junior Coburn	145
50	Julian Stevens	140	49	J. R. Hayman	166
54	Dawin Smart	173	51	Nelson McManus	138
46	James Coburn	167	52	Kenneth McGee	168
39	Sonny Byrd	136	54	Quinton Ikir	140
28	Benny Grant	110	55	Don Parker	170
27	Clenon Eubanks	110	56	Calvin Vickers	115
26	Roger Johnson	139	58	Morris McRae	180
22	Lewis Brown	140	60	John Skinner	180
31	Tommy Sliman	130	61	Dick Burns	135
25	Joe Loftin	130	64	Joe Hext	
	Neal Stephens	115			

1954 Team

1955 Team

1957 Team

189

1957 Team

Refresh at home

LEESVILLE HIGH SCHOOL

No.	Name	Pos.	Wt.	No.	Name	Pos.	Wt.
11	Dee Faircloth	QB	135	38	Chris Bagents	G	165
12	Warren Norris	QB	150	39	Burk Richardson	G	195
13	Romie Byrd	QB	135	40	Carl Thomas	T	155
20	George Smith	WB	145	41	Bobby Craft	T	145
21	Tommy Talley	WB	150	42	Robert Brown	T	180
22	Jim Scogin	WB	130	43	John Williams	T	180
23	Dan Rowzee	WB	150	44	Ronnie McRae	T	165
24	Sid Morris	HB	145	45	Ralph Woods	T	150
25	Robert Pynes	HB	175	46	Doug Marshall	T	175
26	Robert Schwartz	HB	140	47	Kenneth Chaney	T	160
27	John Hail (Capt.)	FB	170	48	Rusty Bailes	T	170
28	Billy Lewis	FB	165	50	Woody Mock	C	145
29	Jerry McClaren	FB	125	51	Charles Wilson	C	170
30	John Simonelli	G	145	52	Chris Smith	C	195
31	Jerry McInnsi	G	150	53	Olan Saunders	C	140
32	Glen Dawson	G	150	60	Joe Scogin	E	165
33	Jim Shapkoff	G	215	61	Hoye Underwood	E	150
34	Joe Woods	G	145	62	Dick Bean	E	145
35	Sherrod Mitcham	G	160	63	Charles Terrell	E	145
36	Tom Smith	G	135	64	Roy Hooker	E	170
37	Felix Tibedeaux	G	160	65	Pat Stewart	E	155

Head Coach: Dalton Faircloth, on Faircloth
Assistants: Richie Bullock, Ted Paris, Billy Bennett.

1958 Team Roster

1960 Team

1962 Team

1963 Team

First District Championship

1964 Team—Playoff Participant

1965 Team

1966 Team

1967 Team

1968 Team

1969 Team

1970 Team

1971 Team

1972 Team

1973 Team

1974 Team

1975 Team

V. Ortiz, R. Kuhlow, R. Schwartz, M. Mallet, and Burgess.

1976 Team

Football Results

Leesville	18	Many	0
Leesville	00	De Ridder	6
Leesville	34	Welsh	14
Leesville	14	Eunice	13
Leesville	7	Jennings	21
Leesville	13	Sam Houston	15
Leesville	7	West Lake	18
Leesville	15	Washington	14
Leesville	7	Marksville	6
Leesville	9	Oakdale	7

1977 Team

1979 Team

1980 Team

First Row: Jimbo Shapkoff, Mike Williams, Clint Ensley, T. J. Moore, Johnny Scott, Reggie Bennett, Kevin West, Fred Schnell, Junior Kerry, Dale Spires, Kik Bruce, Daniel Aboutbahl, Melvin Maxwell, Dowell Green. Second Row: Steve Gunn, Mark Clay, Greg Murphy, Donnie Langford, Chris Robertson, Andrew Robinson, Al East, John Johnson, Stewart Jackson, Odel Miller, Doug Robertson, Tom Crosby, Kevin Fredericks, Sam Hoecker. Third Row: Ernest McQueen, James Schnell, Dickie Fetting, John Clady, Percy Burns, Greg Johnson, Darren Fowler, Dexter Gatewood, James Williams, Eric Rhodes, Craig Robinson, Alan Capello, Jimmy Chamberlain.

1982 Team

1983 Team: First Playoff Appearance since 1964

1984 Team

1985 Team

1986 Team

1987 Team

1988 Team

1989 Team

1990 Team

1991 Team

Landon Dowden, Anthony Gill, Jamal Cooper, Ali Richardson.

Quarterbacks: Corey Davis, Quinton Conner, Andre Middlebrooks.

Offensive Linemen: Ottis Hunt, Justin Lansdale, Pat Parks, Jeremy Rossier, Andrew Maggio, Mark Mawae, Charles Maxie, Robert Frederickson, Rusty Mayo, Bo Everidge, Jason Holt, Joe Rosen, Makato Kuniyoshi, Bryan Webb, Jose Ayala, Scott Mawae, Raphel Sierra, Matt Marrow, Stuart Strain, Quincy Hart, Billy Bullock, Daniel Ford.

Running backs: Willie McNutt, Pat Williams, Ronnie Snapp, Heggie Reynolds, Derrick Smartt, Mark Wilson, Chal-Micah Wilson, Ramone Richardson, Paul Mouton, Andrew Sikes.

1992 Team

1993 Team

Front Row: Peter Smith, Lawrence Powell, Andre Middlebrooks, Robert Robinson, Bruce Billings, Mike Stratton, Jason Green, Thomas Tucker, Greg King, Arland Abbot, Russell Figueroa; 2nd Row: Shannan Cowan, Darrian Davis, Greg Rone, James Higginson, Mike Burks, Shermaine Jones, Rube Ensley, Vernon Lee, Ryan Uta, Virgil Ruffin, Cecil Collins; 3rd Row: Anthony Ford, Matt Glasper, Sedric Clemans, Mike Massing, Mike Lewis, Blake Morrison, Ryan Buckner, Clarence Jones, Landon Dowden, Matt Morrow, Antonelle Goza; 4th Row: Evan Niette, Jared Craft, Greg Orange, Ramone Richardson, Denni Fetting, Rusty Mayo, Sigi Milerski, Carlos Ortiz, Lou Droddy, Phillip Jones, Rodney Honeycutt; 5th Row: Jason Betts, Jeff Kay, Matt Tinker, Justin Lansdale, Larry Catron, Billy Bullock, Andrew Mageo, Neal Williams, Elia Fatuesi, Ottis Hunt, Gene Mann; 6th Row: Adrian Burns, Damian Sweatt, Noka Fatuesi, Trey Tindall, Micah Walker, Jason Williams, Junior Fatuesi, Kevin McCarter, Calvin McCarter, Charles Williams, Jermaine Lee; Managers: Daniel O'Rear (#2), Tim McKisson (#3), Sean Milerski (#4)

1994 Team

1995 WAMPUS CATS
AAAA STATE FINALIST

1996 Team

1997 Team

1998 Team

1999 Team

2000 Team

2002 Team

2003 Team

2004 Team

2005 Team

213

2006 Team

2007 Team

2008 Team

2009 Team

2010 Team

2013 Team

2014 Team

2015 Team

2016 Team

2017 Team

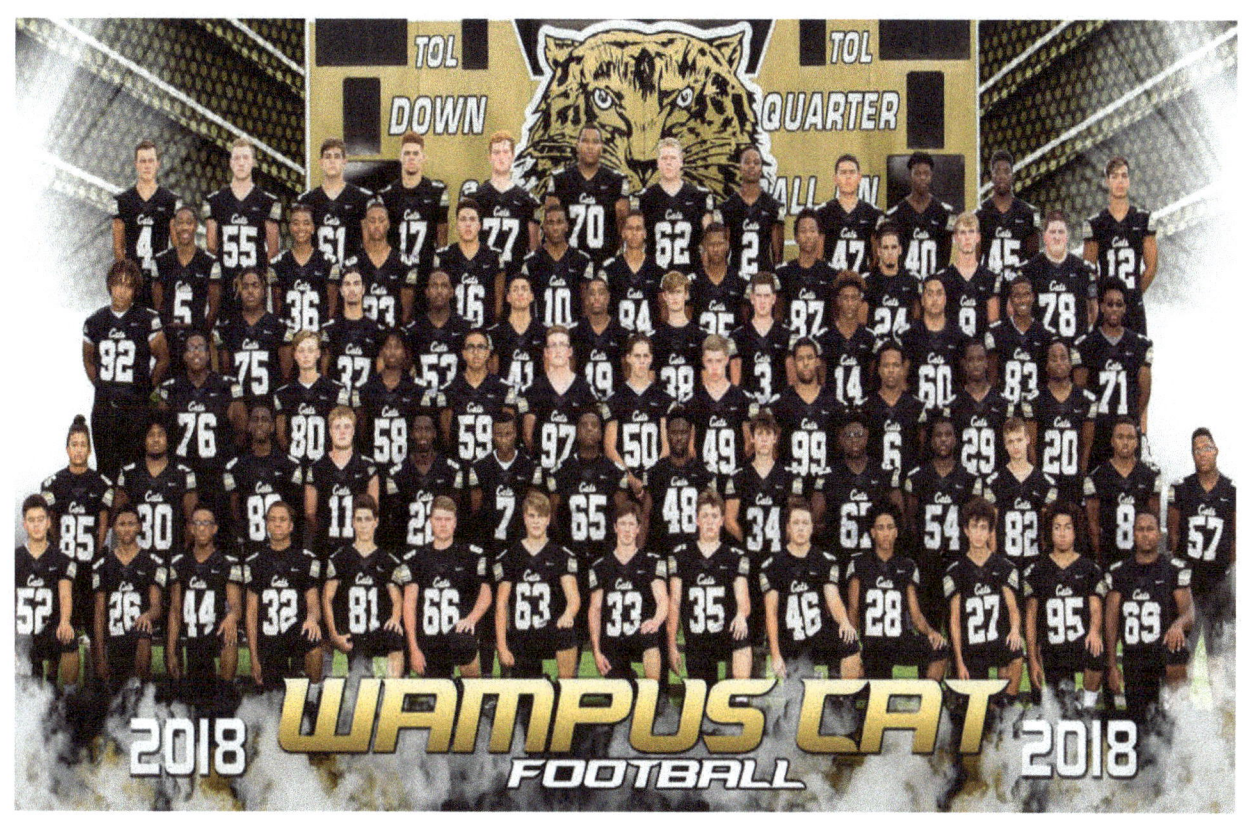

2018 Team

2019 Team

2020 Team

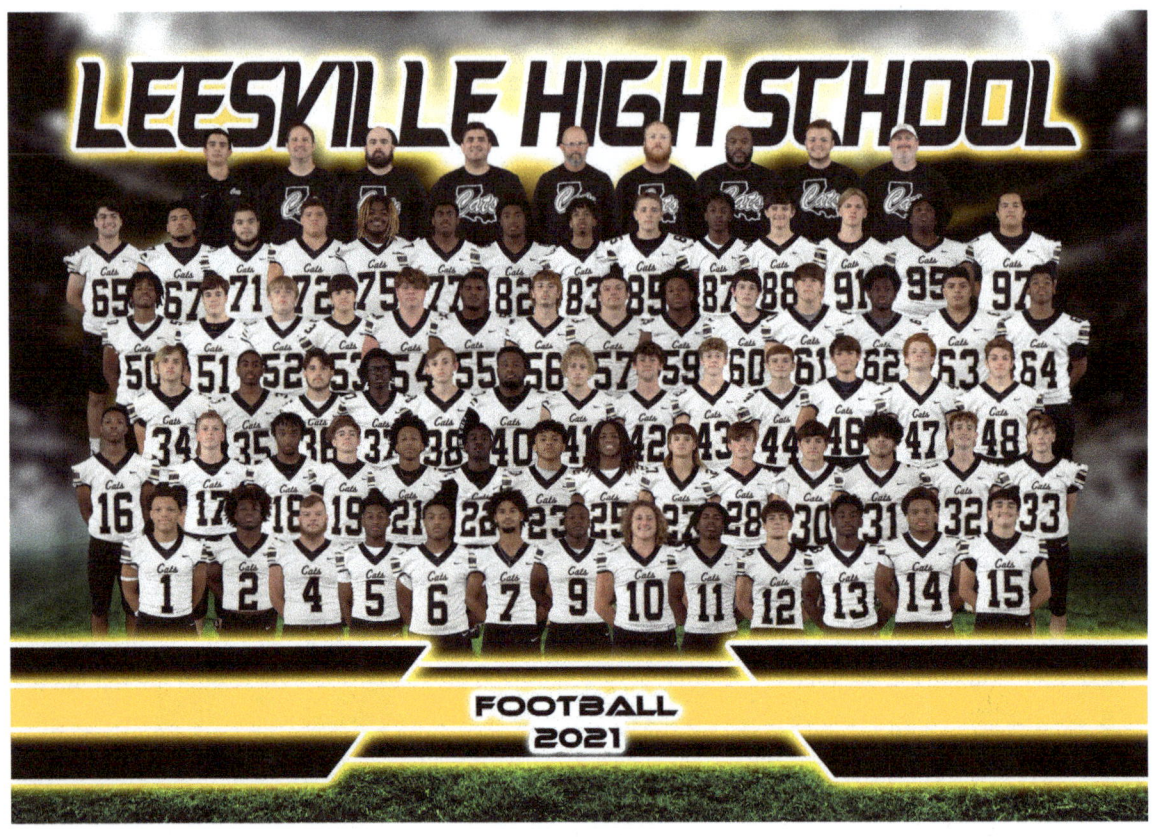

2021 Team

2022 Team

PLAYERS AND COACHES

Wampus Cats Through the Years

Hanson Scobee, 40

CA Hughes, 43

Albert Dunn, 43

Teddy Berry, 47

Sonny, Hoffpauir, 49

Bill Beavers, 49

Ted Paris, 51

Mitch Nicholas, 52

Joe Moses, 52

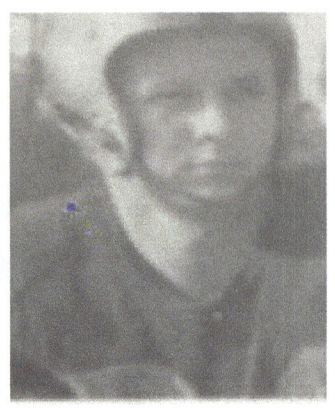
Dawin Smart, 52

Dickie Berry, 53

Kenneth Magee, 53

Julien Stevens, 54

Harles Smart, 54

James Coburn, 54

1953 Wampus Cat Stadium, First Game

1954 Team Action

Lewis Reid Brown, 55

Sam Piranio, 57

Robert Pynes, 58

Jimmy Shapkoff, 58

George Smith, 61

Louis Magee, 62

Paul Nicholas, 63

Don Davis, 65

Darwin Davis, 67

Dennis Kamarales, 66

Rich Morrison, Roger Causey, Dickie Bailes, 66

BobbyCraft, 67

Mike Dudley, 67

CA Hughes and Bo Harris

John Driscoll, 69

Paul Silman, 70

Glover Carter, 70

Sam Burnley, 70

Jakson Mapu, 69

Jimmy Mapu, 71

Johnny Mapu, 72

Raymond Mapu, 73

James Deans, 72

Charlie Hanks, 72

Hubert Knight, 74

Mike Anderson, 74

Max Anthony, 74

Floy Roberts, 74

Football
Dennis Driscoll: All-District Running Back
Mike Anderson: All-District Center
Ray Macias: All-District Tight End
Ralph Ortiz: All-District Defensive Back
Hubert Knight: All-District Linebacker
Bill West: All-District Defensive Tackle
William Dowden: All-District Defensive Tackle

Robert Byrd, 74

Sam Fertita, 75

Jr. Stevens III, 75

Bobby Bordelon, 76

 Terry Haynes, 76
 Bobby Stephens, 77
 Mark Burgess, 77
 Jeff Newsome, 78

 Team Managers, 78
 Tim Cummins, 78
 Jim Tucker, 78

 Tony Jones, 79
 Dana Romano, 79
 Eddie Barber, 80
 Robert Pynes Jr. 81

 Steve Morrison & Michael Deans, 80
 Team Action, 82

Daniel Aboutboul, 82

Oscar Joiner, 82

Team Action, 83

All District 82: Front: JimShapkoff, Sam Hoecker, TJ Moore, Kevin West. - Back: Percy Burns, Mark Clay, Dave Deans, Clint Ensley, Fred Schnell.

Jeff Steel, 83

Charles Buckley, 83

Mark Clay, 83

Percy Burns, 83

1984 Offensive Line

1984 Action

Bo Cryer, 85

Raymond Smoot, 85

Rayford Clayton, 85

Team Managers, 85

Mike Smith, 86

Clint Batterford, 86

1987 Offensive Line

Chip Clark, 88

John Mawae, 87

Kevin Mawae, 88

Scott Mawae, 92

Mark Mawae, 93

Kavika Pittman, 91

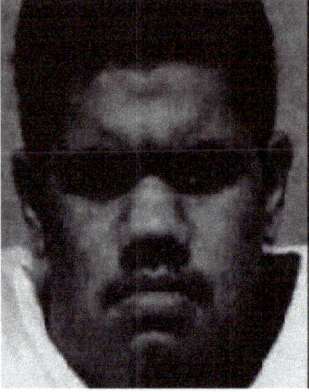
Andrew Mageo, 94

Marcus Lee, Sig Milerski, Vernon Lee, 95

Greg Rone, 95

Vernon Miller & Mark Lewis, 95

Charlie Miller, 96

Roderick Gates & Robbie Carter, 97

Deshun McNeely, 98

Keith Smith, 98

Justin Brown, 2000

Keith Zinger, 2001

Justin Goins, 2002

Lorenzo Garner Jr, 2003

Bernardo Henry, 2003

Josh Andrews, 2004

Frank Larry, 2005

Josh Cryer, 2006

Alan Muse, 2007

Travante Stailworth, 2007

Wes Tunnufu-Sauvo, 2008

Rob Sauvano, 2008

Logan Morrison, 2010

Clinton Thurman, 2010

Diontay Thurman, 2011

Zach Squyres, 2011

Sony Pynes, 2014

Theron Westerchill, 2016

Michael Ciacelli, 2016

Matt Pa inang, 2017

Sabian Matu & Drew Crocker, 2017

Mackenzie Jackson, 2017

Brett Pope, 2018

Duwon Tolbert, 2018

Ryan Ward, 2018

Matthew Anderson, 2018

D'Ante Gallishaw, 2018

Panake Posse, 2018

Khrystian Hoffpauir, 2019

Efosa Evbuoman, 2019

Frank Ford, 2020

Nathan Mawae, 2020

Jeff Keys, 2020

Caleb Gallashaw, 2021

Jayshawn Mayberry, 2021

Marshawn Graham, 2021

Ke'hmari Pruitt, 2021

Andrew Lewis, 2022

Daniel Cheatham, 2022

Christian Henderson, 2022

Xavier Ford, 2022

Head Coaches at Leesville High School

There has been a litany of men who have coached football at Leesville High School. The names of the coaches in the pre-1929 era is nearly non-existent, as are most of the results from those days. But, a gentleman named KS Thompson was discovered as the coach of a team in 1917 in research between the initial and current version of this book. Coach Thompson is credited with 0 wins and a single loss----to DeRidder. The first coach in the post 1929 era is listed as WC Turner, a Vernon native who served the Parish in many capacities, including Sheriff and Clerk of Court. Coach Turner would lead the Cats on two different occasions and serve as both head coach and assistant, at various times. As legend reports, WC Turner paid for the very first set of uniforms when the team was formed up in 1929 as Wampus Cats. In full disclosure, Coach Turner was the great uncle of the author.

In total, twenty-nine names are recorded as the Head Coach of the Leesville High School football team. Seventeen of these coaches are credited with achieving winning records. Eleven have losing records (sub .500) and one has a record of .500. The winningest coach of all time is Robert Causey. At this writing, Causey has completed 7 years at the helm and has achieved 60 wins and suffered only 23 losses. Of the 60 wins credited to his account, 10 of Causey's wins are in the playoffs, easily the highest total in LHS History. The longest tenured coach in Leesville history was Wood Osborne, who led the Cats from 1934-42. The first Cat coach to achieve a playoff win was Jack Andre. The first coach to win a district title was Ted Paris. The average tenure of a head coach at LHS has been 3.2 years.

As a sidelight, two coaches in LHS history led the team with sons on the squad---Robert Causey and Dalton Faircloth. Carter Causey played for his father all four years of high school and Dee Faircloth played for his father for one year (1958); after Dee's freshman year, Coach Faircloth took a coaching job at Many and Dee followed his father there, where he also suited up and played. Dee went on to a full career in coaching high school football. Sadly, Dalton passed away at a young age from a heart attack (while preparing for a game).

Dee Faircloth   Coach Dalton Faircloth   Coach Causey & Carter Causey

Head Coaches

WAMPUS CAT FOOTBALL HISTORY

Ulius Robichaux, 1974-75   Richard Swartz, 1976-78   Ronnie Stephens, 1979-80   Jerry Foshee, 1981-82-99

  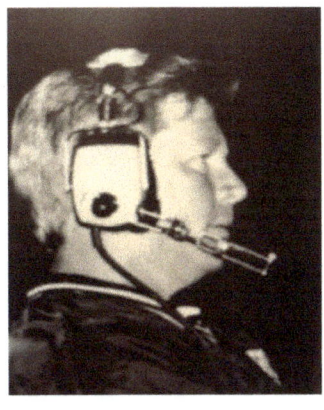 

Jack Andre, 1983-86, 90   Brownie Parmeley, 1987-89   Danny Smith, 1991-98   Kevin Magee, 2000-05

Johnny Cyer, 2006   Terennce Williams, 2007-08   David Feaster, 2009-10

Jimmy Adams, 2011-12   Tommy Moore 2013-15   Robert Causey, 2016-present

Some of the LHS Coaching Staffs Through the Years

Coaches

KEITH MUNYAN
Assistant Coach

TED PARIS
Head Coach

BILL MORGAN
Assistant Coach

1959 Coaching Staff

Norman Soulis
Assistant Coach

Ted Paris
Head Coach

Richie Bullock
Assistant Coach

1963 Coaching Staff

Don Millen; Bobby Craft; Gary Hickman, Head Coach; Francis McDaniel; Claude Patrick

1966 Coaching Staff

Head Coach Charlie Edwards; Coachs: Al Anding, Guy Barr, and Gerald Long

1968 Coaching Staff

LEFT TO RIGHT: Charles Jackson, George Smith, Foster Thomas, Bob Lash, Roland Warren, Richard Schwartz, Douglas Creamer, Head Coach.

1971 Coaching Staff

Front: Ricky Smith, Julius Robichaux, Richard Schwartz; Rear: Ron Burgess, Michael Mallet, George Smith, Rolf Kuhlow
1975 Coaching Staff

1979 Coaching Staff:
Front: Rick Plummer; Ronnie Stephens; Back: Clyde Lloyd, Mike Mallet, Randy Price

Row 1: Rick Wilson, Danny Smith, Jack André — head coach, Hubert (Hub) Jordan, Roger Causey. Row 2: James Williams, Tom Neubert, Troy Howard.

1984 Coaching Staff

Coaches: Williams, Mills, Chamberlain, Camel Stewart, Head Coach-Danny Smith, Cryer.

1992 Coaching Staff

Leesville High School Sports Hall of Fame

In 2012, the Leesville High School Alumni Association created a Leesville High School Sports Hall of Fame. Since that time, the Association has inducted 13 former Wampus Cats into the Hall. The parameters for nomination and induction are listed at the Association's website, www.wampuscats.org. Nominations are open year-round and the induction takes places each year at the LHS Homecoming in the Fall. Athletes and coaches from football, basketball, track, and baseball have been inducted. The athlete/coach and year of induction are below.

Kevin Mawae, 2012
Football

Eddie Fuller 2013
Football

Richard Reese, 2014
Basketball & Coaching

Family of Ted Paris, 2014
Football & Coaching,
Posthumously

Leesville High School Sports Hall of Fame - Continued

Robert Gaines, 2015
Track & Football

Terry Holt, 2016
Football & Track

Grant Westerchil, 2017
Basketball & Coaching

Holly Wentz-Reeves, 2018
Track & Cross Country

TB Porter, 2019
Football

Demond Mallet, 2020
Basketball & Baseball

Leesville High School Sports Hall of Fame - Continued

Greg Fontenot, 2021
Baseball

Nikita Wilson, 2022
Basketball

Donald Mallet & Cordelia Thomas, accepting for
Coach Foster Thomas, 2022
Posthumous Induction

SPECIAL THANKS

This effort came to fruition because of the help, advice and encouragement of a lot of people. God and His son the Lord Jesus are first in my life, so I will say what I said 3 years ago---all the credit for this goes to them. In the previous work, I listed a lot of great people in the first book, and all of those special thanks stand to this day. Sam Hoecker, Bobby Bordelon, Brian Trahan and Daniel Green have my ever-lasting gratitude for their efforts in compiling the data that became this history book.

For this edition, I think VERY Special Thanks needs to two men who have been the VOICES of Wampus Cat Football for over 20 years. Sam Fertitta and Jeff Skidmore have been in the broadcast booth since the mid 1990s and have been the personal witnesses to MUCH of the history I have presented in these pages. I've picked Sam and Jeff's brains for a lot of information and pointers on where to go with this work. They are literally THE witnesses to history and I want to public acknowledge their service to the Wampus Cats. They've traveled to every game the Cats have played in 20+ years as volunteer broadcasters and they have helped make Wampus Cat football a unique thing for our community.

L-4: Jeff Skidmore, Hall of Famer Kevin Mawe, Sam Fertitta, Charles Owen

DEDICATION

This effort & book are STILL dedicated to my sweet and beautiful wife and favorite Golden Cavalier Carolyn, and our adorable daughters, Laura and Emma. Long before Carolyn and I found each other, I was a Wampus Cat and an avid fan of the black and gold. Through the entirety of our marriage and as long as our girls have been around, they will all attest to my unadulterated and unfiltered loyalty to my school. I am grateful they have understood and put up with my intense passions! Our girls have strict instructions that if I pass away before the Cats go back to the State Championship, they are to go to my gravesite and listen to the game on a transistor radio (or reasonable facsimile) and they are to take my helmet. I would instruct them to take my letter jacket to the gravesite, but I will be buried in it.

I also would like to dedicate this work to my sister, Mae Ann and her son, Joseph Creighton Ledet. My sister was a Wampus Cat in every sense of the word. She left a long lasting mark on Leesville High School, and she departed us way too soon. Mae, too was a Golden Cavalier, and proud member of the LHS Marching Band. She was the beloved Librari-an at LHS. Joseph is a good man, and I love him dearly.

Finally, I dedicate this book to my parents, Creighton and Gloria Owen, both mem-bers of the LHS Class of 1942 and the Wampus Cat Marching Band. Mom and dad were Lee-ville people, through and through and they loved LHS.

ABOUT THE AUTHOR

The author of this book wore # 89 and played tight end for the Leesville Wampus Cats. He earned three varsity football letters. He played defense, but wasn't very good. He was also the backup quarterback. He earned four varsity letters in track and three in cross country.

The author was reared in Leesville by two Leesville High School graduates and married a beautiful member of the LHS Danceline, also known as the Golden Cavaliers. #89 has two daughters, and he is very proud of both; his daughters did not attend LHS, but they loved him enough to ensure their high school beat the DeRidder Dragons in basketball on not one, not two, not three, but four occasions. Two of the wins occurred during the high school playoffs, which made the wins all the more delectable for the adoring father.

The author is a proud veteran and retired military officer; he completed college a few times. He and his wife reside in Leesville and he attends every Wampus Cat football game he can. He also helps with radio announcing and other civic activities, including the Leesville High School Alumni Association.

EPILOGUE

Updating this book was a joy. Writing it the first time was grand fun, but when I was nearing publication, I knew there was MUCH more to be compiled, analyzed and disseminated. I think that's where we are right now. In the past 2+ years, I've spent a good bit of time piecing together additional information and statistics on our beloved Wampus Cats. The most time-consuming thing associated with this new effort was compiling the all-time records. I don't know if any of this matters to anyone, but it matters to me. As much as I enjoy the "do you remember when" conversations about teams and achievements from decades gone by, I think there is no replacement for actual, recorded history. There are still deficiencies in terms of some years, but we're approaching 95% solution in terms of recording what has REALLY happened in Wampus Cat history.

Since the last publication, I teamed with some friends in the local area to release two other books: (1) the history of the Hooper Trophy and (2) the history of the Vernon Lions. Both of those books were labors of passion for me, as well. The details and stories about the rivalry between Leesville and DeRidder make great reading. The brief but STORIED history of Vernon High School needed to be documented for a long time. The Lions won 3 x state titles, but when their school was closed in conjunction with Federal Integration, little was ever documented. It's documented now. Both of these books are available on Amazon or from Claitor's Publishing in Baton Rouge, and like THIS book, proceeds go to the Leesville or DeRidder High School. These books are fundraisers for our schools.

See you in a few years

Sources & Methods

This work was created and is carefully and intentionally identified as an "unofficial" history book. This book is not intended to be used as an academic source, nor is it endorsed or validated by any athletic or school governing body. This book was created as a gift to my hometown and is simply an attempt to document what could be found in terms of the history of LHS football. A variety of sources and personal collections and recollections were used to compile this work. Below is a list of sources used in the creation of the book.

1. Butler, Ray, "14-0 Productions: The History of Louisiana High School Sports", retrieved from https://14-0productions.com
2. Leesville Daily Leader, Hard Copy Files and Photographs: Courtesy of Lauren Blankenship, Editor, June 2020
3. Leesville Daily Leader: www.leesvilledailyleader.com, various editions
4. Newspapers.com, Newspaper+Publishers Extra: Retrieved from http://newspapers.com, various dates and various state-wide publications
5. Vernon Parish Library, The Digital Archives Online: Retrieved from: https://vernonparish.advantage-preservation.com/,
- Leesville Daily Leader (1984 – 2019), (1901 – 1984),
- Leesville High School Yearbooks (1950 – 1986),
- High School Yearbooks (1913 – 2017)
6. Smith, Rickie, Photography: Retrieved from https://www.facebook.com/rickie.smith.92
7. Trahan, Brian, Initial Hooper Trophy Rivalry List and Initial Passing, Rushing and Receptions List, 2014
8. Personal Collections and Contributions: Tammy Anderson, Rick Barnickle, Michael Bealer, Callie Berry, Cheryl Browning, Sam Burnley, Edwin Cabra, Billy Crawford, Chip Clark, John Crook, Chris Davis, Darwin Davis, David Detz, Debbie Driscoll, Sam Fertitta, Lisa Berry Franklin, Lorenzo Garner, Daniel Green, Susan Gunter, Amanda Sexson Hughes, Ken Hughes, Lacy Joanne Morris Johnson, Roger Johnson, Dennis Karamales, Tiffany Franklin Koch, Matt Koury, Leroy Lambert, Mark Mawae, Tony McDonald, Sig Milerski, Logan Morrison, Rhonda Morrison, Susie Nuebert, Martha Palmer, Wanda Pynes, Rob Tunuufi Sauvao, Richard Schwartz, Zach Squyres, Danny Smith, Debbie Bailey Smith, Kevin Smith, Roland Stallings. Marilyn Stevens, Carla Wharton, Brenda White, Sheri Wilhelm, Ashley Zinger

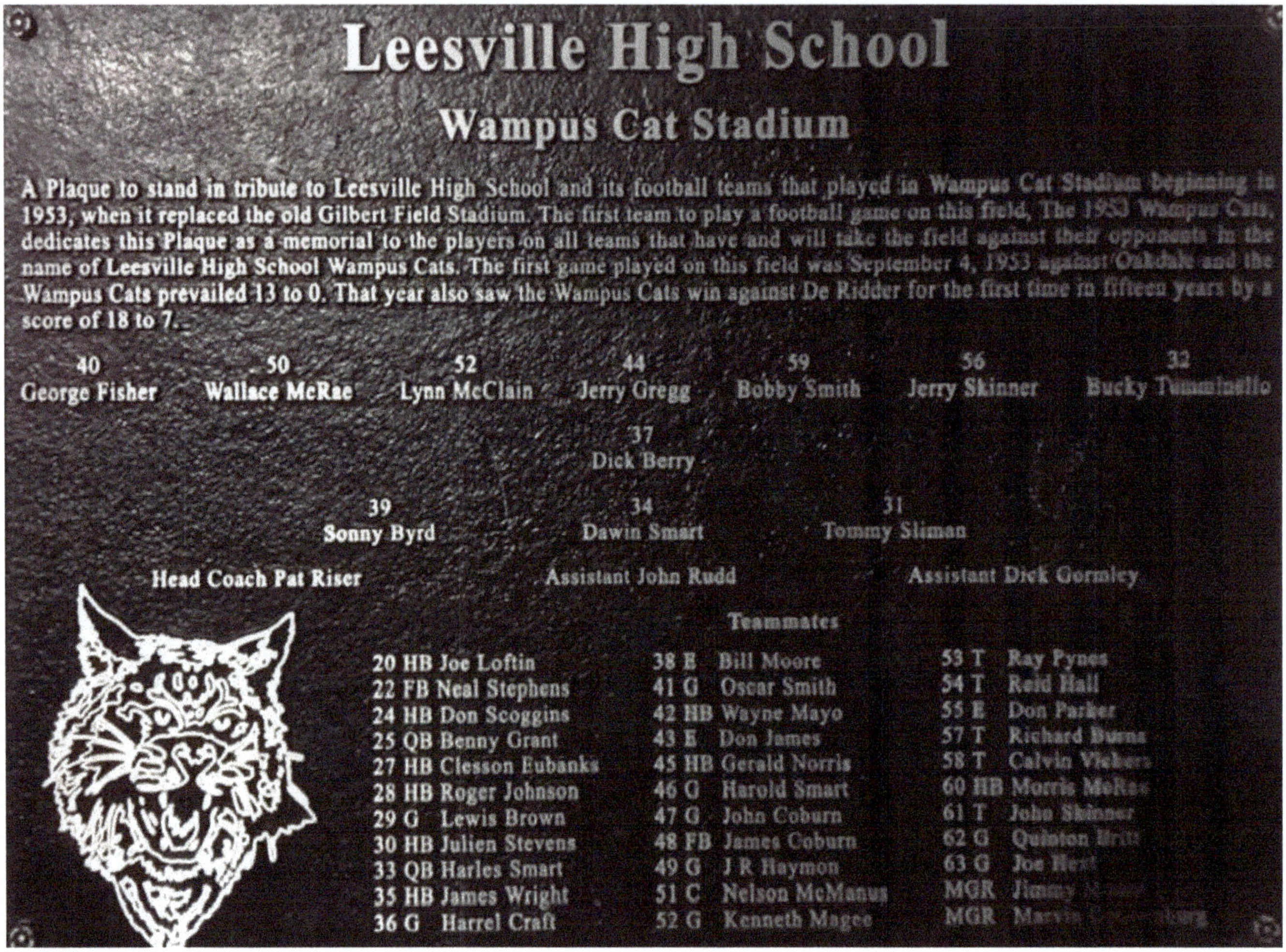

Leesville High School
Wampus Cat Stadium

A Plaque to stand in tribute to Leesville High School and its football teams that played in Wampus Cat Stadium beginning in 1953, when it replaced the old Gilbert Field Stadium. The first team to play a football game on this field, The 1953 Wampus Cats, dedicates this Plaque as a memorial to the players on all teams that have and will take the field against their opponents in the name of Leesville High School Wampus Cats. The first game played on this field was September 4, 1953 against Oakdale and the Wampus Cats prevailed 13 to 0. That year also saw the Wampus Cats win against De Ridder for the first time in fifteen years by a score of 18 to 7.

40	50	52	44	59	56	32
George Fisher	Wallace McRae	Lynn McClain	Jerry Gregg	Bobby Smith	Jerry Skinner	Bucky Tumminello

37
Dick Berry

39	34	31
Sonny Byrd	Dawin Smart	Tommy Sliman

Head Coach Pat Riser   Assistant John Rudd   Assistant Dick Gormley

Teammates

20 HB Joe Loftin	38 E Bill Moore	53 T Ray Pynes
22 FB Neal Stephens	41 G Oscar Smith	54 T Reid Hall
24 HB Don Scoggins	42 HB Wayne Mayo	55 E Don Parker
25 QB Benny Grant	43 E Don James	57 T Richard Burns
27 HB Clesson Eubanks	45 HB Gerald Norris	58 T Calvin Vickers
28 HB Roger Johnson	46 G Harold Smart	60 HB Morris McRae
29 G Lewis Brown	47 G John Coburn	61 T John Skinner
30 HB Julien Stevens	48 FB James Coburn	62 G Quinton Britt
33 QB Harles Smart	49 G J R Haymon	63 G Joe Hext
35 HB James Wright	51 C Nelson McManus	MGR Jimmy
36 G Harrel Craft	52 G Kenneth Magee	MGR Marvin

Index

A

Abbeville, 14, 21, 40, 42, 44, 60, 64, 88, 90, 94
Aboutboul, Daniel, 45
Abrams, Chuck, 45
Adams, 38
  Bill, 53
  Jacob, 27–28, 39
  James, 45
Adron Hackett, 25, 41
African American, 12
  first, 47
Agnes Lewis Hooper, 111
Airline High School in Bossier City, 32
AJ Bush, 37
AJ Green, 27, 39
Alan Muse, 41, 231
Albert Dunn, 223
Allain, 64, 66
  Noah, 28–29, 37
  Simon, 33
All-Conference, 28
All-Conference player, 22
Alleger, 41
Allen, Darius, 29, 37, 69
All-Region, 11
all Star team, 49
All-State honoree, 25
All-State honors, 22–23, 25
All State in track, 43
All-State team, 22
All-Time record, 253, 261
All-Time results, 83
Amazon, 11, 253
American Foundational High School
    Mexico City, 103, 105, 106
American Foundation School Mexico CW, 105
Anders, Tyler, 39
Anderson, 13
  Bill, 8
  Jimmy, 47, 72
  Matthew, 28–29, 37
  Mike 13, 47, 226
  Roger, 45

Andre, Jack, 20, 30–31, 68, 155, 235
Andrew Croker, 28, 37, 39, 69, 127
Andrew Mageo, 21, 43, 230
Ane, EJ 27
Antoinel Goza, 70
Antountel Goza, 21, 43
Arkansas State, 25, 66, 261
Armes, Jake, 8
Arthur, Bobby, 49, 76
ASH, 60–61, 63–64, 86–94, 96
Ashfield, Jack, 10-11, 47
Assumption, 23, 28, 31, 36, 40, 60, 84–85
Atlanta Falcons, 39
Atwater, Demetrius, 39
Auburn, 25, 39, 45
Auvil, Jimmy, 12, 49, 72
Ava Marie University, 261

B

B-1 Boomer, 126–27
Babin, Carl, 8, 51
Bagents, Chris, 9, 49
Bailes, Thad, 49
Bailey, Wes, 22, 43, 70
Baker, James, 25, 41
Barbe, 60, 92–94
Barber, Eddie 227, 235
Barnickle, Rick 126
Barr, 13, 46, 236
Bastedo, Richard, 47, 71
Bastrop, 61, 92–93
Baton Rouge, 11, 14, 23, 25, 135, 253
Batteford, Clint 30, 62
Bealer, Caden 32, 37, 69, 73, 81
Beaver, Bill, 51
Beason, Henry 8, 52, 53
Beebe, Darion 37
Bellamy, Andy 19, 45
Bellhaven, 37, 261
Berry, Dick, 9
Berry, Teddy, 45, 51
Berwick, Hank, 51
Bess, Earnest 47, 66, 71
Bill Beavers, 223
Blackburn, Billy, 51, 75

259

Blackshire, Derrick, 27, 39
Bordelon, Bobby 14, 226, 246
Bobby May, 27, 39
Bobby Stephens, 227
Boerner, Anthony, 43
Bo Harris, 13–14, 225, 261
Bolton, 63–64, 84–87, 89–90, 94, 101
Bonner, David, 45
Borner, Anthony, 20
Bossier, 26, 53, 101, 106–7
Bouves, Wes, 25, 41
Bowl, 9
Boyce, 53, 106
Bradley, Braeden, 37
Brady, Tyler, 69
Breaux Bridge, 21, 40, 60, 88
Breaux, Roland, 62, 64
Brian Trahan, 57, 111, 246
Broadmoor, 44
Brown, Chris, 25, 41
Brown, Devon, 39
Brown, Erwin, 20, 45, 61
Brown, John, 20, 43, 71, 79
Brownie Parmeley, 18, 44, 157, 237
Brown Word, 12
BTW, 91–92
BTW-Shreveport, 60–61
Buckeye, 85–86
Buckley, 17, 58–59, 61
  Charles, 45, 228
Buckner, Cliff, 45
Bucky Tuminello, 9, 49
Bunkie, 100, 103
Burgess, Ron, 240
Burgess, Mark 227
Burkes, James, 24, 41
Burkes, Jeremy, 24, 41
Burnett, Tiasham 39
Burns, Adrian, 22, 43
Burrell, Xavier, 22, 43, 59, 61
Burr family, 7
Burr Ferry, 7
Bush, 65–66

C

Cablevision, 126

Cabra, Percy, 8, 53
Cain Motor Company, 51
Canadian Football League, 16
Capello, 16–17, 45, 62–64
Captain Shreve, 14, 31, 84
Carencro, 61, 92–94
Carr, Larry, 47, 72
Carroll, 21, 88
Carter, 22, 43, 60
  Robert, 22, 43
  Glover 13
Carver, 60
  Keith, 11, 49
Casearez, Leo, 13
Casearez, Lionel, 72
Casetti Brown, 25, 39
Castillo, Ted, 135
Catholic-New Iberia, 60, 84
Catron, Caden 32, 37
Causey, 31, 36, 38, 235
  Carter, 235
  Robbie, 37
  Roger, 11, 16
Cavanaugh, Wayne, 12, 49
Cecil, 22, 58–61
Centenary, 53
Central Florida, 25–26, 41, 261
Chamberlain, Jimmy, 17, 45
Chambers, Jacob, 27, 39
Chancy, 65
Chaney, Josh, 24, 41
Chapman, 37
Cheatam, Daniel, 33
Chene, Beau, 38, 86
Ciachelli, Michael, 28, 37
Cincinnati Bengals, 14
Claitor's Books, 11, 253
Clark, Chip 20, 45, 230
Clark, Lamar, 51
Clark, MG 235
Clarks, 105
Clay, 59, 61
Clayton, 58–60
Clemons, Cedric 22, 43, 70, 79
Clint Batterford, 30, 62-63, 230
Coach Beeson, 53

Coach Causey, 31, 37
Coach Causey & Carter Causey, 235
Coach Causey & Scott Grady, 127
Coach Causey's Cats, 31
Coach Creamer, 47
Coach Cryer, 25
Coach Dalton Faircloth, 9, 235
Coach Danny Smith, 20
Coach Davis Feaster, 26
Coaches Schwartz & Kuhlow, 15
Coach Faircloth, 235
Coach Foster Thomas, 11, 245
Coach Harkins, 32
Coach Hendricks, 51
Coach Jack Andre, 18
Coach Jerry Foshee, 16
Coach Justin Scogin, 28
Coach Kevin Magee, 23
Coach Magee, 25
Coach Magee's Cats, 23
Coach Moore, 39
Coach Osborne, 53
Coach Pat Riser, 9
Coach Robert Causey, 32
Coach Rolf Kuhlow, 15
Coach Smith, 43
Coach Terence Williams, 25
Coach Thompson, 235
Coach Turner, 8, 235
Coach Williams, 26
Coach Wood Osbourne, 8
Cobb, Chris, 70, 80
Cobb, Sam, 22, 43
Coburn, 59
  John, 126
  Junior, 49
Cohen, Mickey, 8, 51
Colbert, 66
Collins, 21, 23, 33, 41, 43, 57, 58-61
Collions, Jason, 43
Combs, Evan, 33, 69
Cong Buddy Leach, 136
Cong Jim McCrery, 136
Conley, Buddy, 51, 75
Cools, Michael, 24, 41
Cooper, Stacy, 18, 45, 71

Cordelia Thomas, 245
Cordell Upshaw, 41
Corey, 59, 62
Cottom McClure, 53
Coushatta, 98–100, 107
Cox, Sam, 136
Coy, Howard, 5
Craft, Bobby, 12, 49, 225
Creamer, 13, 46
Crocker, 232
Croker, 28, 59, 64–65
Crosby, Tom, 17, 45
Cross, Jeremiah, 27, 39, 69, 73, 81
Cross, Solomon, 27, 39, 69, 81
Crowley, 51, 60, 63, 86, 90–92, 103, 105
Cryer, 25, 40
  Bo, 17
  Josh, 41
  Johnny, 25
Cuba, 135
Cummings, Bobby, 41
Cummins, Tim, 227
Curtis, John, 40, 89

D
Daelapp, Mason, 27, 39, 69
Darius, 64–65
Darwin Davis, 225
David, 38
David Detz signs, 41
David Doyle, 32–33
David Feaster, 237
Davion, 65
Davion Clemons, 27, 39, 69
Davion Grubb, 32
Davis, 62
  Chris, 37, 69, 81,115
  Darwin, 12, 72
  Daquan, 28,39
  Dennis, 47
Dawin Smart, 51, 224
Dean, Larry, 72
DeAndre Atwater, 70
Deans, Dave, 228
Deans, Michael 14, 47, 71, 78, 227
DeJuan, 65

Delta State University, 16
Demond and Deshun McNeely, 22, 43
Demond McNeely, 43
Demons, 26
Denni, Harvey, 33
Dennis, Michael, 39
Dennis Fetting, 21–22, 43
Dennis Karamales, 225
Deontay Thurman, 69
Dequincy, 53, 85, 97, 100–106
DeQuincy and Ville Platte, 51
Derek, 66
DeRidder, 7, 9, 13, 16, 20–21, 30–32, 36–54, 60, 63–64, 84–108, 112–15, 252, 261
DeRidder-Leesville football rivalry, 111
Derry Smart, 53
Detz, 25
  David, 25, 41, 70, 73, 80
  Mason, 39
Deval Lewis, 27, 39, 69
Devon Brown. *See* DB
Dhiia, Mustafa 37
DHS, 36, 38–52
DHS forfeit, 114
Dickie Bailes, 11, 12, 49, 72, 77
Dickie Bailies, 11
Dickie Berry, 224
Dickie Fetting, 45
Dietzel, Paul, 9
Dixon, 66
Dantrell Lewis, 27, 37, 39, 41, 43, 45, 47
Don Davis, 225
Don Jackson, 12
Donnie Gill, 12, 49
Doug Creamer, 13, 236
Dowden, Jordan, 37, 69
Dowden, William, 47
Doyle, Cecil 32
Dragons, 10, 31–32, 112
Driscoll, 11,13, 14, 23, 47, 62, 64, 71, 78,
Danny Turick, 45, 47
Dudley, William, 22, 41
Dunlap, 53
Dunn, Alfred, 8, 51
Duwon, 64–65

Duwon Tolbert, 37

E
Earthquake Catch, 261
Easton, Warren, 28
Eddie Barber, 227
Eddie Fuller Offensive MVP, 45
Eddie Herndon Sam Fertitta, 47
Edwards, 46, 48
  Ellis, 69, 81
  Tommy, 23, 41
  Charlie 236
Ellis, Gabe 28, 37
Elysian Fields, 30, 37, 63, 84
Emmy-nominated costume designer, 135
Ensley, Clint, 45, 228
Erwin, 45, 58–59, 61
Estep, 18, 45
Estey, Warren, 18, 45
Eunice, 32, 49, 51, 61, 63, 84, 89–91, 95–97, 99, 105
Evangel, 63, 90
Evans, Terry, 33, 37
Evbuoman, Efosa 29, 37, 233
Ewing, Joe, 47

F
Faircloth, 9, 48
  Dalton, 235
  Dee, 235
Fair Park, 105
Farley, Izaiah, 33, 65
Fatty & Anthony Fertitta, 8
Fatty Fertitta, 53
Feaster, 26, 27, 38
Federal Integration, 253
Feliciano, Jacob, 29, 37
Ferguson, 7, 75
Ferriday, 99–100
Fertitta, Anthony, 53
Fertitta, Ronald, 13
Fertitta brothers, 8
Fisher, 49, 53, 66
  George, 9, 49
Fitzgerald, Mason, 37
Florien, 7, 108

Floy Roberts, 226
Fontenot, Greg, 245
Ford, 25, 33, 39, 58–61, 65, 261
   Anthony, 21, 43
Foshee, 16, 40, 44, 68
Franca, Gilbert, 24
Frances, Gilbert, 41
Frank, Larry, 41
Ford, Frank 30–32, 37, 69, 73, 81, 233
Frank Larry (Ford), 25, 41, 70, 73, 80, 231
Franklinton, 38, 85
Freshley, Robert, 14
Fuller, Eddie, 18, 45, 243, 261
Fuller, Vince, 45
Fuller, Vincent, 19, 45
Funderburk, 66

G

Gaines, Robert, 14, 47
Gallashaw, Caleb, 31–32, 37, 58, 64, 233
Gallashaw, D'Ante 28–29, 37
Gardner, Rodney, 20, 43
Garner, 13, 20, 43, 47, 61
Gaskill, Dylan, 39
Gatewood, Dexter, 17, 45, 71, 73
Gatewood, Nick, 45
Gendron, Joe, 12, 49
George, 59, 66
George Smith, 12–14, 49, 240
Gilbert, Donnie, 13
Gilbert Field, 125
Gill, 21, 66
   Anthony, 43
   Donnie, 12
   Tyler, 25, 41
Glasper, Matt, 21, 43
Glendale Community College, 14, 47
Glenmora, 7, 55, 106, 108
Glover, 60
Goins, 62–63
Golden Cavalier, 250
Goldsby, 47
   Doug, 47
Gonzales, Robert, 45
Grafton, Jimmy, 51
Graham, 65–66

Grambling, 18, 45, 261
Grant, 61, 63, 85–88, 91–92, 95
   Hubert, 71
Green, Daniel, 5, 111, 246
Green, Lowell, 45
Green, Nick, 29, 37
Gregg, Jerry, 9, 51
Grooms, 37
Grubb, 65
Guintini, Jason, 45
Gunn, 17, 45

H

Hadnot, Buddy, 8
Hall, Johnny, 9, 49
Hall of Fame, 8, 13
Hamm, 65
Hanks, 47, 72, 77, 226
Hanley Sanders, 125
Hanna, 52
Hanson Scobee, 223
Hardwood Bowl, 9, 51, 102–3
Harkins, Chad, 32
Harles Smart, 9, 14, 47, 49
Harral, Jamal, 27, 39
Harris, Alton, 21, 43, 70, 73, 79
Harris, Justin, 25, 41
Harris, Michael, 25, 41, 70, 80
Harshaw, Alan, 25, 41
Harvey, 25
   Justin, 70
   Wes, 41, 70
Harville, Dalton, 27, 39, 69
Haughton, 42, 60, 91
Havana Arts Biennial, 135
Haygood, Cindy, BG 135
Haynes, Jerry, 72
Haynes, Terry, 71, 78
Haynie, Frank, 51, 75
Hays, Steve, 47, 72
Head Coaches, 235–36
Heggie, 58
Heggie Smith, 20
Hemphill, 53, 106
Henderson, Christian 33, 37, 233

Henderson, Jaymeion, 37
Hendricks, 50
Henry, Bernardo 25, 41,65 66, 231
Henry, 65–66
Herndon, Eddie, 47, 71
Hickman, 48
High, Junior, 13
Hoecker, Sam, 16, 45, 71, 73, 78, 228, 246
Hoffpauir, 37, 64–65, 223
Holt, 14, 47, 58–59, 61
Holt's Hall of Fame Induction, 15
Honeycutt, Colton, 27, 39
Hooks, Ralph, 51
Hooper, 111–12, 114–15
Hooper Family, 32
Hooper Trophy, 5, 16, 20–21, 31–32,
    111–14, 116, 253, 261
Horlacher, Joe, 39
Hornbeck, 7, 108
Houston, 13, 47, 135
  Sam, 60–61, 64, 87–91, 94–96
Houston Texans, 39
Howard, 58–59, 61
  Carl, 11, 61
Howerton, Jon, BG, 135
Hubert Knight, 226
Hub Jordan, 16
Huell Haymon, 126
Hughes, 8, 13, 51, 223, 225
    Andy, 24–25, 41
    Kenny, 23, 41
Honeycutt, Colton, 27, 39
Hunter, Aaron, 29, 37
Huntington, 44, 87, 94
Huntington-Shreveport, 63
Hurricane Rita, 25, 112, 115
Hurt, Derek, 28, 37, 69

I
Illegal player, 97
Independence Stadium, 31
Iowa, 36, 60, 64, 84, 86
Ivory, 59–60
  Edwin, 41

J
Jack Andre, 237
Jackie Self, 10
Jackson, 11, 65
   Cornelius, 25, 41, 70
   Mackenzie, 69
Jackson, Charles 13
Jacoby Kaiama, 25, 41
Jaelyn Edwards, 27–28, 39, 69, 73, 81
Jackson Mapu, 226
Jamall Harris, 27, 39
James, 59
   Jared, 25, 41
   Stefan, 33, 69, 73, 81
James Burkes, 41
James Coburn, 10, 49
James Deans, 226
James, Stefan 37
James Wintle, 55
Jasper, 107
Javal Chancy, 26, 39
Jayshawn Mabary-Liles, 32, 33, 37, 233
JayShawn Mabry, 37
JC Welch, 49, 76
Jeane, 29
   Larry, 11, 49
   Ruben, 37
Jeff Davis Parish, 30
Jeff Keys, 30–31, 37, 233
Jeff Newsome, 227
Jeff Skidmore, 127, 246
Jeff Steel, 228
Jena, 32, 60, 64, 84, 97–100
Jenkins, 18
   Robert, 45, 71, 78
Jennings, 16, 30–32, 36, 51, 53, 63, 84–85,
    88, 94–97, 104–6
Jennings Listed, 53
Jeron Hamm, 26, 39, 65, 66, 261
Jerry Foshee, 237
Jeval, 65
Jeval Chancy, 39
Jevon Leday, 27, 39
Jimbo Shapkoff, 45, 71, 78
Jim Hawthorne, 125–26
Jimmy Adams, 237

Jimmy Funderburk, 12, 72, 77, 126
Jimmy Mapu, 13–14, 47, 72, 77
Jimmy Shapkoff, 224
Jim Tucker, 227
Joe Moses, 51, 224
John Driscoll, 12, 47, 72
John Martinez, 10–11, 49
John Mawae, 45, 230
Johnny Cryer, 237
Johnny Mapu, 226
Johnson, Anthony, 45, 71, 79
Johnson, Dwayne, 45, 71
Johnson, James, 14, 47
Johnson, Larry, 47
Johnson, Marcus, 24, 41
Joiner, 16, 58–59, 61, 65
  Daryl, 41, 70
  Kobe, 28, 37
  Oscar, 16
Jones, 14
  Corey, 69
  Cornelius, 20, 43
  Derek, 22, 43
  Don, 14, 47
  Kenny, 22–23, 41, 70, 73, 80
  Kory, 27, 39
  Tony, 14, 47, 71
Joseph Creighton Ledet, 250
Josh Andrews, 25, 231
Josh Cryer, 231
Josh Quayhagen, 24, 41, 70, 73, 80
JR Stevens, 53
JR Stevens III, 72
JT Buckley, 13
Julien Stevens, 224
Justin Brown, 22–23, 41, 70, 80
Justin Ford, 25, 41, 58
Justin Goins, 24–25, 41, 231
Juwan Lewtry, 27, 39

K

Karamales, Dennis, 12
Karamales, Mike, 14
Karr, Edna, 38
Katrina, 25
Kavika Pittman, 20, 43, 71, 79, 261

Keedrick Mitchell, 39, 69
Ke'hmari Pruitt, 31, 37, 233
Keith Smith, 22, 43, 70, 73, 261
Keith Zinger, 23, 41, 231, 261
Kendrick, 26
Kennedy, US President John F., 11
Kenneth Magee, 224
Kent State, 135
Kerry, Lyle, 45
Kevin Magee, 237
Kevin Mawae, 20, 45, 243, 261
Keyon, Henry, 25, 41
Khrystian Hoffpauir, 31, 37, 64, 65
King, Clinton, 43
KJAE, 30, 126
KLLA, 125–26
Knight, Hubert, 47, 72, 77
Kole Smith, 27, 39
Kreynbuhl, Logan, 27, 39
Kuhlow, Rolf, 14, 240
KVVP, 126

L

LaGrange, 60, 64, 84, 86, 88–90, 92–94
LaGrange College, 37, 261
Lake Charles, 22, 51, 53, 101, 105–7
Lake Charles Boston, 93
Lake Charles College Prep, 85
Lake Charles press corps, 16
Lake Shore, 36
Lamar University, 37
Leasure, 41
Landry Memorial, 49
Lane Self, 30, 32
Larrie King, 135
Laurent, Larry, 47
Lawhorn, Roderick, 23–24, 41, 70, 80
Layne Self, 37
Leach-Huntoon, Carolyn 136
Leach, Claude, 135
Lee, Jeremiah, 33
Leesville Daily Leader, 183
Leesville High School, 3, 7–8, 11, 83, 111,
  129, 135–36, 183, 235, 250, 252

Leesville High School Alumni Association, 243, 252
Leesville High School Sports Hall of Fame, 11, 20, 243–45
Lefort, Cody, 39
Leftt Nicholas, 53
LeMarcus Thurman, 43
Lemond Leasure, 22, 43
Len Stevens, 125
Leroy Treme, 47
Levander Liggins, 25–27, 39, 57-60, 64=65
Lewis, Andrew, 33
Lewis, Billy, 9, 49
Lewis, Buck, 20, 45
Lewis, Mike, 22, 43, 70
Lewis, Samuel, 32
Lewis Reid Brown, 49, 76
LHSAA (Louisiana High School Athletic Association), 20, 30, 45, 261
LHSAA, named, 43
LHSAA Basketball Hall of Fame, 47
LHSAA Hall of Fame, 14, 20
Lincoln, 18
Lions Club Bowl, 9, 49, 100
Liscicki, Mike, 14
Livingston, 61
Lloyd, Clyde, 240
Logan Morrison, 232
Long, Emanuel, 39
Lord Jesus, 246
Lorenzo Garner, 13, 23, 41, 47, 61, 70
Lorenzo Garner Jr, 231
Louisiana College, 28, 37, 49, 107
Louisiana High School Athletic Association (LHSAA), 20, 30, 45, 261
Louisiana-Monroe, 25
Louisiana National Guard, 135
Louisiana Sports Hall of Fame, 8, 20, 261
Louisiana Sports Writers Association, 17
Louisiana State University, 7
Louisiana Tech, 27, 29, 261
Louis Magee, 225
Louis Magee Hooper Trophy 60th Anniversary Commemoration, 33
Louisville, 22, 261
Lowe, Parker, 37

LSU, 7, 9–10, 14, 18–19, 22, 25, 39, 41, 43, 45, 49, 55, 261
LTG Ronald Clark, 136
Luafalemana, Roger, 27, 39, 69, 73, 81
Lucas, Corey, 71, 73, 79
Lyles, William, 55
Lynch, 29
  Pat, 72

M
Mabry, Jayshawn, 37
Macias, 13. 47. 66
Mackenzie Jackson, 232
Magee, 40
  Kenneth, 9
  Louis, 32, 49
Mageo, 21, 43
Mahoney, Pat, 16, 47
Makenzie Jackson, 81
Maks, 32, 37, 62–64
Maldanado, Michael, 39
Mallet, Demond 244
Mallet, Donald, 245
Mallet, Michael, 240
Mallet, Mike, 14, 240
Mamou, 53
Manns, Greg, 22, 43
Mansfield, 53, 91–92, 102, 107
Mapu, 47
  Jackson, 72, 77
  Johnny, 47, 72, 77
  Raymond, 47
Marbury, Elbert, 27, 39, 69, 81
Marcus, 64–66
Marshall, Doug, 76
Marion, 51, 99–102
Mark Clay, 16, 45, 61, 228
Mark Dowden, 22, 41
Mark Lewis, 230
Mark Mawae, 20, 43
Mark Smith, 14–15, 17, 47, 71, 73, 78
Marksville, 88, 91, 96, 98
Marlon, 63
Marshall, 39
  Doug, 9, 49
Marshawn, 65–66

Marshawn Graham, 33, 233
Martin, 62, 64
  Wayne, 45
Martin Driscoll, 23, 41
Martinez, 11
Martinville, 36
Mason, Ray, 20
Mastracchio, Joe, 47, 71
Matthew Anderson, 232
Mawae, 45, 261
  John, 19
Max Anthony, 226
Maxwell, 16–17, 45, 71, 78
Mayfield, Sean, 45
McCavey, Kevin, 41
McClain, Lynn, 9, 49
McClendon, Charley, 14
McCord, Demarcus, 37
McCoy, 28, 58–59
  Cory 27
  Nigel, 29, 37
McCrery, Jim, 135
McDonald, Tony, 136
Mcelven, Oscar, 53
McKenzie, Cody, 23, 41
McKenzie Jackson, 37
McNeely, 58–61, 65
McNeese, 11, 14, 20, 22, 25–26, 39, 41, 43,
  45, 47
Matt Pajinag Second Team All-State
  Linebacker, 37
McNutt, Willie, 21, 43, 70, 73
McPherson, Arnold, 17, 45
McRae, Glen, 8, 51
McRae, Ronnie, 49
McRae, Wallace, 9, 49, 51, 75
McTear, Eddie, 39
Medina, Thomas, 39
Menard, 51, 86, 94–95, 97–106
Merryville, 51, 53, 101–7
Mexico-American High School, 51, 53
Michael, 38, 58–61
Michael Ciacelli, 232
Michael Ford, 24–25, 33, 39, 41, 261
Michael Toney, 24
Middlebrooks, 21, 43, 62, 65

Mike Dudley, 225
Mike Smith, 18, 45, 71, 73, 79, 229
Miller, Charlie 230
Miller, Odell, 16, 45
Millner, John, 49
Milton, Dante, 37
Minden, 31, 36, 60, 84, 99–100
Mitcham, Jeff, 45
Mitchell, 26
  Curt, 14
  Dennis, 45
Mitch Nicholas, 224
Montae Lynch, 28, 37
Moore, 27, 38, 62, 64
  Johnny, 47
Mo Pointer, 47
Moran, Devin, 25, 39, 41, 70, 81
Morgan City, 49
Morris, Sid, 49
Morris Jean McRae, 49
Morrison, Logan, 27, 39
Morrison, Matt, 41
Morrison, Steve, 17
Morrow, Matt, 21, 43
Morrow, Perry, 13
Morrow, Ron, 77
Morrow, Ronnie, 12, 72
Moses, Johnny, 8, 51
Moses, Lou, 13
Moses, Louis, 8
Mount, Jacob, 37, 62-64

Mundy, Elijah, 28, 39
Muppet, 17
Muse, 25, 64–65
Mustafaa Dhiia, 31

N
NASA's Johnson Space Center, 135
Nash, Chris, 23–24, 41
Natchitoches, 11, 51, 60, 98–107
Nathan Mawae, 37, 233
National Merit Scholarships, 136
National Rodeo Hall of Fame, 8
Naval Academy, 261
Navy Cross, 135–36

NCHS, 88–89, 91–94, 96–97
Nelson, Mike, 25, 41
Neubert, Tommy, 25, 41, 70
Neville, 30, 40, 64, 84, 87, 89
New England, 39
New Iberia, 93
Nicholas, 11, 58–59
  Mitch, 51, 75
Nicholls State, 23, 41, 261
Nichols, Paul, 49
Nickerson, 49
Nick Pollacia, 125
NLIs, 45
NLU, 45
Noah, 64, 66
Noonan, 50
Normal Freshmen, 107
North Caddo, 98, 101
Northeast, 19
Northside, 98–99
Northwestern, 11, 22, 26, 37, 41, 43, 47, 261
Northwestern State, 19, 45, 49
Northwood, 31, 36, 42, 63–64, 84–85, 91, 98
Northwood of Shreveport, 30
Notes, 37–55
NSU, 11, 25, 39, 45, 49, 53
Nunez, Robert, 20, 43

O

Oakdale, 9, 49, 51, 53, 55, 95–103, 105–8
Oberlin, 103
O'Bryan, Chris, 23, 41
O'Bryant, 26
  Demetrius, 39
Old Timers Football Game, 3, 129
Oliver, Matt, 47
Opelousas, 40, 42, 84, 89, 91, 95, 104
Ortiz, 12, 14, 47, 62
  Ralph, 13, 47, 72, 77
Osborne, 8, 50, 52
Oscar, 58–59, 61
Oscar Joiner, 17, 45, 47
Ouachita, 92–93
Ouachita Parish, 30

Owen, 3, 22, 112, 140, 236, 254, 256, 258
Owen, Creighton, 16
Owen, Gloria, 250

P

Pajinag, Matt, 37, 69, 73, 81
Palmer, Dwayne, 11, 49, 76
Pancake Posse, 233
Paris, 9, 51
parish, 12, 19, 30, 35, 235
Parker, 62–64
  Chad, 39
  Cole, 41
Parkway, 61, 92–93
Parmeley, 44
Pat Garner, 12
Pat Riser, 236
Patterson High School, 18
Paul Nicholas, 10–11, 49
Paul Sliman, 225
Payne, Jonathan, 70
Payton, Bruce 14–15, 47
Payton, 66
  Demetrius, 18, 45
Peabody, 37, 39, 60–61, 63–64, 84–94, 97–98
Peevy, Tommy, 47
Pelican, 51, 53, 105, 107
Pelt, John, 53
Percy, 64, 66
Percy Burns, 16, 45, 228
Perry, 26, 39
Pete Hendricks, 236
Peyton Lipps, 29, 37
Phillips, Daniel, 69
Phillips, Tony, 17, 45
Pickering, 126
Pierce, Craig, 17, 45, 71
Pinchback, Bobby, 8, 51
Pineville, 31, 60–61, 63–64, 84–89, 92–94, 97–102
Piranio, Sam 9–10, 49
Pittman, 20, 43
Plaquemine, 14, 47
Pleasant Ferguson, 55
Plummer, Rick, 240

Polk, 20–21
Pollacia, 126
Pollard, Joe, 51
Pope, Brett, 28–29, 37, 232
Pope, Joe, 126
Port Arthur, 51, 104–6
Porter, TB 8
Posthumous Induction, 245
Powell, Lawrence, 21, 43
Price, Jonathan, 27, 39
Price, Randy, 240
Pro-Football, 261
Prologue, 3, 5
Pruitt, 65
Pynes, 9, 58–60

Q
Quan Williams, 37, 69
Quayhagen, 25, 41
Quintiza Scott, 25, 41

R
Ramono, Dana, 227
Ramsey, Michael, 25, 41
Ray, 66
Rayford, 58–60
Rayford Clayton, 18, 45, 58
Raymond Mapu, 226
Raymond Smoot, 19, 45, 229
Rayne, 17, 29, 36, 38, 44–45, 63, 84–86, 94, 96–97
Receiving Leader, 57
Redemptorist, 88
Red Smith, 51, 75
Reese, Richard, 111, 243
Replacing Scogin, 32
Reyes, Xavier, 28, 37
Reynolds, 58
Richard, 46, 66
Richard Schwartz, 10, 14, 49, 237, 240
Rick Morrison, Roger Causey, Dickie Bailes, 225
Rick Barnickle, 127
Ricks College, 47
Riddle, Garland, 135
Riser, Pat, 9, 48, 50

River, Pearl, 36, 60, 84–85
RJ Fertitta, 10, 49, 72, 76
Robbie Carter, 70, 80, 231
Roberick Lawhorn, 41
Roberson, Chris, 45
Robert, 36, 58–60, 65–66
Robert Byrd, 226
Robert Causey, 235, 237
Robert Gaines, 14–15, 47, 71, 78, 244
Robert Pynes, 9–10, 16–17, 45, 47, 49, 71
Robert Pynes Jr, 227
Robertson, Chris, 17, 45, 71
Robichaux, 14, 46–47, 240
Robinson, 66
   Clement, 70, 79
   Homer, 53
   Robert, 70
   Ronnie, 22, 43
Roderick Gates, 231
Rogers, Garrett, 27, 39
Roland, 62, 64
Roland Stallings, 14–15
Ronald Holsomback, 10, 49
Rone, Greg 21–22, 43, 70, 73, 79
Ronnie Stephens, 237
Rosen, Joe, 43
Rosepine, 126
Rowzee, Fred, 8, 53
Roy Hooker, 10, 49
Ruben, 29
Ruffin, Virgil, 43
Rush, 59–60
   Tony, 45, 71
Russell, H. Lynn, 16
Ruston, 44
Ryan Ward, 232

S
Sabian Matu, 28, 37, 69, 81, 232
Sacred Heart, 51, 102–3
Sage, Christian 37, 69
Saints, 26, 39
Salim, 10, 49, 62, 64
Salmen, 21
Sam Burnley, 47, 72, 225
Sam Fertitta, 13, 22, 53, 72, 127, 226, 246

Samuel Staples Lewis, 33
San Jose State, 39
Sapp, Ronnie, 43
SAU (Southern Arkansas University), 41
Sauvao, 24–25
Sawyer, 64–65
   Darius, 29, 37, 66
Schnell, Fred, 228
Schwartz, Richard, 14, 15, 46, 66
Scogin, Jim, 76
Scogin, Joe, 9, 49
Scott, 65
   Richard, 16, 45
   Sam, 22, 43, 115
Scott Mawae, 230
Sedric Clemons, 73
Sepeda, John, 53
Sharper, Brandon, 25, 41
Shaw, Antoine, 20, 43, 71
Shermaine Jones, 21–22, 43, 70
Short, Deshawn, 39
Shreve, 85
Shreveport, 13, 30–31
Shreveport Times, 5, 53
Sig Milerski, 22, 43
Simms, Tyrone, 21, 43
Simonelli, John, 9, 49, 76
Sims, Tyrone, 21, 43, 70
Skidmore, Derek, 24
Skinner, 49, 65
   Jerry, 9, 49, 75
   Jimmy, 49
Slidell, 21
Sliman, Paul, 13
Smart, Albert, 51
Smart, Derrick, 20, 43, 70, 79
Smart, Edwin, 9, 51
Smith, 20, 22, 42–43, 58–59, 62–66
   Bobby, 20, 45
   Damien, 70, 80
   Damion, 25, 41
   Danny, 16, 22, 31, 43, 68, 237
   David, 136
   Donald, 28, 37
   Dustin, 43
   Jacob, 33

   Kevin, 71, 79
   Marshall, 39
   Michael, 25, 41
   Ricky, 240
   Tyron, 20
   Tyrone, 20, 43, 71
Snapp, Ronnie, 20
Sonny Pynes, 232
South Beauregard, 85–86
Southeastern Louisiana University, 25, 261
Southern Arkansas University (SAU), 41
Southern University, 16
Southwood, 92–93
Stallworth, 58–59, 62–64
St. Amant, 44
St. Anthony, 105–7
St. Augustine, 102
Steel, 59, 61
Steele, Jeff, 45
Stefan James, 37
Stephens, 46–47, 63
   Bobby, 14
   Ronnie, 14, 16, 240
Sterlington, 14
Steve Gunn, 17, 45, 71, 73, 78
Steve Morrison, 14, 47, 227
Stevens, Julien, 8–9
Stevens, Stevie, 125
Stevens, Butch (JR III), 47, 77, 226
Stiles, 50
St. Louis, 61, 63, 85, 89, 94
St. Martinville, 28, 44, 61
St. Mary, 95
St. Marys, 61, 95, 104–5
St Michael, 61, 88
Stone, Guy 135–36
Stracner, Greg, 13, 72
St Thomas More, 90
St. Thomas More, 90
Sulphur, 53, 63, 87, 90–94, 105–7
Super Bowl, 14, 261
Superintendent, 16
Symons, Rod, 71

T
100 Tackle Club, 3

Talyn Adams, 28–29, 37, 69
Taylor, 65
  Dejan, 25, 41
TB Porter, 8, 51, 244
Team Records, 3
Teams in Pictures, 3
Team State Runner, 43
Tech, 25, 37, 39, 45, 49
Teddy Berry, 223
Ted Paris, 9, 14, 48, 49 51, 75, 223, 235, 243
Terrence Williams Coach, 38, 39, 40, 237
Terry, 58–59, 61
  John, 9, 49
Terry Haynes, 227
Terry Holt, 14, 47, 58, 244
Thanksgiving Day Game, 106
Tharp, Antonio, 27, 39
Theron Westerchil, 28, 62, 232
Thibodeaux, Dwayne, 22, 43
Thomas, 13
  Foster, 13
  Steven, 28, 37
Thompkins, Corey, 45
Thompkins, Darnell, 23
Thompson, 54
  Darnell, 24, 41
Thurman, 22, 27, 39, 43, 58, 64–66, 70, 73, 232
  Clinton 27, 39, 232
Tidelands Bowl, 49
Tigers, Neville, 30
Tillman, 127
Tioga, 42, 60, 63–64, 84–90, 93–94, 97–99
TJ Moore, 9,16, 45, 228
TL Berry, 9
Tolbert, 29, 64–65
  Moses, 27, 39
Tommy Moore, 27, 237
Tommy Peevey, 45
Tompkins, Corey, 71
Toney, Michael, 24, 41
Tony, 18, 59–60
Tony Jones, 227
Trahan, Brian, 5
Trahan, Roy, 10, 49, 76

Travante, 58–59, 62–64
Travante Stallworth, 63, 231
Tremayne Freeman 26, 39
Treme, Elroy, 72, 77
Trevante Stallworth, 24–25, 39, 41
Trev Stallworth, 39, 41
Tucker, Colonel Tom, 21
Tucker, 27
  Jim, 14
  Kemp 8, 51, 53, 75
Tulane, 10, 12, 22, 43, 45, 49, 261
Tunnifu-Sauvao, Wes, 70, 80
  Rob Saovao, 39, 69, 232
Turick, Danny, 47
Turner, 8, 52
  Bill, 50
  John, 43
  Terrell, 39
Tyler Community College, 29, 37
Tywann Brown, 27, 39

U
ULL, 14, 28, 47
UL Lafayette, 261
ULM, 26, 39, 45
UL Monroe, 261
Upshaw, 41
  Cordell, 24, 70, 80
US Army Team, 49
US Congressmen, 135
US involvement, 8
USL, 14, 47
US service academies, 135

V
Valentine, 53
Vandebilt Catholic, 40, 88
Vargas, Chris, 28, 37, 62–64
  Chris, 28, 37
Vernon, 5, 11, 58, 61, 235
Vernon High School, 253
Vernon-Leesville students, 13
Vernon Lion All State, 14
Vernon Miller, 230
Vernon Parish Library, 183
Vietnam, 11, 49

Vietnam War, 135
Ville Platte, 51, 98–99, 102–5
Vincent, 58–60
Vinson, Casey, 24, 41
Vinton, 100–102
Vivian, 51, 103

W
Walker, 23, 90
Wallace, Earl, 45
Walters, James, 16
Wampus Cat Club, 17
Wampus Cat Marching Band, 136, 250
Wampus Cat Stadium, 21, 27, 125, 129, 224
Washington, 95–97
Washington-Marion, 60–61, 63–64, 84–87, 89–92, 94, 95
Watley, Stan, 45, 71
Watts, 63
WC Turner, 235
Webster Parish, 31
Wego, Mike, 49
Well, James, 10, 49
Welsh, 61, 95–96
Wentz-Reeves, Holly 244
West, Bimbo, 14
West, Bill, 13, 47
West, Kevin, 45, 228
West, Ricky, 71
West brothers, 13
Westerchil, 62, 644
Westfall, Caleb, 29
Westgate, 36
Westlake, 60, 64, 85–86, 94–102, 104
West Monroe, 87–88
West Point, 14, 47, 261
Wes Tunnufu-Sauvo, 24, 41, 231
Wheeler, Caden, 27, 39, 62
White, Chris, 24, 41, 70
White, James, 22, 41
William Noonan, 236
Williams, 38, 48, 50, 59, 61, 66
  Dante, 70
  James, 16
  Joe, 45
  Marcus, 25, 41
  Mike, 47
  Stacy, 47, 71, 78
  Terry, 47
  Willie, 20, 43
Williamson, Danny, 25, 41
Williamson, Dante, 24, 41
Wilson, 61
  Charles, 49
  Larry, 47, 72
  Nikita, 245
  Rick, 16
  Micah 21, 43
Winnfied, Daniel, 39
Winnfield, 32, 39, 51, 53, 86, 97–98, 103–7
  Daniel, 39, 69, 73, 81
Winslow, Steven, 37
Wintle, 7
Wise, Eddie 5
Wisner, 14
Wood, 14, 50, 52
  Johnny, 76
Woodlawn, 14, 23, 40, 85, 91
Wood Osborne, 235, 236
Woods, Adam, 27, 39
Woods, Demetrius, 70
World Champion Cowboy, TB Porter 8
World War II, 8
Wossman, 21, 42–44, 94

X
Xavier, 22, 58–61
Xavier Ford, 33, 37, 233

Y

Z
Zachary, 38, 60
Zach Squyres, 27, 39, 57
Zack, 62–64
Zinger, 41, 64, 66, 261
Zolon, 50
Zolon Stiles, 50, 236

www.ingramcontent.com/pod-product-compliance
Lightning Source LLC
Chambersburg PA
CBHW061210230426
43665CB00032B/2975